IN THE NAME OF

ALLAH

THE ALL-COMPASSIONATE, ALL-MERCIFUL

Weakness of Faith

- Title: Weakness of Faith
- Author: Muhammad Sâlih al-Munajjid
- English Edition 1 (1999)
- New Revised English Edition 3 (2011)
- Layout Design: IIPH, Riyadh, Saudi Arabia
- Filming and Cover Design: Samo Press Group

New and revised edition

WEAKNESS OF FAITH

ظاهرة ضعف الإيمان

Muhammad Salih al-Munajjid

الدار العالمية للكتاب الإسلامي

INTERNATIONAL ISLAMIC PUBLISHING HOUSE

Copyright © 2011 International Islamic Publishing House
King Fahd National Library Cataloging-in-Publication Data

Al-Munajjid, Muhammad Salih
  Weakness of faith / Muhammad Salih al-Munajjid - 3.
.- Riyadh, 2011

  112 p ; 21 cm

  ISBN Hardcover: 978-603-501-120-4

  1- (Faith) Islam   I- Title

  243 dc   1432/7773

Legal Deposit no. **1432/7773**
ISBN Hardcover: **978-603-501-120-4**

International Islamic Publishing House (IIPH)
P.O. Box 55195 Riyadh 11534, Saudi Arabia
Tel: 966 1 4650818 / 4647213 — Fax: 966 1 4633489
E-mail: iiph@iiph.com.sa — iiphsa@gmail.com
www.iiph.com.sa

LIST OF CONTENTS

ARABIC HONORIFIC SYMBOLS USED IN THIS BOOK

(﷾): *Subḥânahu wa ta'âlâ* — 'The Exalted'

(ﷺ): *Ṣalla-Allâhu 'alayhi wa sallam* — 'Blessings and peace be upon him'

(ﷵ): *'Alayhis-salâm* — 'Peace be upon him'

(﷜): *Raḍiya Allâhu 'anhu* — 'May Allah be pleased with <u>him</u>'

(﷝): *Raḍiya Allâhu 'anhâ* — 'May Allah be pleased with <u>her</u>'

PRONUNCIATION AND TRANSLITERATION CHART

Arabic script	Pronunciation	Transliterated form
أ	short 'a', as in *cat*	a
آ – ى	longer 'a', as in *cab* (not as in *cake*)	â
ب	/b/ as in *bell*, *rubber* and *tab*	b
ت	/t/ as in *tap*, *mustard* and *sit*	t
ة	takes the sound of the preceding diactrical mark sometimes ending in h (when in pausal form): ah, ih, or ooh; or atu(n), ati(n) or ata(n) when uninterrupted	h or t (when followed by another Arabic word)
ث	/th/ as in *thing*, *maths* and *wealth*	th
ج	/j/ as in *jam*, *ajar* and *age*	j
ح	a 'harsher' sound than the English initial /h/, and may occur medially and in word-final position as well	ḥ
خ	as in *Bach* (in German); may occur initially and medially as well	kh
د	/d/ as in *do*, *muddy* and *red*	d
ذ	as in *this*, *father*, and *smooth*	dh
ر	/r/ ás in *raw*, *arid* and *war*; may also be a rolled 'r', as pronounced in Spanish	r

Arabic script	Pronunciation	Transliterated form
ز	/z/ as in *zoo*, *easy* and *gaze*	z
س	/s/ as in *so*, *messy* and *grass*	s
ش	as in *ship*, *ashes* and *rush*	sh
ص	no close equivalent in English, but may be approximated by pronouncing it as /sw/ or /s/ farther back in the mouth	ṣ
ض	no close equivalent in English, but may be approximated by pronouncing /d/ farther back in the mouth	ḍ
ط	no close equivalent in English, but may be approximated by pronouncing it as /t/ farther back in the mouth	ṭ
ظ	no close equivalent in English, but may be approximated by pronouncing 'the' farther back in the mouth	<u>dh</u>
ع	no close equivalent in English: a guttural sound in the back of the throat	'
غ	no close equivalent in English, but may be closely approximated by pronouncing it like the French /r/ in 'rouge'	gh
ف	/f/ as in *fill*, *effort* and *muff*	f

Arabic script	Pronunciation	Transliterated form
ق	no close equivalent in English, but may be approximated by pronouncing it as /k/ farther back in the mouth	q
ك	/k/ as in *king*, *buckle* and *tack*	k
ل	/l/ as in *lap*, *halo*; in the word *Allah*, it becomes velarized as in *ball*	l
م	/m/ as in *men*, *simple* and *ram*	m
ن	/n/ as in *net*, *ant* and *can*	n
‍ه‍ – ه – ـه	/h/ as in *hat*; unlike /h/ in English, in Arabic /h/ is pronounced in medial and word-final positions as well	h
و	as in *wet* and *away*	w
و	long 'u', as in *boot* and *too*	oo
ي	as in *yard* and *mayo*	y
ي	long 'e', as in *eat*, *beef* and *see*	ee
ء	glottal stop: may be closely approximated by pronouncing it like 't' in the Cockney English pronunciation of *butter*: *bu'er*, or the stop sound in *uh-oh!*	' (Omitted in initial position)

Diphthongs:

Arabic script	Pronunciation	Transliterated form
وَ ، أو	long 'o', as in *owe*, *boat* and *go*	au, aw
يَ ، أي	long 'a', as in *aid*, *rain* and *say*	ay, ai, ei

Diacritical marks (*tashkeel*):

Name of mark	Pronunciation	Transliterated form
´ fatḥah	very short 'a' or schwa (unstressed vowel)	a
ˏ kasrah	shorter version of ee or schwa (unstressed vowel)	i
ˊ Ḍammah	shorter version of oo	u
˞ shaddah	a doubled consonant is stressed in the word, and the length of the sound is also doubled	double letter
˚ sukoon	no vowel sound between consonants or at the end of a word	absence of vowel

ABOUT THE WORD 'LORD'

The word *lord* in English has several related meanings. The original meaning is 'master' or 'ruler', and in this sense it is often used to refer to human beings: 'the lord of the mansion' or 'Lord So-and-So' (in the United Kingdom, for example). The word *Lord* with a capital L is used in the lexicon of Islam to refer to the One and Only God — Allah. In Islam, there is no ambiguity about the meaning of this word. While it is true that one may occasionally use the word *lord* (whether capitalized or not) to refer to a human being, in Islamic discourse the reference of this term is always clear from the context. Whereas for Christians, Hindus and other polytheists, the word *Lord* with a capital 'L' may refer to Allah, to Jesus or to some imagined deity, for Muslims, there can be no plurality of meaning. Allah alone is the Lord, and the Lord is Allah — not Jesus, not Rama, not any other being.

The Editor

WHEN 'JIHAD' REFERS TO FIGHTING

$\mathcal{A}$lthough jihad is often translated into English as 'holy war', it must be noted that war has never been described as 'holy' in any of Islam's primary texts or even early Islamic literature. Linguistically speaking, jihad is an Islamic term that applies to a broad spectrum of activities, ranging from daily striving to meet the day's challenges, to the striving against one's desires and self, to the struggle to provide for one's family. Its basic definition is 'the act of striving or struggling in the way of Allah'. Therefore, jihad is not limited to war; it includes struggling with one's soul, speech, body and wealth so that the message of Allah reaches all humans willing to receive it.

Islamic scholars have referred to different types of jihad, such as jihad against the self (to understand Islam, act upon it, call others to it and be patient with the difficulties of making this call), jihad against the Devil (repelling Satanic whispers, doubts and lusts), jihad against the tongue (controlling it, using it to enjoin what is good, forbid what is wrong, spread the correct teachings of Islam and answer false ideologies), jihad against aggression (with the purpose of protecting Islam and the lives, honour and property of Muslims) and other types of jihad like jihad against the hypocrites, jihad against oppressors and jihad against mischief makers.

Jihad — in the context of fighting — has specific rules and conditions that need to be met before jihad is initiated. The first

rule is that people are not to be fought because of what they believe, or to coerce them to accept Islam. The second rule is to 'fight only those who fight you' and never initiate unprovoked aggression *(Qur'an 2: 190)*. That means that Muslims are only allowed to fight back, rather than initiating fighting; but 'fighting back' includes fighting against actual aggression as well as proactively addressing real threats of aggression. In both cases, Muslims are instructed to be prepared and ready to defend their nation before they actually engage in military conflict. There are additional conditions, but the above-mentioned conditions are vital for putting jihad in its broader meaning in the proper context.

Another condition of the sort of jihad which involves fighting is that it should take place only under an Islamic authority that 'raises the banner' for such jihad. It is not following the Sunnah at all for any individual or self-appointed group of Muslims to wage war on behalf of a nation. Instead, Muslims should be united under the single authority of an imam or khaleefah (caliph), except in the case where an individual needs to defend his own family and property, or to help his neighbour to do so. This is proved by the example of the early Muslims as well as texts in the Qur'an and the Sunnah:

《When there comes to them [the hypocrites] a matter related to [public] safety or fear, they spread it about; if only they had referred it to the Messenger and to such of them as are in authority, those among them who are able to think through the matter would have understood it.》 *(Qur'an 4: 83)*

«Ḥudhayfah ibn Yaman asked the Prophet (ﷺ): What if (the Muslims) have no single leader (they are divided into disputing groups)? The Prophet (ﷺ) answered: If they have no single leader

or unified group, then leave all these disputing groups, even if you have to bite on a tree until your death.» (part of a longer hadith recorded by Bukhari)

There are other conditions for jihad. In general, the rules laid out for war in Islam should be upheld unless there is some legitimate need or strategy when fighting occurs that would necessitate going against those rules. A Muslim should not kill himself or herself *(Qur'an 4: 29)* nor kill another Muslim, except by accident *(Qur'an 4: 92)*. Women, children, the elderly and other non-combatants should not be harmed. Land should not be destroyed, nor trees cut down. Corpses should not be mutilated. Islam should not be imposed upon non-believers. Rather, if combatant non-Muslims choose on their own to embrace Islam, even if only as a deceitful trick, it should be accepted by the Muslim leadership, and fighting should stop. Peace should be sought before lives are lost. Treaties and agreements should be upheld. Prisoners should be well-treated. Above all, justice must be done.

❨Fight in the path [according to the rules set by Allah] of Allah only those who fight you, but do not commit aggression [transgress limits]. Allah does not love aggressors. ...And fight them until persecution is no more, and religion is [freely embraced] for [the individual's faith in] Allah. But if they desist, then let there be no aggression except against transgressors.❩

(Qur'an 2: 190, 193)

❨Allah does not forbid you from being good, kind, just, and fair to those who have not fought you because of religion nor driven you from your homeland. Allah loves those who are just. Allah forbids you from giving allegiance to those who have fought you because

of religion and have driven you from your homeland, and those who supported your expulsion...﴾   *(Qur'an 60: 8-9)*

In addition, the Muslim nation is encouraged to maintain strong military capabilities to promote justice and to deter acts of war and aggression.

﴿And make ready for them [their potential aggression] all you can of power, including steeds of war, to deter the enemy of Allah and your enemy, and others besides, whom you may not know but whom Allah knows.﴾   *(Qur'an 8: 60)*

The Editor

THE ISLAMIC VIEWPOINT ON SLAVERY

Slavery existed before the coming of Prophet Muhammad (ﷺ). Islam did not abolish slavery, though it put limits on it and made it a virtuous act to free slaves.

In Islam, there is only one way a person may become enslaved and that is by being a non-Muslim among people who have been captured after raising arms and fighting against the Muslim nation. When such people have been conquered, the Muslim ruler has the option of enslaving them or releasing them (with or without ransom), and he makes this decision based upon the best interests and safety of the state. The Prophet (ﷺ) strongly rebuked any other means of enslaving a person. Thus, no person may become enslaved due to poverty, debt, kidnapping, committing a crime, voluntarily submitting to slavery, or any other means.

Islam encourages the freeing of slaves and has made the freeing of a slave a form of expiation for sins such as accidental manslaughter, the breaking of a vow, or voiding a fast by engaging in sexual intercourse. The freeing of slaves is also one of the categories upon which the zakâh funds should be spent *(Qur'an 9: 60)*. The Qur'an calls the freeing of a slave an act of righteousness that may be performed at any time:

❲Righteous are those who believe in Allah, the Last Day, the angels, the scripture, and the prophets; and they give money, cheerfully, to the relatives, the orphans, the needy, the wayfarer, the beggars, and to free the slaves.❳ *(Qur'an 2: 177)*

In regards to the treatment of slaves, the Prophet Muhammad (ﷺ) said: «They are your brothers whom Allah has put under your authority, so if Allah has put a person's brother under his authority, let him feed him from what he eats and clothe him from what he wears, and let him not overburden him with work, and if he does overburden him with work, then let him help him.» (Bukhari)

«Whoever accuses his slave when he is innocent of what he says will be flogged on the Day of Resurrection.» (Bukhari)

«Whoever slaps his slave or beats him, his expiation is to manumit him.» (Muslim)

«If a man had a slave woman whom he fed — and fed her well, and taught her — and taught her well, then he set her free and married her — he will have a double reward.» (Bukhari and Muslim)

The male owner of a female slave has the right to have sexual intercourse with her as long as he, or the slave's previous owner, has not married her to another person. This is a right exclusive to the slave's owner. No one, including the owner's sons, may touch the woman unless the owner marries her to him. If the slave woman bears her owner a child, then her owner may never sell her and she automatically becomes a free woman upon his death, if he has not released her before that.

As can be seen from this evidence, slavery in Islam is far different from the institution of slavery as known in many non-Muslim countries.

The Editor

PUBLISHER'S NOTE

All praise and thanks belong to Allah alone, the One, the Almighty and All-Merciful. Blessings and peace be upon Prophet Muhammad, the last of His Messengers and Prophets, and upon his family, his Companions and all those who follow in his footsteps until the end of time.

The human heart, called *qalb* in Arabic, is constantly in motion. It alternates between a weak and a strong level of faith which, in turn, is reflected in one's deeds.

Weakness of faith may be caused by committing evil deeds, being separated from righteous people and environments, seeking worldly pleasures and so on. In this book, the author discusses in detail the causes and goes on to prescribe remedies. You may be sick, but you will be unable to diagnose your disease by yourself; this is why it is important for all of us to read such a valuable book written by an experienced and knowledgeable author.

One of many beneficial works written by Shaykh al-Munajjid, this is a book which no Muslim should be without. It is a pleasure for IIPH to present it to our brothers and sisters, and we pray to Allah that it will be a source of great benefit to them.

May Allah accept the efforts of all those who contributed to the production of this book, and may it be acceptable to Him, *âmeen.*

Muhammad ibn Abdul Mohsin Al-Tuwaijri

Managing Director
International Islamic Publishing House
Riyadh, Saudi Arabia.

INTRODUCTION

*A*ll praise is for Allah (*Subhânahu wa Ta'âlâ* — Glorified and Exalted is He). We praise Him and seek His help; we also seek refuge with Allah (ﷻ) from the evil of our own selves and from our evil deeds. No one can misguide the one whom Allah (ﷻ) leads to the straight path, and no one can guide the one whom He allows to go astray. I bear witness that there is no true god except Allah (ﷻ) alone, with no partner or associate. I also bear witness that Muhammad (*salla Allâhu 'alayhi wa sallam* — blessings and peace be upon him) is His slave and messenger.

﴿يَـٰٓأَيُّهَا ٱلَّذِينَ ءَامَنُوا۟ ٱتَّقُوا۟ ٱللَّهَ حَقَّ تُقَاتِهِۦ وَلَا تَمُوتُنَّ إِلَّا وَأَنتُم مُّسْلِمُونَ ۝﴾

(سورة آل عِمرَان: ١٠٢)

◆O you who have believed, fear Allah as He should be feared and do not die except as Muslims [in submission to Him].▷

(Qur'an 3: 102)[1]

﴿۞ يَـٰٓأَيُّهَا ٱلنَّاسُ ٱتَّقُوا۟ رَبَّكُمُ ٱلَّذِى خَلَقَكُم مِّن نَّفْسٍ وَٰحِدَةٍ وَخَلَقَ مِنْهَا زَوْجَهَا وَبَثَّ مِنْهُمَا رِجَالًا كَثِيرًا وَنِسَآءً ۚ وَٱتَّقُوا۟ ٱللَّهَ ٱلَّذِى تَسَآءَلُونَ بِهِۦ وَٱلْأَرْحَامَ ۚ إِنَّ ٱللَّهَ كَانَ عَلَيْكُمْ رَقِيبًا ۝﴾

(سورة النِّسَاء: ١)

---

[1] The translations of the meanings of the Qur'anic verses in this book have been adapted from: Ṣaḥeeḥ International. *The Qur'an: Arabic Text with Corresponding English Meanings*. Jeddah: Abul Qasim Publishing House, 1997.

❨O humankind, fear your Lord, who created you from one soul and created from it its mate and dispersed from both of them many men and women. And fear Allah, through whom you ask one another, and the wombs [in regard to relations of kinship]. Indeed Allah is ever, over you, an Observer.❩   *(Qur'an 4: 1)*

﴿يَتأَيُّهَا ٱلَّذِينَ ءَامَنُواْ ٱتَّقُواْ ٱللَّهَ وَقُولُواْ قَوْلًا سَدِيدًا ۝ يُصْلِحْ لَكُمْ أَعْمَلَكُمْ وَيَغْفِرْ لَكُمْ ذُنُوبَكُمْ وَمَن يُطِعِ ٱللَّهَ وَرَسُولَهُ فَقَدْ فَازَ فَوْزًا عَظِيمًا ۝﴾

(سورة الأحزَاب : ٧٠–٧١)

❨O you who have believed, fear Allah and speak words of appropriate justice. He will [then] amend for you your deeds and forgive you your sins. And whoever obeys Allah and His Messenger has certainly attained a great attainment.❩

(Qur'an 33: 70-71)

The manifestation of weakness in faith has become widespread among Muslims. Many people complain about the harshness in their hearts, uttering such expressions as: "I feel a hardness in my heart," "I don't find pleasure in worship," "I feel that my faith is at an all-time low," "I am not affected by the recitation of the Qur'an," and "I fall into sin easily." Signs of this disease are visible upon many, and indeed this disease is the basis of every disaster and the cause of every subsequent deficiency and affliction.

The subject of hearts is sensitive but important. The heart has been named *al-qalb* [in Arabic] because of the speed with which it turns over and changes [*taqallub*].

In one *hadith* (a statement or action of Prophet Muhammad that was remembered and recorded by his Companions and followers), the Prophet (ﷺ) said: «The heart was named as such

due to its fluctuation. The example of the heart is like a feather caught on a tree trunk, with the wind turning it over and over.»[2] (Aḥmad; al-Albâni graded it as sound)

In another narration, he (ﷺ) stated: «The example of the heart is like a feather caught on open ground, with the wind turning it over and over.» (Recorded by Ibn Abi ʿÂṣim; al-Albâni graded it as sound)

The Prophet (ﷺ) described it as being extremely changeable: «The heart of the son of Adam goes up and down faster than a violently boiling pot.» (Recorded by Ibn Abi ʿÂṣim; al-Albâni graded it as sound)

In another narration: «...it turns over more than [the contents of] a pot when boiling.» (A sound hadith recorded by Aḥmad, at-Tirmidhi and an-Nasâ'i)

Without a doubt, it is Allah (ﷺ) who transforms the hearts and controls them. ʿAmr ibn al-ʿÂṣ (*raḍiya Allâhu ʿanhu* — may Allah be pleased with him) reported that he heard the Messenger of Allah (ﷺ) say: «All the hearts of Adam's children are between the two fingers of the Most Merciful, as if they were one heart that He controls as He wills.» Then the Messenger of Allah (ﷺ) supplicated: «O Allah, turner of hearts, turn our hearts to your obedience.» (Muslim)

Given that:

﴾ ... أَنَّ ٱللَّهَ يَحُولُ بَيْنَ ٱلْمَرْءِ وَقَلْبِهِ ... ﴿٢٤﴾ ﴿   (سورة الأنفال: ٢٤)

﴾...Allah intervenes between a person and his heart...﴿

(Qur'an 8: 24),

---

[2] Literally, from top to bottom.

and that none will escape punishment on the Day of Resurrection

﴿إِلَّا مَنْ أَتَى ٱللَّهَ بِقَلْبٍ سَلِيمٍ ۩﴾ (سورة الشُّعَرَاء: ٨٩)

﴿But only one who comes to Allah with a sound heart﴾

(Qur'an 26: 89),

as well as the fact that Allah (ﷻ) promises destruction

﴿ ... فَوَيْلٌ لِّلْقَـٰسِيَةِ قُلُوبُهُم مِّن ذِكْرِ ٱللَّهِ ... ۩﴾ (سورة الزُّمَرِ: ٢٢)

﴿...to those whose hearts are hardened against the remembrance of Allah...﴾ *(Qur'an 39: 22)*,

while the promise of paradise is for those

﴿مَّنْ خَشِىَ ٱلرَّحْمَـٰنَ بِٱلْغَيْبِ وَجَآءَ بِقَلْبٍ مُّنِيبٍ ۩﴾ (سورة قَ: ٣٣)

﴿Who feared the Most Merciful unseen and came with a heart returning [in repentance]﴾ *(Qur'an 50: 33)*

— it is necessary for the believers to probe their hearts and be aware of the location and cause of any sickness. After this acknowledgement, they should hasten to treat it before their hearts are overcome by a stain[3] and destroyed. The matter is both important and urgent, because Allah (ﷻ) has warned us about hearts that are hard, locked, diseased, blind, covered, inverted and sealed.

---

[3] ﴿No! Rather, the stain has covered their hearts of that which they were earning.﴾ *(Qur'an 83: 14)*. The Prophet (ﷺ) explained: «When a person commits a sin, a black mark is etched onto his heart; if he ceases and seeks forgiveness, his heart is wiped clean. If he repeats it, the black stain increases until it eventually envelops the heart. This is the stain that Allah has mentioned in His Book.» (An authentic hadith recorded by Aḥmad, at-Tirmidhi and an-Nasâ'i).

What follows is an effort to make the reader familiar with the symptoms of the disease called 'weak faith,' along with its causes and its treatment. I ask Allah (ﷻ) to benefit my Muslim brothers and sisters and me through this work and to fully reward those who have participated in its publication. We ask Him to soften our hearts and to guide us. Allah (ﷻ) is the best ally; He is sufficient for us and is the best disposer of our affairs.

Chapter 1

Symptoms of weak faith

$\mathcal{W}$eak faith is a disease that has numerous symptoms and indications, including:

1. Falling into sin and performing actions that are unlawful

Some people are persistent with evil deeds; they commit one sin after another with the result that they end up committing a variety of sins. Repetition of a sin leads to its becoming a habitual practice; eventually, its shamefulness is removed from the heart, and it is committed openly. Thus, the offender is included in the following hadith: «All of my *Ummah* (the global community of Muslims) may be forgiven except those who show sin openly. Among these is a man who committed a sin at night and Allah concealed it for him, but when morning came, he said: O so-and-so, yesterday I did this and that — while his Lord had spent the night concealing it for him. In the morning, he removed Allah's cover from himself.» (Bukhari)

2. Feelings of hardness and harshness in the heart

People might even reach a point where they feel their hearts have turned into rigid stones, issuing nothing and affected by nothing, as Allah (جَلَّ جَلَالُهُ) says:

$$\langle\!\langle \stackrel{\text{\tiny ۷٤}}{\bigcirc} \rangle\!\rangle ... \text{ فَسَوَةً} \text{ أَشَدُّ} \text{ أَوْ} \text{ كَالْحِجَارَةِ} \text{ فَهِيَ} \text{ ذَلِكَ} \text{ بَعْدِ} \text{ مِنْ} \text{ قُلُوبُكُم} \text{ فَسَتْ} \text{ ثُمَّ}\rangle\!\rangle$$

(سورة البَقَرَة: ٧٤)

❮Then your hearts became hardened after that, being like stones or even harder...❯   *(Qur'an 2: 74)*

The hard-hearted are not affected by admonitions about death or by the sight of dead people or funerals. They may have carried the body themselves and buried it in the ground, but for them, walking among graves is the same as walking among stones.

3. Carelessness during acts of worship

An example is the wandering of the mind during prayer, Qur'anic recitation, supplication, and the like. When people do not reflect upon the meaning of what they are saying, they recite in an automatic way — assuming that they are doing these acts regularly to begin with. Also, if they become accustomed to reciting a specific supplication at a specific time according to the *Sunnah* (the practice and collected sayings of Prophet Muhammad that together with the Qur'an forms the basis of Islamic law), they will not think about its meaning.

The Prophet (ﷺ) said: «Allah does not accept supplication from a heart that is heedless and distracted.» (Recorded by at-Tirmidhi; al-Albâni graded it as reliable)

4. Laziness about performing acts of obedience and worship, or neglecting them altogether

In this case, even if they are performed, they are simply empty movements, without spirit. Allah, the Mighty and Majestic, has described hypocrites as follows:

﴾ ... وَإِذَا قَامُوٓاْ إِلَى ٱلصَّلَوٰةِ قَامُواْ كُسَالَىٰ ... ﴿ (١٤٢) ﴾ (سورة النِّسَاء: ١٤٢)

﴾...And when they stand for prayer, they stand lazily...﴿

(Qur'an 4: 142)

Also included in this is the failure to take advantage of special seasons and times of worship, which shows that the people are not particularly concerned with obtaining any reward. They might postpone performing *Hajj* (the major pilgrimage to Makkah, a pillar of Islam that must be undertaken by every able Muslim at least once in his or her lifetime) even though they have the ability to do so, or pass up *jihad* (struggle or striving in the cause of Allah), or miss the congregational prayer and perhaps even the Friday congregational prayer.

The Messenger of Allah (ﷺ) said: «Some people will continue to lag behind [joining] the first row until Allah keeps them behind in the fire.» (Recorded by Abu Dâwood; al-Albâni graded it as sound)

Such people experience no guilt when they sleep through an obligatory prayer. If they miss one of the regular *sunnah* (recommended, but not mandatory) prayers or other acts of worship, they have no desire to make it up. Eventually, they will come to neglect acts that are sunnah or are communal duties (meaning that the obligation is satisfied if anyone in the Muslim community performs it, but if no one does, then the entire community is blameworthy). They may, therefore, miss the prayer of *Eid*[4] (one of two Islamic celebrations that take place at the end of the fasting month of *Ramadan* and at the culmination of the

---

[4] Most scholars consider the Eid prayer a sunnah prayer, although some say that it is an obligation.

Hajj), the eclipse prayer or the funeral prayer. They are aware of the rewards, yet they choose to forgo them. This is quite contrary to those whom Allah (ﷻ) has described in His book, saying:

﴾... إِنَّهُمْ كَانُوا يُسَٰرِعُونَ فِى ٱلْخَيْرَٰتِ وَيَدْعُونَنَا رَغَبًا وَرَهَبًا وَكَانُوا لَنَا خَٰشِعِينَ ۝﴿   (سورة الأنبياء: ٩٠)

❨...Indeed, they used to hasten to good deeds and supplicate Us in hope and fear, and they were to Us humbly submissive.❩

(Qur'an 21: 90)

They might also show laziness about performing the sunnah prayers, the optional late night prayers, and the optional mid- to late morning prayer, as well as the two-unit prayers for repentance or for guidance (when seeking the help of Allah in making a decision).

5. Depression, moodiness and reclusiveness

The individuals feel as if they are carrying a heavy burden; as a result, they become easily irritated, complaining about the smallest things. They become annoyed by the behaviour of the people around them and lose their tolerance with them.

The Prophet (ﷺ) described faith by saying: «Faith is patience and tolerance.» (Recorded by aṭ-Ṭabarâni; al-Albâni graded it as sound)

He (ﷺ) described the believer as someone who: «befriends and is befriended, and there is no good in the one who neither befriends nor is befriended.» (Recorded by Ibn Ḥibbân with a sound chain of narrators)

6. Indifference to the verses of the Qur'an

These people are not affected by the Qur'an's promises or its threats, by its commands or its prohibitions, or by its description of the resurrection. Those whose faith is weak grow bored with hearing the Qur'an and are unable to continue reading it for very long; every time they open the Qur'an, they close it soon after.

7. Heedlessness concerning Allah, the Mighty and Majestic, and failure to remember Him and supplicate to Him

They find it difficult to remember to mention the name of Allah (ﷻ); their supplications are fleeting and superficial. Allah (ﷻ) has described the hypocrites as:

(سورة النِّسَاء: ١٤٢)   ﴿...وَلَا يَذْكُرُونَ ٱللَّهَ إِلَّا قَلِيلًا ۝﴾

❴...not remembering Allah except a little.❵   *(Qur'an 4: 142)*

8. Complacency when Allah's prohibitions are violated

Because the flames of concern and anger have been extinguished, these persons no longer deplore evil. They neither order what is right nor forbid what is wrong; their faces will not change for the cause of Allah, the Mighty and Majestic. The Messenger of Allah (ﷺ) described such a heart afflicted with weakness in the following hadith: «Hearts will be exposed to trials like straws in a mat, one by one, so any heart that absorbs it is spotted with a black spot...» until it becomes as the Prophet (ﷺ) informed us at the end of the hadith: «...black and speckled like a clay mug that has tipped over, neither recognising right nor deploring wrong except what suits its own desire.» (Muslim)

The love of right and the dislike of wrong have been removed from the hearts of such people. Since both wrong and right are the same to them, what could motivate them to order or forbid anything? They might even hear that a wrong has been committed in the land and approve of it, thereby earning a sin similar to that of a person who actually witnessed and accepted it. This is similar to what the Prophet (ﷺ) mentioned in an authentic hadith: «When a sin is committed in the land, the one who was present and disliked it [and once he said: deplored it] is like one who was absent from it. And one who was absent from it but approved of it is like one who was present during it.» (Recorded by Abu Dâwood; al-Albâni graded it as reliable)

Their approval, which is a deed of the heart, put them in the same position as one who was present and participating in the sin.

9. Love of prominence

There are several types:

a) Desire for a position of leadership without any consideration given to its responsibility and significance. This is what the Messenger of Allah (ﷺ) warned about when he said: «Indeed, you will covet leadership, and it will be a regret [for you] on the Day of Resurrection. The first of it is [seemingly] good, and the last of it is evil.» (Bukhari)

That is because in the beginning, leadership brings wealth, influence and enjoyment, while it ends in being either killed or removed. Its consequences will be incurred on the Day of Resurrection.

The Prophet (ﷺ) also said: «If you like, I will inform you about leadership and what it is. The first of it is criticism, the second is

regret, and the third is punishment on the Day of Resurrection, except for the one who was just.» (Recorded by al-Haythami and Ibn Ḥajar al-'Asqalâni; al-Albâni graded it as reliable)

However, it is possible that an individual is genuinely concerned about performing his or her duty and shouldering the responsibility in a position for which there is no better candidate. Once the person gets the position of leadership, he or she exerts sincere effort, gives beneficial advice and practices justice, similar to Prophet Joseph (*'alayhi as-salâm* — peace be upon him). In such cases, acquisition of leadership is good and noble. More often than not, though, the motivating factor is a wilful desire for leadership and for taking precedence over the more qualified. This desire manifests itself in usurping the rights of others and monopolising the centre of the government.

b) A liking for prominence in gatherings and a tendency to dominate conversations, forcing others to listen: This liking extends to being the one who decides and commands. Such 'pulpits' are what the Messenger of Allah (ﷺ) warned us about when he said: «Beware of those slaughterhouses.» (Recorded by al-Bayhaqi; al-Albâni graded it as sound)

c) Desiring that others stand up when they enter, in order to satisfy the love of grandeur in their diseased souls. The Messenger of Allah (ﷺ) has said: «Whoever is pleased that the servants of Allah should stand up for him, let him take his place in a house of hellfire.» (Bukhari)

When Mu'âwiyah (ﷺ) went to Ibn az-Zubayr (ﷺ), Ibn 'Âmir rose, while Ibn az-Zubayr remained seated. Mu'âwiyah (ﷺ) said to Ibn 'Âmir: Be seated, for I heard the Messenger of Allah (ﷺ) say: «Whoever likes that men stand up for him, let him take his seat in hellfire.» (Abu Dâwood and Bukhari)

Such people are seized with anger if the Sunnah is practiced, as when someone begins from the right (in greeting or serving, for example). Upon entering a gathering, they also expect others to get up and give them their places, despite the Prophet's prohibition in the following hadith: «Let no one remove a man from his seat and then sit in it.» (Bukhari)

10) Stinginess and miserliness

Allah (﷾) has praised the *Anṣâr* (the Muslim citizens of Madinah who gave refuge to the Prophet and the other Muslim emigrants from Makkah), saying:

$$﴾ ... وَيُؤْثِرُونَ عَلَىٰٓ أَنفُسِهِمْ وَلَوْ كَانَ بِهِمْ خَصَاصَةٌ ... ۝ ﴿$$

(سورة الحَشر: ٩)

❲...They...give [them] preference over themselves, even though they are in privation...❳ *(Qur'an 59: 9)*

This makes it clear that the successful are those who are protected from the stinginess of their souls. There is no doubt that weakness of faith generates stinginess; in fact, the Prophet (ﷺ) said: «Stinginess and faith are never combined in the heart of a servant.» (an-Nasâ'i; al-Albâni graded it as reliable)

The danger of stinginess and its effects upon a person were outlined by the Prophet (ﷺ): «Beware of stinginess, for those before you were destroyed by stinginess. It ordered them to withhold, so they withheld; it ordered them to cut off relations, so they cut them off; and it inclined them towards immorality, so they became immoral.» (Abu Dâwood; al-Albâni graded it as sound)

The person with weak faith can hardly ever spend for the cause of Allah (﷾), even when voluntary charity is being encouraged,

the poverty of their Muslim brothers and sisters is evident, and calamities have struck many. There is nothing more profoundly accurate than Allah's words about this matter:

﴿هَٰأَنتُمْ هَٰٓؤُلَاءِ تُدْعَوْنَ لِتُنفِقُوا۟ فِى سَبِيلِ ٱللَّهِ فَمِنكُم مَّن يَبْخَلُ وَمَن يَبْخَلْ فَإِنَّمَا يَبْخَلُ عَن نَّفْسِهِۦ وَٱللَّهُ ٱلْغَنِىُّ وَأَنتُمُ ٱلْفُقَرَآءُ وَإِن تَتَوَلَّوْا۟ يَسْتَبْدِلْ قَوْمًا غَيْرَكُمْ ثُمَّ لَا يَكُونُوٓا۟ أَمْثَٰلَكُم ٣٨﴾   (سورة محمَّد: ٣٨)

❴Here you are — those invited to spend in the cause of Allah — but among you are those who withhold [out of greed]. And whoever withholds only withholds [benefit] from himself; and Allah is the free of need, while you are the needy. And if you refuse, He will replace you with another people; then they will not be the likes of you.❵   *(Qur'an 47: 38)*

11) Preaching [claiming or ordering] what they do not practice

Allah (﷾) said:

﴿يَٰٓأَيُّهَا ٱلَّذِينَ ءَامَنُوا۟ لِمَ تَقُولُونَ مَا لَا تَفْعَلُونَ ٢ كَبُرَ مَقْتًا عِندَ ٱللَّهِ أَن تَقُولُوا۟ مَا لَا تَفْعَلُونَ ٣﴾   (سورة الصَّف: ٢-٣)

❴O you who have believed, why do you say what you do not do? Great is hatred in the sight of Allah that you say what you do not do.❵   *(Qur'an 61: 2-3)*

Undoubtedly, this is a kind of hypocrisy; those whose speech is contrary to their deeds are blameworthy in the sight of Allah (﷾) and disliked by others. The people of hellfire will discover the reality of the ones who used to order what was right in this

world but did not practice it themselves. Similarly, they would forbid what was wrong, while indulging in those very deeds.

12. Feeling pleased at the affliction of their Muslim brothers or sisters, whether it concerns a failure, loss, disaster or cessation of a blessing

Their pleasure is based on the fact that the others are no longer in a better condition than they are.

13. Judging matters merely on the basis of whether or not they are actually prohibited, and not caring if they are disliked

Some people, when they want to do something, do not ask if the deed is righteous. They only check to see whether or not that particular deed will be counted as a sin: "Is it actually forbidden, or merely disapproved of?" Such a mentality leads them to fall into the trap of doubtful and disapproved matters, which can eventually drag them towards what is prohibited. This is exactly what the Prophet (ﷺ) stated: «He who falls into doubtful matters will fall into what is prohibited, just as a shepherd who pastures his sheep around a private property can hardly prevent their crossing over into it.» (Bukhari and Muslim)

In fact, some people, when they seek a ruling about something and are told that it is prohibited, will even ask: "Is it a strong prohibition?" or "How much sin does it entail?" Such people do not really care about avoiding wrongdoing or bad deeds; they are prepared to commit lesser degrees of prohibited actions. Carelessness about small sins results in an attitude of audacity towards the prohibitions of Allah (ﷻ) in general, and in the removal of inhibitions against disobedience. That is why the

Messenger of Allah (ﷺ) said: «I will certainly know people of my community who come on the Day of Resurrection with good deeds as great as the white mountains of Tihâmah, but Allah, the Mighty and Majestic, will render them as dust dispersed. Thawbân (ﷺ) said: O Messenger of Allah, describe them to us; make them clear to us so that we will not be among them without knowing. He (ﷺ) said: Indeed, they are your brothers and of your race, and they take a portion of the night [for worship] as you do, except that they are people who violate the prohibitions of Allah when they are alone.» (Ibn Mâjah; al-Albâni graded it as sound)

Thus, you will find them falling into the prohibitions without reserve or hesitation. Such people have an easygoing attitude about sins as a result of their weak faith; they refuse to accept that they have done anything wrong.

Ibn Mas'ood (ﷺ) compared the state of the believer and the state of the hypocrite by saying: "Indeed, the believer sees his sins as if he were sitting at the foot of a mountain, fearing that it would fall upon him, while the wicked person sees his sins as a fly passing by his nose which is brushed away." (Bukhari)[5]

14. Considering good deeds to be insignificant, and showing no concern for smaller ones

Imam Ahmad narrated: «Abu Jariy al-Hujaymi said that he approached the Messenger of Allah (ﷺ) and said: O Messenger of Allah, we are people of the desert, so teach us something by which Allah, the Blessed and Exalted, will benefit us. He (ﷺ) said: Do not perceive any good deed as insignificant — even pouring from

---

[5] See also: Ahmad ibn 'Ali Ibn Hajar al-'Asqalâni, *Taghleeq at-Ta'leeq* (Beirut: al-Maktab al-Islâmi).

your bucket into the container of one seeking water, and speaking to your brother with a pleasant face.» (Muslim and Aḥmad)

Drawing water from a well and pouring it for someone else might seem to be a small deed, but it should not be thought of as insignificant. The same is true of greeting a brother or sister with a pleasant face, or removing litter and dirt from the mosque, even if it is only a piece of straw. Perhaps that small deed might cause your sins to be forgiven. Such good deeds may seem too simple to be noteworthy, but Allah (ﷻ) appreciates such deeds from His servants and thereby forgives them.

Consider that the Prophet (ﷺ) said: «A man came upon a tree branch in the road and said: By Allah, I will remove this so it will not harm the Muslims. Thus he entered paradise.» (Muslim)

A person who looks down upon small good deeds is in error. A sufficient penalty for that is being deprived of a great bounty. This is apparent from the following hadith, in which the Prophet (ﷺ) said: «Whoever removes something harmful from the road has recorded a good deed, and whoever has a good deed at his or her disposal will enter paradise.» (Bukhari)

«Once Muʻâdh (ﷺ) was walking with a man. When he removed a rock from the path, the man asked him why. Muʻâdh (ﷺ) replied: I heard the Messenger of Allah (ﷺ) say: One who removes a rock from the road has recorded a good deed, and whoever has a good deed will enter paradise.» (aṭ-Ṭabarâni; al-Albâni graded it as sound)

15. Indifference to the problems of Muslims

Those who are not moved by supplication, voluntary charity, or any other kind of help, are cold and indifferent towards the

affliction of their brothers and sisters in every corner of the earth, whether they are suffering from oppression, persecution by an enemy or other disasters. Such people are satisfied as long as they are free from such afflictions themselves, and that is due to a weak level of faith. The believer is quite different, as the Prophet (ﷺ) said: «The believer among the people of faith is like a head to the body. The believer feels pain for the people of faith, just as the body feels pain from what is in the head.» (Aḥmad and as-Suyooṭi; al-Albâni graded it as reliable)

16. Loosening of the ties of brotherhood and sisterhood

The Prophet (ﷺ) said: «No two persons hold affection for each other in the way of Allah, the Mighty and Majestic, or in Islam, but that the first sin separates them. [In another narration: They are separated by a sin that one of them commits.]» (Bukhari)

This proves that the evil of disobedience can affect and undo the ties of brotherhood and sisterhood. The estrangement that people sometimes feel between themselves and their brothers and sisters is a result of a decrease in faith. This is caused by acts of disobedience, because Allah (ﷻ) removes the one who disobeys Him from the hearts of His servants. Hence, they live among them in the worst way, having lost their worth and having become objects of disdain and disrespect. They also lose the company of the believers and subsequently the defence of Allah (ﷻ), for:

(سورة الحَجّ : ٣٨)   ﴿ ۞ إِنَّ ٱللَّهَ يُدَٰفِعُ عَنِ ٱلَّذِينَ ءَامَنُوٓاْ ... ۝ ﴾

﴿Indeed, Allah defends those who have believed...﴾

(Qur'an 22: 38)

17. Lack of motivation to work for the religion, not striving to spread it or serve it

This is contrary to the example of the Prophet's Companions (may Allah be pleased with them); when they entered the religion, they immediately felt responsible for striving to both promote and protect it. After at-Ṭufayl ibn 'Amr (ﷺ) accepted Islam, how long did it take him to go and invite his people to Allah, the Mighty and Majestic? As soon as he entered the religion, he became aware of his great responsibility, so he asked the Messenger of Allah (ﷺ) for permission to return to his people to invite them to Allah (ﷺ). Today, after adhering to the religion, people remain dormant for a long period of time before they reach the stage of inviting others to Allah (ﷺ).

The Companions of Prophet Muhammad (ﷺ) practiced what was required by those entering the religion: animosity toward the disbelievers, disassociation from them, and breaking away from them. When Thumâmah bin Athâl, chief of the Yamâmah people, was taken prisoner [by the Muslims] and tied up in the mosque, the Messenger of Allah (ﷺ) presented Islam to him. Allah (ﷺ) enlightened his heart; he accepted Islam and went to perform *'umrah* (the minor pilgrimage). When he reached Makkah, he said to the disbelievers of *Quraysh* (the dominant tribe there at the time, whose society was based on polytheism): "You will not receive a single grain of wheat from Yamâmah unless the Messenger of Allah (ﷺ) allows it." (recorded by Bukhari, *Fath al-Bâri*)

His break from and economic boycott of the disbelievers, and his employment of every available means to serve the cause of Allah (ﷺ), were immediate because his firm faith required these deeds from him.

18. Panic and fear at the time of an affliction or problem

When struck with misfortunes or trials, some people will be found trembling, unbalanced, distracted with a fixed gaze, and confused. In their view, all the ways out are closed, so anxieties pile up on them, leaving them unable to face reality with firm and strong hearts. All this is due to the weakness in their faith; if their faith was strong, they would have been steadfast and faced the greatest misfortunes and severest trials with strength and determination.

19. An abundance of arguments and disputes, which hardens the heart

The Prophet (ﷺ) said: «No people went astray after they had been upon guidance except that they were given to argument.» (at-Tirmidhi; al-Albâni graded it as reliable)

Arguing without proof and without valid intentions leads to distancing themselves from the straight path. It is very sad that people today bicker profusely about falsehood, confronting each other without knowledge or guidance from the enlightening book (the Qur'an) and the Sunnah. Even if they had such knowledge, the following hadith should be sufficient motivation for them to give up this blameworthy trait.

The Prophet (ﷺ) said: «I am responsible for a house in the fields of paradise for the one who ceases disputing even though he or she is right.» (Abu Dâwood; al-Albâni graded it as reliable)

20. Attachment to and love of the world, and feeling ease therein

The hearts are attached to this world to the extent that their owners feel pain when they miss any of its pleasures, such as

wealth, influence, position or homes. They also consider themselves to be deprived and unfortunate because they cannot obtain what others have obtained. They are further hurt and distressed when they see their Muslim brothers and sisters having gained some of the shares of this world that they themselves missed out on. As a result, they might envy them and wish that those blessings were taken away from the other person. This is inconsistent with faith, according to the Prophet's saying: «Envy and faith are not combined in the heart of a servant.» (an-Nasâ'i; al-Albâni graded it as reliable)

21. Complete rationalisation of speech and behaviour, and loss of any impression of belief

One can hardly find in the words of such people any trace of reference to the Qur'an or the Sunnah or even the words of the early scholars (may Allah have mercy upon them).

22. Exaggerated self-interest

People pay excessive attention to food, drink, clothing, the home, means of transport and various luxuries. They embellish their personalities and exert themselves in order to purchase fine clothes and adornments for the house, spending too much time and money upon unnecessary improvements while some of their fellow Muslims are in greater need of that money. Eventually, they drown themselves in luxury and extravagance, which has been prohibited. Mu'âdh ibn Jabal (رضي الله عنه) related that when the Prophet (صلى الله عليه وسلم) sent him to Yemen, he instructed him to: «Beware of luxury, for the servants of Allah are not those who live in luxury.» (Aḥmad; al-Albâni graded it as reliable)

Chapter 2

Causes of weak faith

There are many reasons for weakness in faith, some of which are associated with symptoms that we have discussed previously, such as falling into sins and excessive preoccupation with worldly pursuits. The following are some additional causes.

1. Remaining distant from an atmosphere of faith for a long period of time

Allah, the Mighty and Majestic, has said:

﴿۞ أَلَمْ يَأْنِ لِلَّذِينَ ءَامَنُوٓاْ أَن تَخْشَعَ قُلُوبُهُمْ لِذِكْرِ ٱللَّهِ وَمَا نَزَلَ مِنَ ٱلْحَقِّ وَلَا يَكُونُواْ كَٱلَّذِينَ أُوتُواْ ٱلْكِتَٰبَ مِن قَبْلُ فَطَالَ عَلَيْهِمُ ٱلْأَمَدُ فَقَسَتْ قُلُوبُهُمْ وَكَثِيرٌ مِّنْهُمْ فَٰسِقُونَ ۝﴾

(سورة الحَديد: ١٦)

《Has the time not come for those who have believed that their hearts should become humbly submissive at the remembrance of Allah and what has come down of the truth? And let them not be like those who were given the scripture before, and a long period passed over them, so their hearts hardened; and many of them are defiantly disobedient.》 *(Qur'an 57: 16)*

The verse clearly states that being away for a long time from the environment of belief is conducive to the weakening of faith in the heart. For example, those who leave their fellow Muslims for a

long period due to travel, work or other reasons, miss the atmosphere of belief that they used to enjoy and from which they drew strength of heart. This is because believers are in a minority by themselves and in the majority when they are together with their fellow Muslim brothers and sisters.

Al-Ḥasan al-Baṣri said: "Our brothers are dearer to us than our families; our families remind us of the world, while our brothers remind us of the hereafter."

Prolonged absence leads to estrangement, which, after some time, turns into distaste for the atmosphere of faith. Subsequently, the hearts become hardened and darkened, with the light of faith extinguished. This partly explains the change in some people when they travel during the holidays or are transferred to another place of work or study.

2. Distance from righteous examples

Some people learn from good and pious men and women, acquiring from them beneficial knowledge, strength of faith and motivation to do good deeds. They commit themselves to this person and take him or her as a role model, so if they are away from that individual for a while, they will experience a hardening of the heart.

When the Messenger of Allah (ﷺ) passed away and was covered by the earth, the Companions said: "Our hearts denied us." They were afflicted with gloom because their educator, teacher and example had died. Their description of themselves was recorded as: "like sheep during a rainy winter night." The Prophet (ﷺ), however, left behind him men like mountains, all of them suitable as successors, who became role models for one

another. Today the Muslim Ummah is in dire need of good examples like them.

3. Failure to seek religious knowledge and interact with the books of the early scholars and other books that liven the heart

There are books that stir faith in the hearts of the readers and motivate their souls. The foremost of these is the book of Allah (鑑), then books of *Hadith* (the collected statements and actions of Prophet Muhammad that, with the Qur'an, form the basis of Islamic law), followed by the books of recognised scholars explaining and giving their advice on delicate matters. There are books by those scholars who excel in presenting the religious tenets and required beliefs in a manner that awakens the heart, such as Ibn al-Qayyim, Ibn Rajab and others.

Being cut off from such books, while confining their reading to intellectual matters, rulings without any sources given, linguistics and fundamentals, for example, can sometimes harden the hearts. This is not to condemn books of language, fundamentals and other subjects; my intention is to alert those who neglect the books of Qur'anic commentary and Hadith, because these are the books that connect the heart to Allah, the Mighty and Majestic. Reading the *Ṣaḥeeḥs* of Bukhari and Muslim, for example, makes the readers feel as though they are living with the Messenger (鑑) and his Companions (may Allah be pleased with them all) in the atmosphere of the first generation of Muslims; they sense the fragrance of faith through their life stories and the incidents that took place during their time.

A poet said:

The people of Hadith are the family of the Prophet.
Even if they were not companions to his person,
they are, to his style, companions.

The effect of neglecting these books is evident upon those who study subjects that are unrelated to Islam and formulated without any reference to Islam. The same is true of those who are devoted to fiction and love stories, as well as those who habitually follow, with great concern and interest, unimportant affairs in newspapers and magazines.

4. Presence of a Muslim in an environment saturated with disobedience to Allah

In such a scenario, one person is proudly talking about a sin he has committed, another is absorbed in the words and melodies of a song, a third is smoking, a fourth is spreading open a pornographic magazine, and a fifth is cursing and insulting — not to mention the gossiping and backbiting and so on.

Some surroundings do not remind people of anything except worldly affairs. Most office meetings and other gatherings are focused on commerce, jobs, finance, consultations, work problems, advances, promotions, assignments, and so on, which are among the main concerns of many people and the subjects of their conversation.

As for homes, one can speak easily about the deluge of calamities and evils that bring perspiration to the brows of true Muslims and break their hearts. Brazen songs and immoral films fill the homes of Muslims, and there is unlawful social mixing between the sexes. In such environments, the hearts undoubtedly become diseased and hardened.

5. Excessive preoccupation with this world, to the point that the heart becomes a slave to it

The Messenger (ﷺ) said: «Miserable is the slave of the *dinar* and the *dirham* (gold and silver coins).» (Bukhari)

He also said: «Sufficient for one of you from worldly things is the equivalent of the provisions of a rider.» (Recorded by as-Suyooṭi and aṭ-Ṭabarâni; al-Albâni graded it as sound)

This essentially means that a small amount, just enough to enable one to reach his or her destination, is sufficient. The opposite is obvious in these days of materialism and greed for more and more worldly goods: people are running after business ventures, professions, corporate shares, and so on. This is in accordance with what the Prophet (ﷺ) informed us: «Indeed Allah, the Mighty and Majestic, said: We sent wealth for the establishment of prayer and giving of charity. If a son of Adam had a valley [of wealth], he would like to have another; and if he had two valleys, he would want to add a third to them. Nothing will [truly] fill the inside of a son of Adam except earth. Then Allah (ﷻ) will forgive the one who has repented.» (Bukhari and Aḥmad)

6. Excessive preoccupation with property, spouse and children

Allah, the Mighty and Majestic, has said:

﴿وَٱعْلَمُوٓا۟ أَنَّمَآ أَمْوَٰلُكُمْ وَأَوْلَٰدُكُمْ فِتْنَةٌ ... ۝﴾   (سورة الأنفال: ٢٨)

﴿And know that your properties and your children are but a trial...﴾   *(Qur'an 8: 28)*

He (ﷺ) has also said:

﴿زُيِّنَ لِلنَّاسِ حُبُّ ٱلشَّهَوَٰتِ مِنَ ٱلنِّسَآءِ وَٱلْبَنِينَ وَٱلْقَنَٰطِيرِ ٱلْمُقَنطَرَةِ مِنَ ٱلذَّهَبِ وَٱلْفِضَّةِ وَٱلْخَيْلِ ٱلْمُسَوَّمَةِ وَٱلْأَنْعَٰمِ وَٱلْحَرْثِ ذَٰلِكَ مَتَٰعُ ٱلْحَيَوٰةِ ٱلدُّنْيَا وَٱللَّهُ عِندَهُۥ حُسْنُ ٱلْمَـَٔابِ﴾ (سورة آل عِمرَان: ١٤)

◆Beautified for people is the love of that which they desire — of women and sons, heaped-up sums of gold and silver, fine branded horses and cattle, and tilled land. That is the enjoyment of worldly life, but Allah has with Him the best return [meaning paradise].◆

(Qur'an 3: 14)

This verse warns that if the love of such things, the foremost of these being spouses and children, takes precedence over obedience to Allah (ﷻ) and His Messenger (ﷺ), it is repugnant and blameworthy. However, if the love of these things is within the limits of what is lawful, while obedience to Allah (ﷻ) is observed, then it is good and praiseworthy.

The Prophet (ﷺ) said: «I have been given from this world the love of wives and good scent, but my greatest pleasure is in prayer.» (Aḥmad and an-Nasâ'i; al-Albâni graded it as reliable)

Many people follow the wishes of their spouses in unlawful matters and allow their children to distract them from obeying and worshipping Allah, despite the Prophet's saying: «A child is a cause of grief, cowardice, ignorance and stinginess.» (aṭ-Ṭabarâni; its chain of narrators is acceptable)

Stinginess: When individuals intend to spend in the cause of Allah (ﷻ), the devil reminds them of their children, so they refrain from spending, saying: "My children have more right to this money... they will need it when I am gone, so I will keep it for them."

Ignorance: Parents are kept away from seeking and obtaining knowledge. They are prevented from attending meetings and reading books that will provide them with it.

Cowardice: When men want to fight in the cause of Allah (ﷻ), the devil comes to them and says: "You will be killed, and your children will become orphans in distress." Consequently, they refrain from going for jihad.

Grief: When their child is ill, the parents grieve for them; when children ask for something that the parents are unable to provide, the parents are saddened. When they grow up and are undutiful to their parents, this is a continual source of grief and distress.

All this does not mean that one should not marry and have children, or that one should abandon the raising of children. It is only a warning against being preoccupied with them in prohibited ways and neglecting the remembrance of Allah (ﷻ).

As for the trial through wealth, the Prophet (ﷺ) said: «For every community is a trial, and the trial for my community is wealth.» (Recorded by at-Tirmidhi with a sound chain of narrators)

Greed for wealth is more corrupting for the religion than a wolf prevailing in a pen of sheep. That is the meaning of the Prophet's saying: «Two hungry wolves released among sheep are no more ruinous to them than the greediness of a person for wealth and status is to his religion.» (An authentic hadith recorded by at-Tirmidhi)

This is why the Prophet (ﷺ) encouraged people to be satisfied with what is sufficient for them, without striving for the excesses that distract them from the remembrance of Allah (ﷻ).

The Messenger (ﷺ) said: «It is enough wealth for you to have a servant and transport to use in the way of Allah.» (Aḥmad; al-Albâni graded it as reliable)

He also threatened those who collect and amass wealth – with the exception of those who give in charity: «Woe to the hoarders, except for one who did with his wealth such-and-such and such-and-such, four: on his right, on his left, in front of him and behind him.» (Ibn Mâjah; al-Albâni graded it as reliable)

He meant giving wealth through various kinds of charities and kindnesses.

7. Extended hope and expectation that one will still be alive at a future time

Allah (ﷻ) said:

$$﴿ذَرْهُمْ يَأْكُلُوا۟ وَيَتَمَتَّعُوا۟ وَيُلْهِهِمُ ٱلْأَمَلُ فَسَوْفَ يَعْلَمُونَ ۝﴾$$

(سورة الحجر: ٣)

﴿Let them eat and enjoy themselves and be diverted by [false] hope, for they are going to know.﴾   *(Qur'an 15: 3)*

'Ali (ﷺ) said: "The most frightening thing I fear for you is the following of one's desires and extended hope. Following desires averts one from the truth, and extended hope makes one forget the hereafter." (Recorded by Bukhari in *Fatḥ al-Bâri*)

Some Companions were quoted as saying: "Four things belong to wretchedness: indifference of the eye, hardness of the heart, extended hope, and greediness for what is in the world."

Extensive expectation of continuity generates laziness in worship, postponement of repentance, desire for this world,

neglect of the hereafter and hardness in the heart. This is because sensitivity and clarity in the heart come from being reminded of death and the grave, of rewards and penalties, and of the terrors of the resurrection. Allah (ﷻ) said:

(سورة الحَديد: ١٦)   ﴿ ... فَطَالَ عَلَيْهِمُ ٱلْأَمَدُ فَقَسَتْ قُلُوبُهُمْ ... ۝ ﴾

﴿...And a long period passed over them, so their hearts hardened...﴾
(Qur'an 57: 16)

It has been said: "Those who limit their expectations also lessen their anxiety and enlighten their heart, because when they bring death to mind, they exert effort in obedience." (*Fath al-Bâri*)

8. An excess of food, sleep, staying up late, and talking and mixing with people

Overeating slows down the brain and burdens the body, keeping it from worshipping Allah (ﷻ) and instead nourishing the currents of Satan in a person. It has been said: "Whoever eats too much and drinks too much will sleep too much and lose much reward."

Talking too much hardens the heart; too much socialising prevents people from being alone with their own souls, taking them to account and considering how to deal with them. Too much laughter causes the life (sensitivity) of the hearts to be extinguished, as the Prophet (ﷺ) said: «Do not be excessive in laughter, for too much laughter deadens the heart.» (Ibn Mâjah; al-Albâni graded it as sound)

Time that is not filled with obedience to Allah (ﷻ) brings about barren hearts, which benefit neither from the admonitions of the Qur'an nor the exhortations of faith.

The causes of weak faith are too many to enumerate. An intelligent reader, however, may receive guidance from what has been mentioned here, as well as what has not been mentioned. We ask Allah (ﷻ) to purify our hearts and protect us from the evil within ourselves.

Chapter 3
Curing weak faith

$\mathcal{A}$l-Ḥâkim narrated in his *Mustadrak,* and at-Ṭabarâni in his *Mu'jam,* that the Prophet (ﷺ) said: «Faith becomes worn out inside one of you just as a garment becomes worn out, so ask Allah to renew the faith in your hearts.» (al-Ḥaythami graded it as reliable)

By that, he meant that faith deteriorates as a garment does when it becomes old and threadbare. The hearts of believers are sometimes overcome by the clouds of disobedience; thus, they become dark, as the Messenger of Allah (ﷺ) illustrated in an authentic hadith: «Among hearts, there is no heart that does not have a cloud like that of the moon, in that the moon shines but is darkened when covered by a cloud, and when it passes away from it, it gives light.» (aṭ-Ṭabarâni; al-Albâni graded it as reliable)

The moon's light is covered by a passing cloud, which disperses after a time. Similarly, the hearts of the believers are sometimes covered by a dark cloud of disobedience, blocking the light and leaving the people in darkness and desolation. When they exert themselves towards increasing their faith, seeking help from Allah (ﷺ), the clouds are dispersed, and the light of their heart shines once again.

When trying to understand weakness of faith and plan its treatment, it is important to focus on the knowledge that faith

increases and decreases. Among the basic beliefs of *Ahl as-Sunnah wal-jamâ'ah* (people of the Sunnah and the community) are that faith comprises pronunciation by the tongue, belief in the heart, and deeds by the body, and also that faith increases through obedience and decreases through disobedience. The following are some of the proofs from the Qur'an and Sunnah:

(سورة الفَتح: ٤)   ﴾... لِيَزْدَادُوٓاْ إِيمَٰنًا مَّعَ إِيمَٰنِهِمْ ...﴿

﴾...that they would increase in faith along with [that is, in addition to] their [present] faith...﴿   *(Qur'an 48: 4)*

﴾... أَيُّكُمْ زَادَتْهُ هَٰذِهِۦٓ إِيمَٰنًا فَأَمَّا ٱلَّذِينَ ءَامَنُواْ فَزَادَتْهُمْ إِيمَٰنًا وَهُمْ يَسْتَبْشِرُونَ ﴿

(سورة التَّوبَة: ١٢٤)

﴾...which of you has this increased faith? As for those who believed, it has increased them in faith, while they are rejoicing.﴿
(Qur'an 9: 124)

The Prophet (ﷺ) said: «Whoever among you sees a wrong, let him change it by his hand; if he is unable to do so, then by his tongue; and if he is unable to do that, then in his heart; and that is the weakest level of faith.» (Muslim)

The effect of obedience and disobedience on the extent of faith is a matter that is well known, witnessed and experienced. For instance, a man goes out to the market, where he gazes at women who are not properly covered and hears the shouting and improper speech of the people. He then goes to a graveyard; entering and contemplating there, he soon feels his heart softening. He surely finds a manifest difference between these two states, for the heart changes quickly.

This concept was also stated by one of the early scholars, who said that people have understanding when they pay attention to their faith and what has decreased thereof, when they know whether their faith is increasing or decreasing, and when they recognise how the suggestions of the devil come to them.[6]

It should be known that abandoning obligatory acts or committing unlawful acts because of a decrease in faith is a dangerous condition, and the persons who do so are at fault. They must repent to Allah and immediately begin to correct themselves. Sometimes, though, a weak level of faith does not lead people to abandon what is mandatory or engage in what is unlawful; it only makes them discontinue an optional meritorious deed, for example. If this happens, they must take control, focus upon what is appropriate, and improve themselves until they return to their regular state of activity and exertion in worship. This is what one infers from the Prophet's statement: «You do deeds with enthusiasm, but for every enthusiasm, there is an intermission. One whose intermission is towards my Sunnah has succeeded, and one whose intermission is toward something else is destroyed.» (Recorded by Aḥmad with a sound chain of narrators)

Before discussing the treatment, it should be noted that many of those who feel harshness in their hearts search for cures outside themselves. They want to depend upon others to help them, whereas it is within their capacity, if they wish, to treat themselves. This is the primary and proper way to go about it, because faith is a relationship between the servants and their Lord. The following are a number of lawful Islamic methods that can enable Muslims to cure themselves of weak faith and a hard heart,

---

[6] Ibn Qayyim al-Jawziyah, *Sharḥ al-Qaṣeedat an-Nooniyah* (Beirut: al-Maktab al-Islâmi, 1962).

but this will happen only when they depend upon Allah (ﷻ) and begin to exert effort.

1. Reflection upon the meanings of the noble Qur'an,

which Allah, the Mighty and Majestic, has revealed as clarification for all things. It is a light through which the Exalted guides whom He wills among His servants, and it undoubtedly contains a significant and effective treatment. Allah (ﷻ) has said:

$$ ﴿وَنُنَزِّلُ مِنَ ٱلْقُرْءَانِ مَا هُوَ شِفَآءٌ وَرَحْمَةٌ لِّلْمُؤْمِنِينَ ... ﴿٨٢﴾﴾ $$

(سورة الإسرَاء: ٨٢)

﴿And We send down of the Qur'an that which is a healing and a mercy for the believers...﴾   *(Qur'an 17: 82)*

Treatment is through thought and reflection.

«The Messenger of Allah (ﷺ) used to reflect upon the book of Allah (ﷻ) and repeat it while standing in the night prayers. One night, he stood repeating one verse from Allah's book while praying, not going beyond it until morning appeared. The words were as follows:

$$ ﴿إِن تُعَذِّبْهُمْ فَإِنَّهُمْ عِبَادُكَ وَإِن تَغْفِرْ لَهُمْ فَإِنَّكَ أَنتَ ٱلْعَزِيزُ ٱلْحَكِيمُ ﴿١١٨﴾﴾ $$

(سورة المَائدة: ١١٨)

﴿If you should punish them — indeed they are Your servants; but if You forgive them — indeed it is You who is the Exalted in Might, the Wise.﴾   *(Qur'an 5: 118)*»
(Ibn Mâjah and an-Nasâ'i; al-Albâni graded it as sound)

The Prophet (ﷺ) used to reflect upon the Qur'an a great deal. Ibn Ḥibbân narrated in his *Ṣaḥeeḥ* with a sound chain from 'Aṭâ',

who said: «I entered the house of 'Â'ishah (*raḍiya Allâhu 'anhâ* — may Allah be pleased with her) with 'Ubaydullâh ibn 'Umayr, and he said: Tell us about the most wondrous thing you observed from Allah's Messenger (ﷺ).

She wept and said: He got up one night, saying: O 'Â'ishah, let me worship my Lord.

I said [to him]: By Allah, I like to be near you, but I like what pleases you.

So he got up and purified himself [made ablution]; then he stood in prayer and wept until his chest was wet. He continued weeping and did not cease until the ground was wet. Bilâl came to make the call for [the dawn] prayer, and when he saw him weeping, he asked: O Messenger of Allah, you weep while Allah has forgiven all your past and future sins?

He replied: Then should I not be a grateful servant? Some verses were revealed to me tonight; woe to one who recites them and does not reflect upon them:

﴿إِنَّ فِى خَلْقِ ٱلسَّمَـٰوَٰتِ وَٱلْأَرْضِ وَٱخْتِلَـٰفِ ٱلَّيْلِ وَٱلنَّهَارِ لَأَيَـٰتٍ لِّأُوْلِى ٱلْأَلْبَـٰبِ ۝ ٱلَّذِينَ يَذْكُرُونَ ٱللَّهَ قِيَـٰمًا وَقُعُودًا وَعَلَىٰ جُنُوبِهِمْ وَيَتَفَكَّرُونَ فِى خَلْقِ ٱلسَّمَـٰوَٰتِ وَٱلْأَرْضِ ... ۝﴾   (سورة آل عِمرَان: ١٩٠-١٩١)

❰Indeed, in the creation of the heavens and the earth and the alternation of the night and the day are signs for those of understanding — who remember Allah while standing or sitting or [lying] on their sides and give thought to the creation of the heavens and the earth...❱   *(Qur'an 3: 190-191)*»
(Muslim and Ibn Ḥibbân)

This proves that it is a duty of a Muslim to reflect upon such verses.

The Qur'an contains verses about the oneness of Allah, as well as promises and threats, rulings, information, narratives, manners and morals. Its effects upon the soul are wide-ranging; there are some chapters that frighten the soul more than others, as illustrated by the Prophet's words: «*Soorah* (Chapter) *Hood* and its sisters have given me grey hair prematurely.» (Recorded by at-Tirmidhi with a sound chain of narrators)

In another narration, he said: «*Hood, al-Wâqi'ah, al-Mursalât, 'Amma Yatasâ'aloon* [soorat *an-Naba'*] and *at-Takweer*» (at-Tirmidhi; al-Albâni graded it as sound)

These chapters of the Qur'an turned the hair of Allah's Messenger (ﷺ) grey because they describe the realities of the faith and the great responsibilities that come with it. Their burden filled the heart of the Messenger (ﷺ) to the extent that the effects appeared on his hair and body.

$$﴾فَٱسْتَقِمْ كَمَآ أُمِرْتَ وَمَن تَابَ مَعَكَ ... ﴿١١٢﴾﴾ \qquad (سورة هُود: ١١٢)$$

❴So remain on a right course as you have been commanded, [you] and those who have turned back with you [to Allah]...❵

(Qur'an 11: 112)

His Companions would also recite, reflect and be affected. Abu Bakr (ﷺ) was a compassionate man with a sensitive heart. When he led the people in prayer and recited the words of Allah (ﷺ), he could not restrain himself from weeping. 'Umar (ﷺ) once fell ill from the impact of Allah's words:

$$﴾إِنَّ عَذَابَ رَبِّكَ لَوَٰقِعٌ ﴿٧﴾ مَّا لَهُۥ مِن دَافِعٍ ﴿٨﴾﴾ \qquad (سورة الطُّور: ٧-٨)$$

❨Indeed, the punishment of your Lord will occur. Of it there is no preventer.❩   *(Qur'an 52: 7-8)*[7]

His sobbing could be heard behind the rows when he recited Allah's quotation from the Prophet Jacob (ﷺ):

(سورة يُوسُف: ٨٦)   ❨... إِنَّمَآ أَشْكُوا بَثِّى وَحُزْنِىٓ إِلَى اللَّهِ ...❩ (٨٦)

❨...I only complain of my suffering and my grief to Allah...❩
(Qur'an 12: 86)[8]

'Uthmân (ﷺ) said: "If our hearts were pure, we could not get enough of the words of Allah." He was later martyred, a victim of injustice, with his blood on his Qur'an. (al-Bayhaqi)

There are numerous narrations about the Companions in this regard. Ayyoob (ﷺ) related that he heard Sa'eed bin Jubayr repeat this verse in prayer more than twenty times:

(سورة البَقَرَة: ٢٨١)   ❨وَاتَّقُوا يَوْمًا تُرْجَعُونَ فِيهِ إِلَى اللَّهِ ...❩ (٢٨١)

❨And fear a day when you will be returned to Allah...❩
(Qur'an 2: 281)[9]

It is the last verse of the Qur'an that was revealed; it ends:

❨... ثُمَّ تُوَفَّىٰ كُلُّ نَفْسٍ مَّا كَسَبَتْ وَهُمْ لَا يُظْلَمُونَ (٢٨١)❩

(سورة البَقَرَة: ٢٨١)

---

[7] The narration and its sources are found in Abu al-Fidâ' 'Imâd ad-Deen Isma'eel ibn 'Umar Ibn Katheer, *Tafseer Ibn Katheer* (Dâr ash-Sha'b), 7:406.

[8] Abul-Faraj Ibn al-Jawzi, *Manâqib 'Umar*.

[9] Muhammad ibn Ahmad ad-Dhahabi, *Siyar A'lam an-Nubalâ'* (Cairo: Dar El Hadith).

❨...Then every soul will be compensated for what it earned, and they will not be treated unjustly.❩   *(Qur'an 2: 281)*

Ibrâheem ibn Bashar said: "The verse during which 'Ali ibn al-Fadheel died was:

﴿وَلَوْ تَرَىٰٓ إِذْ وُقِفُواْ عَلَى ٱلنَّارِ فَقَالُواْ يَٰلَيْتَنَا نُرَدُّ ... ﴿٢٧﴾ ﴾   (سورة الأنعام: ٢٧)

❨If you could but see when they are made to stand before the fire and will say: Oh, would that we could be returned [to life on earth]...❩   *(Qur'an 6: 27)*

He died in that place, and I was among those who prayed at his funeral — may Allah have mercy upon him."[10]

Even during the prostrations of recitation (prostrations that the Prophet used to make after reciting specific verses), they were affected. Take the story of the man (may Allah have mercy upon him) who recited:

﴿وَيَخِرُّونَ لِلْأَذْقَانِ يَبْكُونَ وَيَزِيدُهُمْ خُشُوعًا ۩ ﴿١٠٩﴾ ﴾   (سورة الإسراء: ١٠٩)

❨And they fall upon their faces weeping, and the Qur'an increases them in humble submission.❩   *(Qur'an 17: 109)*

He prostrated there, then said, rebuking himself: "This is the prostration, but where is the weeping?"

It is most important to reflect upon the examples given in the Qur'an. This is because whenever Allah (ﷻ) gives us examples in the Qur'an, He encourages thinking and remembrance. In one place, He has said:

﴿...وَيَضْرِبُ ٱللَّهُ ٱلْأَمْثَالَ لِلنَّاسِ لَعَلَّهُمْ يَتَذَكَّرُونَ ﴿٢٥﴾ ﴾   (سورة إبراهيم: ٢٥)

---

[10] Ibid.

❨...And Allah presents examples for the people that perhaps they will be reminded.❩ *(Qur'an 14: 25)*

He has also said:

﴿ ... وَتِلْكَ ٱلْأَمْثَلُ نَضْرِبُهَا لِلنَّاسِ لَعَلَّهُمْ يَتَفَكَّرُونَ ۝ ﴾

(سورة الحَشر: ٢١)

❨...And these examples We present to the people, that perhaps they will give thought.❩ *(Qur'an 59: 21)*

One of the pious predecessors contemplated an example from the Qur'an, but its meaning was not clear to him, so he wept. When asked why, he said: "Allah, the Mighty and Majestic, says:

﴿وَتِلْكَ ٱلْأَمْثَلُ نَضْرِبُهَا لِلنَّاسِ وَمَا يَعْقِلُهَآ إِلَّا ٱلْعَلِمُونَ ۝﴾

(سورة العَنكبوت: ٤٣)

❨And these examples We present to the people, but none will understand them except those of knowledge.❩ *(Qur'an 29: 43)*

I have not understood the example, and I weep for the loss of knowledge."

Allah (ﷻ) has presented many examples to us in the Qur'an. Some of them are: the one who kindled a fire, the one who shouts at that which does not hear, the grain seed which grows seven spikes, the dog that pants, the donkey that carries volumes of books, the fly, the spider, the blind seeing and the deaf hearing, ashes blown by a strong wind, a sound tree and a rotten tree, rain falling from the sky, a niche within which is a lamp, a slave who is owned and incapable of doing anything by himself, a man owned by two quarrelling partners, and so on. We should return to the verses containing examples and give them special attention and

care, seeking to derive the lessons that Allah (ﷻ) has placed therein for us to ponder and to implement in our own lives.

Ibn al-Qayyim has summarised what a Muslim should do to treat hardness of heart with the Qur'an:

> The basis of that is in two things: first, to transfer your heart from the habitat of this world to that of the hereafter, and then to put it completely in confrontation with the meanings of the Qur'an, the elucidation of them and reflecting on them, comprehending what was intended by their revelation while taking your share from each of its verses and letting it descend upon the disease in your heart. When it has descended on the disease in your heart, it will be cured by the permission of Allah (ﷻ).

2. Consciousness of Allah's greatness, knowledge of His names and attributes; reflecting upon them and understanding their meanings

This knowledge must settle in the heart and spread to other body parts, whose deeds will express what the heart has perceived. This is because the heart is their sovereign, and they are its soldiers; thus, they are sound when it is sound, and they are corrupt when it is corrupt.

The words from the Qur'an and Sunnah concerning Allah's grandeur are many. When the Muslims contemplate them, their hearts tremble and their souls become humble before the Most High, the Most Great. The limbs submit to the All-Hearing and All-Knowing, and they increase in humility before the Lord of the first and last generations. This is due to the awareness of His many names and attributes, for He is the Most Great, the Controller, the Compeller, the Superior, the Powerful, the Prevailing, the Grand

and the Exalted. He is the Living who does not die, while the *jinn* (non-human, rational beings created by Allah from fire, often referred to as 'demons' or 'devils') and humankind die. He is the Subjugator over His servants. Even the angels and the thunder praise Him, from fear of Him. He is the Mighty Avenger, the Sustainer who sleeps not, who encompasses all things in His knowledge and who knows what deceives the eyes and what the breasts conceal. He has described the vastness of His knowledge by saying:

﴿۞ وَعِندَهُۥ مَفَاتِحُ ٱلْغَيْبِ لَا يَعْلَمُهَآ إِلَّا هُوَ وَيَعْلَمُ مَا فِى ٱلْبَرِّ وَٱلْبَحْرِ وَمَا تَسْقُطُ مِن وَرَقَةٍ إِلَّا يَعْلَمُهَا وَلَا حَبَّةٍ فِى ظُلُمَٰتِ ٱلْأَرْضِ وَلَا رَطْبٍ وَلَا يَابِسٍ إِلَّا فِى كِتَٰبٍ مُّبِينٍ ٥٩﴾

(سورة الأنعام: ٥٩)

﴿And with Him are the keys of the unseen; none knows them except Him. And He knows what is on the land and in the sea. Not a leaf falls but that He knows it. And no grain is there within the darkness of the earth and no moist or dry [thing] but that it is [written] in a clear record.﴾ *(Qur'an 6: 59)*

Of His greatness is what He informed us about Himself:

﴿وَمَا قَدَرُوا۟ ٱللَّهَ حَقَّ قَدْرِهِۦ وَٱلْأَرْضُ جَمِيعًا قَبْضَتُهُۥ يَوْمَ ٱلْقِيَٰمَةِ وَٱلسَّمَٰوَٰتُ مَطْوِيَّٰتٌ بِيَمِينِهِۦ سُبْحَٰنَهُۥ وَتَعَٰلَىٰ عَمَّا يُشْرِكُونَ ٦٧﴾

(سورة الزُّمَر: ٦٧)

﴿They have not appraised Allah with true appraisal [appreciation of His attributes], while the earth entirely will be [within] His grip on the Day of Resurrection, and the heavens will be folded in His right hand.﴾ *(Qur'an 39: 67)*

Allah's Messenger (ﷺ) said: «Allah will take hold of the earth on the Day of Resurrection and fold up the heavens in His right hand. Then He will say: I am the Sovereign. Where are the kings of the earth?» (Bukhari)

The mind dissolves and the heart trembles when contemplating the story of Moses (ﷺ), when he said:

$$ \text{﴿...رَبِّ أَرِنِي أَنظُرْ إِلَيْكَ قَالَ لَن تَرَانِي وَلَٰكِنِ أَنظُرْ إِلَى ٱلْجَبَلِ فَإِنِ ٱسْتَقَرَّ مَكَانَهُ فَسَوْفَ تَرَانِي فَلَمَّا تَجَلَّىٰ رَبُّهُ لِلْجَبَلِ جَعَلَهُ دَكًّا وَخَرَّ مُوسَىٰ صَعِقًا ... ﴿١٤٣﴾﴾} $$

(سورة الأعراف: ١٤٣)

❴...My Lord, show me [Yourself] that I may look at You. So Allah said: You will not see Me, but look at the mountain; if it should remain in place, then you will see Me. But when his Lord appeared to the mountain, He rendered it level and Moses fell unconscious...❵   *(Qur'an 7: 143)*

When the Prophet (ﷺ) explained this verse, he recited it and said, gesturing with his hand: «Thus [and he put his thumb on the highest joint of the little finger and then said:] the mountain sank.» (at-Tirmidhi; al-Albâni graded it as sound)

This means that Allah (ﷺ) only appeared to that small extent, yet this was enough to cause the mountain to sink into the ground.

The Prophet (ﷺ) described Allah (ﷺ) thus: «His screen is light; if He should remove it, the splendour of His Face would burn His creation to the extent of His vision.» (Muslim)

The Messenger (ﷺ) spoke of Allah's grandeur, saying: «When Allah decrees a matter in the heavens, the angels beat with their wings in compliance with His word like a chain upon stone until:

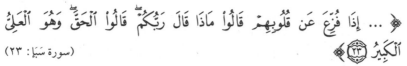

(٢٣ :سَبَإٍ سورة)

❨...when terror is removed from their hearts, they will say [to one another]: What has your Lord said? They will say: The truth — and He is the Most High, the Grand.❩ *(Qur'an 34: 23)* »(Bukhari)

There are many more texts on this subject; the bottom line is that consciousness of Allah's grandeur through contemplation of these texts and others is among the most beneficial components in the treatment of weak faith.

Ibn al-Qayyim described the greatness of Allah (ﷻ) in sweet and beautiful words. He said:

> He manages the affairs of His subjects; He orders and prohibits, He creates and provides, He causes death and life, He honours and humiliates, and He rotates the night and the day. He alternates days [of varying conditions] among the people, and He overthrows nations, doing away with one and producing another. His command and authority are in effect throughout the regions of the heavens and on the earth and whatever is upon it and beneath it or in the seas or the air. He has encompassed everything in knowledge and counted all things in number. His hearing is inclusive of all sounds; no voice is unrecognised by Him or obscure to Him. He hears the clamour in their different languages for their various needs, and He is not distracted by hearing one from hearing another. He is not confused by numerous requests and is not weary of the persistent demand of those in need. His vision encompasses all that is visible; He sees the movement of a black ant upon a massive rock during a dark night. The unseen to Him is seen, and the secret to Him is known.

﴿يَسۡـَٔلُهُۥ مَن فِي ٱلسَّمَٰوَٰتِ وَٱلۡأَرۡضِۚ كُلَّ يَوۡمٍ هُوَ فِي شَأۡنٍ ٢٩﴾   (سورة الرّحمٰن : ٢٩)

﴾Whoever is within the heavens and earth asks Him; each day He is bringing about a matter [for each of His creatures].﴿

(Qur'an 55: 29)

— forgiving a sin, relieving an anxiety, removing a distress, comforting a broken individual, enriching a poor person, guiding one who is lost, directing one who is confused, helping one who is in trouble, feeding one who is hungry, clothing one who is naked, curing one who is ill, freeing one from a trial, accepting one who repents, rewarding one who does good, supporting one who is oppressed, breaking a tyrant, covering a fault, relieving a fear, and raising the positions of some and lowering others.

If all the inhabitants of His heavens and earth, from the first of His creation to the last of them, humans and jinn, were as righteous as the heart of the most righteous man among them, it would not increase anything of His dominion. By the same token, if the first of His creation and the last of them, humans and jinn, were as wicked as the heart of the most wicked man among them, it would not decrease anything of His dominion. If all the inhabitants of His heavens and earth, humans and jinn, whether alive or dead, moist or dry, stood in one place and asked something of Him, and He gave all of them what they asked for, it would not decrease what He has by even an atom's weight.

He is the First, preceded by nothing, and the Last, followed by nothing; the Ascendant, with nothing above Him; and the Intimate, with nothing nearer than Him. Blessed and exalted is He, having the most right to be remembered and worshipped, the most worthy of gratitude, most gracious of rulers, and most generous of anyone asked. He is the Sovereign having no partners, the unique

with no equal, the Eternal Recourse without [need of] offspring, the Sublime with nothing resembling Him. Everything will be destroyed except His countenance, and everything will cease except His sovereignty.

He cannot be obeyed except by His permission and cannot be disobeyed except according to His knowledge; He rewards obedience and forgives disobedience. Every affliction from Him is just, and every blessing from Him is a favour. He is the nearest witness and the closest guardian. He controls all creatures, registers all effects, and decrees all life spans. Hearts are manifest to Him, and a secret is the same as an announcement. His gift is a word, and His punishment is a word:

$$﴿إِنَّمَآ أَمْرُهُۥٓ إِذَآ أَرَادَ شَيْئًا أَن يَقُولَ لَهُۥ كُن فَيَكُونُ ۝﴾ \quad (سورة يَس: ٨٢)$$

❴His command is only when He intends a thing that He says to it: Be, and it is.❵ *(Qur'an 36: 82)*[11]

3. Seeking religious knowledge

This knowledge leads to imbibing fear of Allah (ﷻ) and additional faith in Him as He, the Exalted, has said:

$$﴿ ... إِنَّمَا يَخْشَى اللَّهَ مِنْ عِبَادِهِ الْعُلَمَٰٓؤُاْ إِنَّ اللَّهَ عَزِيزٌ غَفُورٌ ۝﴾$$

$$(سورة فَاطِر: ٢٨)$$

❴...Only those fear Allah, from among His servants, who have knowledge...❵ *(Qur'an 35: 28)*

---

[11] Adapted from Ibn Qayyim al-Jawziyah, *Al-Wâbil as-Sayyib wa Râfi' al-Kalim aṭ-Ṭayyib* (Maktaba Dâr al-Bayyân).

Not equal in faith are those who know and those who do not know. Consider the state of the one who knows the details of Islamic law; the meaning of the two testimonials of faith (that there is none worthy of worship other than Allah and that Muhammad is the Messenger of Allah) and their requirements; the details of what occurs after death, the torment in the grave, the terrors and scenes of the resurrection and gathering; the pleasure of paradise and torment of hellfire; the wisdom of Islamic law regarding what is permitted and prohibited; the details of the Prophet's biography; and so on. Compare such an individual with the one who has little or no knowledge of Islam. How could such a person be equal to the ones who are ignorant of the religion: its rulings and its revelations regarding matters that are not apparent? Their share of religion is merely imitation, and their knowledge is of poor quality.

﴿ ... قُلْ هَلْ يَسْتَوِى ٱلَّذِينَ يَعْلَمُونَ وَٱلَّذِينَ لَا يَعْلَمُونَ ... ﴾   (سورة الزُّمَر : ٩)

◖...Say: Are those who know equal to those who do not know?...◗
(Qur'an 39: 9)

4. Regular attendance at circles of dhikr (remembering Allah through praising and supplicating to Him)

This leads to an increase of faith for several reasons, among which are: the remembrance of Allah (ﷻ), being covered by mercy, the descent of tranquillity, being surrounded by the angels, Allah's mention of the group among the highest company, His pride with them before the angels, and His forgiveness of their sins, as mentioned in authentic hadiths such as: «No group sits remembering [or mentioning] Allah except that the angels surround them, mercy covers them, tranquillity descends upon

them, and Allah mentions them among those with Him.»
(Muslim)

Sahl ibn al-Handhaliyah (رضي) reported that the Messenger of
Allah (ﷺ) said: «No people meet for remembrance and then
separate but that they are told: Arise forgiven.» (aṭ-Ṭabarâni and
Aḥmad; al-Albâni graded it as sound)

Ibn al-Ḥajar said: What is meant by the remembrance of Allah
and intended from it is perseverance in doing the deeds that He
made obligatory and that He encouraged, such as recitation of the
Qur'an, reading Hadith and group study.[12]

Another evidence that gatherings of remembrance increase
faith is a hadith related from Handhalah al-Usaydi (رضي), who said:
«Abu Bakr (رضي) met me and asked: How are you, Handhalah?

I replied: Handhalah has become a hypocrite.

IIc exclaimed: *Subḥân Allâh!* (Glory be to Allah!) What are
you saying?

I explained: When we are with the Messenger of Allah (ﷺ), he
reminds us of hellfire and paradise as if we were eyewitnesses;
after we leave him, though, our wives, children and occupations
overcome us, so we forget much.

Abu Bakr (رضي) said: By Allah, the same happens to me.

Abu Bakr (رضي) and I went to the Messenger of Allah (ﷺ). I
said: Handhalah has become a hypocrite, O Messenger of Allah.

---

[12] Aḥmad ibn 'Ali Ibn Ḥajar al-'Asqalâni, *Fatḥ al-Bâri Sharḥ Ṣaḥeeḥ al-
Bukhâri.* (Riyadh: Darussalam). Incessant group repetition of particular names
of Allah (ﷺ) or other formulas, which has been named 'dhikr' by the Sufis
and their followers among the common people and supposedly serves to
'empty the heart of all else', was not known to be a practice of the Prophet
(ﷺ) or his Companions. (Editor)

He asked: And how is that?

I replied: When we are with you, you remind us of hellfire and paradise as though we are eyewitnesses. After we leave you, though, our wives, children and occupations overcome us, so we forget much.

The Messenger of Allah (ﷺ) said: By Him in whose Hand is my soul, if you should always be as you are with me and in constant remembrance, the angels would shake your hands in your homes and streets. But Handhalah, there is a time for this and a time for that. [He repeated it three times].» (Muslim)

The Companions (may Allah be pleased with them) were very keen to sit together and remember Allah (ﷺ). They would refer to this as belief, as Mu'âdh (ﷺ) said to a man: "Let us sit and believe for a while." [13]

5. Doing many righteous deeds and filling one's time with them

This is an important matter, as its effect on strengthening faith makes it one of the greatest cures. A great example is found in Abu Bakr aṣ-Ṣiddeeq (ﷺ).

«One day, the Messenger (ﷺ) asked his Companions: Who among you began his morning today by fasting?

Abu Bakr (ﷺ) replied: I did.

He inquired: Who among you accompanied a funeral procession today?

Abu Bakr (ﷺ) said: I did.

---

[13] An authentic narration quoted by al-Albâni, *Arba' Masâ'il fil-Eemân,* 72.

He queried: Who among you fed a poor person today?

Abu Bakr (رضي) answered: I did.

He asked: Who among you visited a sick person today?

Abu Bakr (رضي) replied: I did.

The Messenger of Allah (ﷺ) said: These [virtues] are not combined in a person but that he will enter paradise.» (Muslim)

This narration shows that aṣ-Ṣiddeeq (رضي) was eager to take advantage of opportunities and practice different kinds of worship. Since the question came unexpectedly from the Prophet (ﷺ), it showed that Abu Bakr's days were filled with good deeds. The members of the three best generations after the Prophet (ﷺ) attained a high degree in the additional performance of righteous deeds, as illustrated by what was reported about some of them. For instance, Imam 'Abdur-Raḥmân ibn Mahdi said that if Ḥammâd ibn Salâmah was told that he was going to die tomorrow, he would not be able to increase his deeds at all.[14]

A Muslim should observe certain etiquette pertaining to righteous deeds:

a) Hastening to perform them. Allah, the Exalted, has said:

$$ \text{﴿} \circledast \text{ وَسَارِعُوٓا۟ إِلَىٰ مَغْفِرَةٍ مِّن رَّبِّكُمْ وَجَنَّةٍ عَرْضُهَا ٱلسَّمَـٰوَٰتُ وَٱلْأَرْضُ} $$

$$ \text{...} \circledast \text{﴾} \qquad (سورة آل عِمرَان: ١٣٣) $$

❴And hasten to forgiveness from your Lord and a garden [meaning paradise] as wide as the heavens and earth...❵

(Qur'an 3: 133)

---

[14] ad-Dhahabi, *Siyar A'lam an-Nubalâ'*.

$$﴾سَابِقُوٓا إِلَىٰ مَغْفِرَةٍ مِّن رَّبِّكُمْ وَجَنَّةٍ عَرْضُهَا كَعَرْضِ ٱلسَّمَآءِ وَٱلْأَرْضِ ...﴿$$

(سورة الحديد: ٢١)   ﴿۲۱﴾

﴿Race toward forgiveness from your Lord and a garden whose width is like the width of the heavens and earth...﴿

(Qur'an 57: 21)

The meaning behind these verses motivated the Prophet's Companions to compete with each other in terms of doing good deeds. Anas ibn Mâlik (ﷺ) related this hadith about the battle of Badr, when the polytheists had come close to victory: «The Prophet (ﷺ) said: Arise to paradise, which is as wide as the heavens and earth!

'Umayr ibn al-Humam al-Anṣâri asked: O Messenger of Allah, paradise as wide as the heavens and earth?

He replied: Yes.

'Umayr exclaimed: Great!

The Messenger of Allah (ﷺ) asked: What made you say: Great?

He answered: By Allah, it was only the hope that I could be among its inhabitants.

He said: Indeed, you are among its inhabitants.

'Umayr took out some dates from his container and began to eat them, then said: If I live to eat these dates of mine, it will indeed be a long life. He threw aside his dates and fought until he was martyred.» (Muslim)

Previously, Prophet Moses (ﷺ) had hurried to the meeting with his Lord and said:

﴿ ... وَعَجِلْتُ إِلَيْكَ رَبِّ لِتَرْضَىٰ ﴿٨٤﴾ ﴾   (سورة طه: ٨٤)

﴿...I hastened to You, my Lord, that You be pleased.﴾

(Qur'an 20: 84)

Allah (ﷻ) has also praised Zachariah (ﷺ) and his family, saying:

﴿ ... إِنَّهُمْ كَانُوا يُسَـٰرِعُونَ فِي ٱلْخَيْرَٰتِ وَيَدْعُونَنَا رَغَبًا وَرَهَبًا
وَكَانُوا لَنَا خَـٰشِعِينَ ﴿٩٠﴾ ﴾   (سورة الأنبياء: ٩٠)

﴿...Indeed, they used to hasten to good deeds and supplicate Us in hope and fear, and were to Us humbly submissive.﴾

(Qur'an 21: 90)

The Prophet (ﷺ) said: «Deliberation in all things is good unless it is in doing a deed for the hereafter.» (Abu Dâwood; al-Albâni graded it as sound)

b) Continuing to perform them

The Messenger (ﷺ) quoted the following from his Lord in a sacred hadith: «My servant does not cease drawing near to Me through additional worship until I love him.» (Bukhari)

The words 'does not cease' show continuation.

The Prophet (ﷺ) said: «Follow up between Hajj and 'umrah.» (Muslim)

This also means continuation. This is an important principle regarding the strengthening of faith and caring for the soul, and preventing it from inactivity and stagnation. Continual worship, even if it is a little, is preferable to a great amount that is discontinued after a couple of times. Consistent performance of good deeds strengthens one's faith.

When the Prophet (ﷺ) was asked which deeds are most loved by Allah, he said: «The most regular of them, even if they are few.» (Bukhari)

«When he practiced an act of worship, he made it permanent.» (Muslim)

c) Expending effort

Treatment for hard-heartedness cannot be a temporary one, where faith improves for a while and then returns to weakness. Instead, there must be a constant renewal of faith, and this is not possible unless effort is spent in worship.

Allah (ﷻ) has mentioned in His book the efforts of those who are close to Him and their conditions:

﴿إِنَّمَا يُؤْمِنُ بِـَٔايَٰتِنَا ٱلَّذِينَ إِذَا ذُكِّرُواْ بِهَا خَرُّواْ سُجَّدًا وَسَبَّحُواْ بِحَمْدِ رَبِّهِمْ وَهُمْ لَا يَسْتَكْبِرُونَ ۩ تَتَجَافَىٰ جُنُوبُهُمْ عَنِ ٱلْمَضَاجِعِ يَدْعُونَ رَبَّهُمْ خَوْفًا وَطَمَعًا وَمِمَّا رَزَقْنَٰهُمْ يُنفِقُونَ ۝﴾ (سورة السَّجْدَة: ١٥-١٦)

❝Only those believe in Our verses who, when they are reminded by them, fall down in prostration and exalt [Allah] with praise of their Lord, and they are not arrogant. They arise from [their] beds; they supplicate their Lord in fear and aspiration, and from what We have provided them, they spend.❞   *(Qur'an 32: 15-16)*

﴿كَانُواْ قَلِيلًا مِّنَ ٱلَّيْلِ مَا يَهْجَعُونَ ۝ وَبِٱلْأَسْحَارِ هُمْ يَسْتَغْفِرُونَ ۝ وَفِىٓ أَمْوَٰلِهِمْ حَقٌّ لِّلسَّآئِلِ وَٱلْمَحْرُومِ ۝﴾ (سورة الذَّارِيَات: ١٧-١٩)

❝They used to sleep but little of the night, and in the hours before dawn they would ask forgiveness, and from their properties was

[given] the right of the [needy] petitioner and the deprived.﴾

(Qur'an 51: 17-19)

Observing the state of our righteous predecessors and how they attained the attributes of worshippers brings about wonder and motivates one to follow their footsteps. They used to complete one-seventh of the Qur'an daily and stay up during the nights before campaigns and battles, praising Allah (ﷻ) and praying. Even when imprisoned, they would align their feet, their tears would fall, and they would contemplate the creation of the heavens and earth.

One of them would pretend to sleep — as a woman does with her child — and when he was sure his wife was asleep, he would slip out of her bed for night prayers. They would divide the night between their families and themselves, and spend their days fasting, learning, teaching, accompanying funerals, visiting the sick, and helping people. Some of them would go years without missing a prayer in congregation with the imam. Their hearts were attached to the mosques; they would await one prayer after another. One of them looked after his brother's family for years after his brother's death, spending to maintain them; this increased his faith.

d) Keeping the soul from becoming weary

Consistency in worship and effort therein does not mean exposing oneself to monotony and boredom; it only means not discontinuing worship. Muslims can strike a balance between the two extremes by taking upon themselves only those acts of worship that they can sustain. They aim to pursue them and work hard when they find themselves enthusiastic, while remaining moderate during intermissions. A collection of hadiths points to

these concepts, among them: «Indeed, the religion is ease, and anyone who overdoes the religion will be defeated by it, so aim for and pursue a middle course...» (Bukhari)

In another narration: «...and you will reach the objective.» (Bukhari)

In a chapter on what is disliked regarding exaggeration in worship, Bukhari (may Allah have mercy upon him) reported that Anas (رضي الله عنه) said: «The Prophet (صلى الله عليه وسلم) once entered the mosque and found a rope tied between two pillars. He asked: What is this rope? They replied: It is a rope for Zaynab — when she becomes tired, she grasps it for support. The Prophet (صلى الله عليه وسلم) said: No, untie it. Let people pray when they are energetic, but when they become tired, they should sit down.» (Bukhari)

When the Prophet (صلى الله عليه وسلم) found out that 'Abdullâh ibn 'Amr ibn al-'Âs (رضي الله عنه) prayed the whole night and fasted consecutively for many days, he forbade him from that and clarified the reason, saying: «For if you do that, your eyes will become sunken and your soul fatigued.» (Bukhari, Muslim, an-Nasâ'i and Ahmad)

The Messenger of Allah (صلى الله عليه وسلم) also said: «Take upon yourselves whatever deeds you can sustain, for Allah, the Mighty and Majestic, does not become uninterested although you do. Indeed, the deeds most loved by Allah are the most regular, even if few.» (Bukhari, an-Nasâ'i, Ahmad and Abu Dâwood)

e) Making up for what was missed

'Umar ibn al-Khattâb (رضي الله عنه) reported that the Prophet (صلى الله عليه وسلم) said: «If one sleeps without reciting his portion of the Qur'an at night, or part of it, but then recites it between the dawn prayer and the noon prayer — it will be recorded for him as though he had recited it during the night.» (Muslim)

'Â'ishah (ﷺ) said: «When the Messenger of Allah (ﷺ) prayed a prayer, he would be regular about it; and when he missed getting up for prayer at night, having been overcome by sleep or pain, he would pray twelve *raka'ât* (units of formal prayer) during the day.» (Aḥmad and Muslim)

In another narration: «When he slept at night or was ill, he prayed twelve raka'ât during the day.» (Muslim)

When Umm Salamah (ﷺ) saw him praying two raka'ât after the late afternoon prayer, she asked him about it, and he (ﷺ) replied: «O daughter of Abu Umayah, you asked about two raka'ât after the late afternoon prayer. Some people from 'Abdul-Qays came and kept me occupied so that I missed the two raka'ât after the noon prayer; they are those two.» (Bukhari)

When he did not pray four raka'ât before the noon prayer, he prayed them after it. (at-Tirmidhi; al-Albâni graded it as 'reliable but odd')

These hadiths are evidence for making up sunnah prayers.

Ibn al-Qayyim has mentioned three meanings concerning the Prophet's fasting in Sha'bân more than other months. Two of them are:
(a) he used to fast three days of every month; perhaps during some months he was prevented from fasting, so he combined them and fasted them all in Sha'bân instead,
(b) in order to do it before the obligatory fast of Ramadan. (Muslim and Abu Dâwood)

Also, during the last ten days of Ramadan, the Prophet (ﷺ) used to stay in the mosque for the purpose of worship. One year, he was unable to do so due to travelling, so he did it the following year for twenty days. (Bukhari)

f) Hoping for acceptance while fearing the opposite

After doing their best in acts of obedience, believers should still fear that their deeds might not be accepted due to some fault in performance, intent or attitude known only to Allah (ﷻ).

«'Â'ishah (ﺭ) reported: I asked the Messenger of Allah (ﷺ) about this verse:

(سورة المؤمنون: ٦٠)   ﴿وَٱلَّذِينَ يُؤْتُونَ مَآ ءَاتَوا۟ وَّقُلُوبُهُمْ وَجِلَةٌ ... ۝﴾

﴾And they who give what they give while their hearts are fearful...﴿   *(Qur'an 23: 60)*

Are they the ones who drink intoxicants and steal?

He replied: No, O daughter of aṣ-Ṣiddeeq, they are those who fast and pray and give charity while fearing that it will not be accepted from them. Those are the ones who race to good deeds.» (at-Tirmidhi; al-Albâni graded it as sound)

Abu ad-Dardâ' (ﺭ) was quoted as saying: "To be certain that Allah had accepted from me a single prayer would be more pleasing to me than the world and whatever is in it, for He says:

(سورة المَائدة: ٢٧)   ﴿ ... إِنَّمَا يَتَقَبَّلُ ٱللَّهُ مِنَ ٱلْمُتَّقِينَ ۝﴾

﴾...Allah only accepts from the righteous [who fear Him].﴿
(Qur'an 5: 27)"[15]

Among the attributes of believers is that they consider themselves unworthy before Allah (ﷻ).

The Prophet (ﷺ) said: «If a man were to be dragged on his face from the day he was born to the day he died in old age, seeking the

---

[15] Ibn Katheer, *Tafseer Ibn Katheer.*

pleasure of Allah (🕮), he would see it as insignificant on the Day of Resurrection.» (Aḥmad; al-Albâni graded it as reliable)

Those who know Allah (🕮) as well as themselves will be certain that whatever they have to offer is not sufficient, even if they could bring together all the deeds of human beings and jinn. They know that Allah (🕮) accepts them because of His generosity and favour and rewards them out of His generosity and favour.

6. Diversifying types of worship

It is from Allah's mercy and His wisdom that He has varied for us the kinds of worship we can do. Some are done with the body, such as prayer; some through wealth, like giving charity; some with both, like Hajj; and some by the tongue, such as praise and supplication.

Even within one type are both obligations and desirable sunnahs. For example, within the different types of prayers, there are prayers of different ranks: such as the regular sunnah prayers of twelve units in a day and some of lower rank, such as the four sunnah before the late afternoon prayer and the optional mid- to late morning prayer. There are some of higher rank, such as the optional late night prayers, which take different forms as well; within them there is prayer of two or four raka'ât at a time, followed by a single raka'ah of supererogatory prayer and sometimes five, seven or nine units, with only one sitting in the prayer, and so on.

The one who keeps track of the acts of worship will find great diversity in their numbers, times, forms, attributes and rulings. Perhaps the wisdom behind this is to prevent the soul from becoming bored and to enable it to find something new. In

addition, not everyone is equal in terms of concentration and ability. Some may enjoy the performance of certain kinds of worship more than others. Perfect is He who has assigned the doors to paradise according to the types of worship, as mentioned in the hadith of Abu Hurayrah (رضي الله عنه) where the Messenger of Allah (ﷺ) said: «Whoever spends repeatedly in the cause of Allah will be called from the doors to paradise: O servant of Allah, this is good! Those of the people of prayer will be called from the door of prayer; those of the people of jihad will be called from the door of jihad; those of the people of fasting will be called from the door named ar-Rayyân, and those of the people of charity will be called from the door of charity.» (Bukhari)

This hadith refers to those people who continuously perform additional, voluntary worship of each kind specified in the hadith. Obligatory duties, of course, must be done by everyone.

The Prophet (ﷺ) said: «The parent is the central door to paradise.» (A sound hadith recorded by at-Tirmidhi)

Kindness to parents, which is another form of worship, can increase faith. It is also simple to implement continuously.

One may benefit from this diversity in the treatment of weak faith by increasing those forms of worship to which the soul is inclined, while regularly performing the obligations ordained by Allah (ﷻ). When inspecting texts about worship, Muslims will find that there are unique things that can be done to increase faith. These have subtle meanings and effects on the soul, and through them, people can single out their weaknesses and focus on improving their ability to strengthen their faith. Here are two examples:

a) Abu Dharr (رضي الله عنه) narrated that the Prophet (ﷺ) said: «There are

three whom Allah loves and three whom Allah hates. Among those whom Allah loves is a man who confronts the enemy in a company and plants himself firmly, fighting against them until he is killed or his companions are granted victory. Another is the one who is travelling with people far into the night until they long to touch ground [to rest]; when they halt, he foregoes [sleep] and prays and then awakens them for departure. And [the third is] a man who has a neighbour who annoys him, and he patiently bears his annoyance until they are separated by death or departure.» (Aḥmad; al-Albâni graded it as sound)

b) A man came to the Prophet (ﷺ) complaining of harshness in his heart. He said to him: «Would you like your heart to be softened and to attain your need? Show mercy to the orphan, stroke his head and feed him from your food. Your heart will be softened, and you will get what you need.» (Recorded by Aḥmad with a sound chain of narrators)

This is a direct attestation concerning the treatment of weak faith.

7. Fear of a bad end,

which motivates Muslims to obediently do acts of worship and renews faith in their hearts. A bad end [while dying] has many causes. Among them is a weak level of faith, leading to preoccupation with disobedient ways. The Prophet (ﷺ) illustrated such deaths in the following hadith: «Whoever kills himself with an iron [knife or sword] will have it in his hand, thrusting it into himself in hellfire forever. Whoever drinks poison and kills himself will sip it in hellfire eternally. Whoever throws himself from a mountain and kills himself will be falling [continuously] in hellfire forever.» (Muslim)

Such occurrences did take place during the time of the Prophet (ﷺ). «There was a man who fought most bravely on behalf of the Muslims in a battle. The Prophet (ﷺ) looked at him and said: If anyone would like to see a man from the people of the fire, let him look at this (brave man). One of the Muslims followed him, and he was fighting fiercely against the pagans until he was wounded. Then he hastened to end his life by placing his sword between his breasts and throwing his weight onto it until it came out between his shoulders.» (Bukhari)

The scholars have recorded a number of incidents where bad endings affected people. Ibn al-Qayyim mentioned in his book *ad-Dâ' wad-Dawâ' (The Disease and the Medication)*:

Someone was told at the time of death to say *Lâ ilâha illâ Allâh* (there is no God worthy of worship besides Allah), but he replied: "I cannot." Another was told to say *Lâ ilâha illâ Allâh*, but he began to sing deliriously. A businessman whose commerce had diverted him from the remembrance of Allah (ﷺ) was told, when death approached him, to say *Lâ ilâha illâ Allâh*, but he started saying: "This piece is good; this is up to your standards; this can be bought cheaply," until he died.

It is also related:

One of the soldiers of the king, an-Nâṣir, was on the verge of death, so his son told him to say *Lâ ilâha illâ Allâh*, but he said: "An-Nâṣir is my lord." The son repeated it again to him, but his father kept on saying: "An-Nâṣir is my lord, an-Nâṣir is my lord;" then he died.

Someone else was told to say *Lâ ilâha illâ Allâh*, but he started saying: "Fix such-and-such in that house, and do such-and-such in that garden." A usurer was told at death to say *Lâ ilâha illâ Allâh*,

but he said: "Ten for eleven," repeating it until he died. Some people also turn blackish or turn their faces away from the direction of prayer.[16]

Ibn al-Jawzi said: "Indeed, I heard someone whom I thought had much goodness saying on the eve of his death: 'It is my Lord who was unjust to me.' Exalted is Allah above what he said — on his deathbed, he accused Allah of injustice!"

Then Ibn al-Jawzi said: "I have not ceased to be disturbed and preoccupied with making preparations to meet that day."[17]

Subhân Allâh! How many lessons of this sort have people witnessed? And what is hidden from them of the dying person's condition is even greater.[18]

8. Frequent remembrance of death

The Messenger (ﷺ) has said: «Remember often the destroyer of pleasures: death.» (at-Tirmidhi; al-Albâni graded it as 'reliable but odd')

Remembering death inhibits disobedience and softens the hard heart. For everyone who remembers it during life's restrictions, things become easier. For everyone who remembers it during ease, things become restrictive. One of the greatest reminders of death is visiting graves; therefore, the Prophet (ﷺ) ordered visiting the graveyards and said: «I had prohibited you from visiting graves; however, visit them [now], for it makes the heart

---

[16] Ibn Qayyim al-Jawziyah, *Ad-Dâ' wad-Dawâ'* (Beirut: Dar at-Tawzee wan-Nashr ul-Islamia).

[17] Abul-Faraj Ibn al-Jawzi, *Sayd al-Khâṭir* (Al-Maktabat-ul-Asriya, 2004).

[18] al-Jawziyah, *ad-Dâ' wad-Dawâ'*.

tender, enables the eye to shed tears, and reminds one of the hereafter. Do not say anything evil.» (Recorded by Aḥmad with an acceptable grade)

It is even permissible for Muslims to visit the cemeteries of non-Muslims for the purpose of being admonished and warned. The proof of that is in the authentic narration in which the Prophet (ﷺ) visited his mother's grave; he wept and caused those around him to weep as well. Then he said: «I asked the permission of my Lord to seek forgiveness for her, but He did not give it to me. And I asked His permission to visit her grave, and He permitted me. So visit the graves, for it reminds one of death.» (Muslim)

Visiting graves is among the greatest means of softening the heart; it benefits the visitor with the remembrance of death and benefits the dead through the supplication of the living for them. Among the supplications from the Sunnah is that of the Prophet (ﷺ): «Peace be upon you, people of the abode from the believers and Muslims, and may Allah have mercy upon those who have gone before and those who went later. And we will be joining you, Allah willing.» (Muslim)

Those who decide to visit should adopt proper manners and ensure that their presence is heartfelt; the intention should be to seek Allah's acceptance. They should also seek to purify the corruption in their hearts by deriving a lesson from those who are now under the ground, severed from family and friends.

Let the visitors contemplate the state of those who have left their brothers, sisters and associates, who had once entertained hopes and collected wealth — how their hopes ended and their wealth was of no avail; how the ground erased the beauty of their faces; how they disintegrated in the graves; and how their spouses

are now widowed and their children orphans. Let them remember the peril of being deceived by material means, good health, youth and fondness for diversions and amusements. Let the visitors remember that they will certainly become like the ones whom they loved and who are now deceased. Let them think about the state of a dead person: how his legs are destroyed, his eyes melt and ooze, the worms eat his tongue and the dust consumes his teeth.[19]

O you who listens to the caller to misery
While having been called by two announcers of death:
  grey hair and old-age,
If you should not hear the reminder
Then for what are two attentive ones in your head:
  the ears and the eyes?
The deaf and blind is not but a man
Unguided by two guides: vision and narration.
Neither time will remain nor the world
Nor the highest heavenly bodies nor the shining
  of the sun and moon.
The two residents: desert and city dwellers,
Will surely travel from the world, even if unwilling to leave it.[20]

Those who remember death often will be favoured with three things: quick repentance, a satisfied heart and energetic worship. Those who forget death will be penalised with three things: procrastination of repentance, discontentment with what is sufficient, and laziness in worship.

---

[19] Abu 'Abdullâh al-Qurtubi, *at-Tadhkirah* (Egypt: Dâr al-Manârah).

[20] Verses [in Arabic] by 'Abdullâh ibn Muhammad al-Andulusi ash-Shantreeni in Ibn Katheer, *Tafseer Ibn Katheer*.

The soul is also affected by observing those who are dying. When one looks at dying persons, witnessing their agonies and struggles and reflecting upon their form after death, he or she will find that which deprives the soul of pleasures, prevents the eye from sleeping and the body from resting, motivates good work and increases effort.

Al-Ḥasan al-Baṣri (may Allah have mercy on him) once visited a sick man and found him in the throes of death. After observing his distress and the severity of his affliction, he returned to his family with changed colour. They said to him: "Eat, may Allah have mercy upon you." He said: "O people, take your food and drink. By Allah, I have seen a death such as I will continue to work [in preparation] for, until I encounter it."[21]

To complete one's perception of death is performance of the funeral prayer, carrying the body, taking it to the graveyard, burying the deceased, and covering him or her with earth, which brings to mind the hereafter. The Prophet (ﷺ) said: «Visit the sick and accompany funerals; it will remind you of the hereafter.» (Recorded by Aḥmad with a strong chain of narration)

In addition, there is a great reward for accompanying a funeral procession. The Prophet (ﷺ) mentioned: «Whoever is present at a funeral from its house [and in another narration: Whoever follows the funeral of a Muslim out of faith and seeking Allah's reward] until he prays the funeral prayer will have one measure, and whoever is present until burial will have two measures of reward. Someone asked: O Messenger of Allah, what are the two measures? He (ﷺ) replied: As much as two great mountains. [And

---

[21] al-Qurtubi, *at-Tadhkirah.*

in another narration: Each measure is like Mount Uḥud.]»
(Bukhari and Muslim)[22]

When the early scholars gave advice to people who had
committed sins, they used to remind them of death. During the
assembly of one of these scholars, a man mentioned another in a
bad way. The scholar said to the man who was backbiting:
"Remember the cotton they will place over your eyes!" referring
to the time of shrouding after death.

9. Remembering the stations of the hereafter

Ibn al-Qayyim said:

When one's thought is sound, it imposes vision upon him and
it is light within the heart. With it, he will perceive Allah's
promise and threat, paradise and hellfire, and what Allah (ﷻ)
has prepared therein for His dear ones and for His enemies. He
will visualise the people when they have been brought out of
their graves, racing toward the call of truth while the angels of
the heavens have descended and surrounded them and Allah
(ﷻ) has come and established His place for the final
judgement. The earth will shine with His light.

The book of deeds will be placed, and the prophets and
witnesses will be brought. The scale will be erected, and the
records will be spread. Opponents will be brought together,
and every creditor will cling to his debtor. The pool will appear
with its cups nearby; many will be thirsty, but few will come to
it. The bridge will be placed [over hell] to be crossed, and the
people will press towards it. Lights will be apportioned for

---

[22] The wording is from several different narrations. See Muhammad Nâṣiruddin
al-Albâni, *Aḥkâm al-Janâ'iz*, 4th ed. (Beirut: al-Maktab al-Islâmi).

crossing through its darkness while the fire crushes in on itself below; and those falling into it are many, many times those who escape it.

Thus, an eye is opened in his heart, by which he sees all that, and his heart becomes a witness to the hereafter, showing it to him with its eternity and showing him the world with its quick extinction.[23]

Within the magnificent Qur'an, scenes from the last day are mentioned frequently, such as in soorahs *Qâf*, *al-Wâqi'ah*, *al-Qiyâmah*, *al-Mursalât*, *an-Naba'*, *al-Muṭaffifeen* and *at-Takweer*. The same is true for volumes of Hadith, under chapters with names like 'Resurrection', 'Sensitising the heart', 'Paradise', 'Hellfire', and the like. Another important source is books written by scholars for that purpose, such as *Prompter of Souls* by Ibn al-Qayyim, *The Ultimate in Tortures and Massacres* by Ibn Katheer, *The Reminder about Conditions of the Dead and Matters of the Hereafter* by al-Qurtubi, *The Great Resurrection, Paradise and Hellfire* by 'Umar al-Ashqâr, and others. The intention is to increase faith through knowledge of aspects of the hereafter: the resurrection, the gathering, the intercession, the accounting, the reward and punishment, the retribution, the scale, the pool, the bridge, and the final home — paradise or hell.

10. Interaction with the signs of the universe

«It is narrated that when the Messenger of Allah (ﷺ) saw a cloud or wind, it showed on his face. 'Â'ishah (﵂) asked: O Messenger of Allah, I notice that when people see a cloud, they rejoice expecting rain; but when you see it, I recognise discomfort

---

[23] Ibn Qayyim al-Jawziyah, *Madârij as-Sâlikeen* (California: Dar al-Kitab al-Arabi, 2004).

in your face. He replied: O 'Â'ishah, how can I be sure that it does not contain a punishment? A people were punished by the wind, and though they saw the punishment [coming], they said:

(سورة الأحقاف : ٢٤)　　　　　　﴿ ... هَـٰذَا عَارِضٌ مُّمْطِرُنَا ... ﴾

《...This is a cloud bringing us rain...!》 *(Qur'an 46: 24)》* (Muslim)

The Prophet (ﷺ) would jump up in alarm when he saw an eclipse.

Abu Moosâ (رضي الله عنه) related: «The sun eclipsed, and the Prophet (ﷺ) got up alarmed, fearing that it was the hour [of resurrection].» (Bukhari)

During a solar or lunar eclipse, He ordered Muslims to seek refuge in prayer, announcing that they were two signs from Allah (عزّ وجلّ) with which He warns His servants. Undoubtedly, through being affected by these phenomena and feeling terrified by them, faith is renewed in the heart, as it reminds one of Allah's punishment, His assault, His grandeur, His ability, His power and His vengeance. 'Â'ishah (رضي الله عنها) related: «The Messenger of Allah (ﷺ) took my hand and then pointed to the moon and said: O 'Â'ishah, seek refuge in Allah from its evil, for indeed, it is darkness when it becomes dark.» (Recorded by Ahmad with a sound chain of narrators)

Other examples include being affected when passing by places where the earth has caved in and torment has occurred, or passing the graves of oppressors.

Ibn 'Umar (رضي الله عنهما) narrated that the Messenger of Allah (ﷺ) said to his Companions when they arrived at al-Hijr: «Do not enter upon those tortured ones unless you are weeping. If you are not weeping, do not enter upon them lest you are struck by that which struck them.» (Bukhari)

In spite of this, people today go there for tourism and photography. Imagine how delicate their position is in the sight of Allah (ﷻ)!

11. Remembrance of Allah (ﷻ)

This is one of the most important means of treating weak faith because it polishes the heart, cures it and heals it when it is ailing. It is the essence of righteous deeds and has been ordained by Allah (ﷻ), who says:

﴿يَٰٓأَيُّهَا ٱلَّذِينَ ءَامَنُوا۟ ٱذۡكُرُوا۟ ٱللَّهَ ذِكۡرًا كَثِيرًا ۝﴾   (سورة الأحزاب: ٤١)

﴿O you who have believed, remember Allah with much remembrance﴾   *(Qur'an 33: 41).*

He has promised success for those who do it frequently:

﴿ ... وَٱذۡكُرُوا۟ ٱللَّهَ كَثِيرًا لَّعَلَّكُمۡ تُفۡلِحُونَ ۝﴾   (سورة الأنفال: ٤٥)

﴿...and remember Allah much that you may be successful.﴾
(Qur'an 8: 45)

The remembrance of Allah (ﷻ) is greater than all else, as He said:

﴿ ... وَلَذِكۡرُ ٱللَّهِ أَكۡبَرُ ... ۝﴾   (سورة العنكبوت: ٤٥)

﴿...and the remembrance of Allah is greater...﴾   *(Qur'an 29: 45)*

It was also advised by the Prophet (ﷺ) for the one who was overwhelmed by the commandments of Islamic law. He said: «Let your tongue remain moist through the mention of Allah.» (at-Tirmidhi; al-Albâni graded it as sound)[24]

---

[24] The hadith begins: «A man said: O Messenger of Allah, the ordinances of Islam have become many for me, and I am now old. Tell me something to which I may attach myself...»

It is a means of pleasing the Most Merciful, driving away Satan, eliminating anxiety and distress, obtaining provision, opening doors to knowledge, planting the garden of paradise, and ridding the tongue of its evils. It is also a comfort for the poor who feel saddened by having nothing to give in charity. Allah (﷾) has substituted for them the mention of Him, in contrast to the financial means of worship He may have blessed others with.

Failure to mention or remember Allah (﷾) is a cause of harshness of the heart. It has been said:

Forgetting Allah is death to the hearts,
Their bodies, before the graves, are their graves
Their souls incompatible with their forms,
For them, until resurrection, there is no revival.

Thus, it is necessary for those who want to treat their weakness of faith to frequently remember Allah (﷾), who said:

﴿ ... وَٱذۡكُر رَّبَّكَ إِذَا نَسِيتَ ... ۝ ﴾ (سورة الكهف: ٢٤)

❴...And remember your Lord when you forget...❵ *(Qur'an 18: 24)*

Allah (﷾) also said, showing its effect on the heart:

﴿ ... أَلَا بِذِكۡرِ ٱللَّهِ تَطۡمَئِنُّ ٱلۡقُلُوبُ ۝ ﴾ (سورة الرّعد: ٢٨)

❴...Unquestionably, by the remembrance of Allah hearts are assured.❵   *(Qur'an 13: 28)*

Ibn al-Qayyim stated on the subject: "Within the heart is a hardness that is only melted by the remembrance of Allah (﷾), so the servant should treat the harshness of his heart by remembering Allah."

Someone remarked to al-Ḥasan al-Baṣri: "I complain to you of my hard heart." He said: "Soften it with remembrance."

This is because the more heedless the heart, the harder it becomes; when it remembers Allah (ﷻ), the hardness is melted just as lead melts in fire. Remembrance is healing for the heart and a remedy, while heedlessness is its disease and malady. Makhul said, "Remembrance of Allah, the Exalted, is a cure, while the remembrance of people is an illness."[25]

Through remembrance, a servant can bring down the devil just as the devil brings down the heedless and forgetful. An early scholar said:

When a heart is full of Allah's remembrance, if the devil comes near, it will throw him down. Then the other devils will gather around him and exclaim: "What's this?" They will be told: "He has been afflicted by a human!"[26]

Most of the people who are afflicted by devils are those who are heedless and do not protect themselves with recitations and supplications. For this reason, the devils can easily get involved with them.

Some of those who complain of weak faith find difficulty in certain methods of treatment, such as night prayers and additional worship. For these people, it would be suitable to begin with the following remedies, taking care to do them regularly. Some of these include memorising and continually repeating various recitations, such as these words of praise that were often spoken by the Prophet (ﷺ) and have been narrated by Bukhari and others: «*Lâ ilâha illâ Allâhu waḥdahu lâ shareeka lah, lahul-mulku wa lahul-ḥamdu wa huwa 'alâ kulli shay'in qadeer.* (There is no god

---

[25] al-Jawziyah, *Al-Wâbil as-Sayyib wa Râfi' al-Kalim at-Ṭayyib.*

[26] al-Jawziyah, *Madârij as-Sâlikeen.*

but Allah alone, having no partner. To Him belongs dominion, and to Him is due (all) praise. He is over all things competent.)»

«*Subḥân Allâhi wa biḥamdihi. Subḥân Allâhil-'adheem.* (Exalted is Allah, and [I affirm it] by praise of Him. Exalted is Allah, the Most Great.)»

«*Lâ ḥawla wa lâ quwwata illâ billâh.* (There is no power and no strength except in Allah.)»

— and so on.

They might also memorise the supplications from the Sunnah which are related to a time or place, such as those for the morning and the evening; when going to sleep and waking up; after having dreams; when eating; when relieving oneself; while travelling; at the time of rain; when entering the mosque; when seeking the decision of Allah (﷾); at the time of a disaster; when visiting the graves; during a strong wind; when seeing a new moon; when mounting a riding animal; when greeting someone; after sneezing; when hearing the crowing of a rooster, the braying of a donkey or the barking of a dog; for expiation of sins at the end of a gathering; when seeing people afflicted by misfortune, and so on. Undoubtedly, those who carefully observe these will find them directly affecting and creating an impression on their heart.[27]

12. Addressing Allah (﷾) privately and showing humility before Him

This revives faith in the heart, because the more humble and submissive the servants, the closer they become to Allah (﷾).

---

[27] Taqi ad-Deen Ibn Taymiyah, *Al-Kalim aṭ-Ṭayyib* (condensed and edited by Shaykh al-Albâni).

The Messenger of Allah (ﷺ) said: «The closest a servant can be to his Lord is while he is in prostration, so make much supplication then.» (Muslim)

The reason is that the state of prostration involves humility and subjection more than any other posture or position. When the servants of Allah press their foreheads — the highest part of them — to the ground, they show great humility and subservience to their Creator. Hence, they are the closest to their Lord in this posture. Ibn al-Qayyim expresses the beautiful words of the repentant, broken and humbled individual before his Lord:

> How sweet to Allah are the words of the one in this condition who says: I ask You by Your strength and my weakness, and by Your self-sufficiency and my need for You.[28] My deceitful sinning forelock is before You; Your servants other than me are numerous [while You are my only Lord]. There is no refuge and no safety from You except in You. I ask You with the plea of a poor man and implore You in submission and humility; I supplicate to You with the supplication of a fearful blind man, that of the one who has bowed his neck [exposing his vulnerability] to You and thrust his nose into the ground for You [debasing himself], whose eyes have wept and whose heart has deferred to You.

As the servants offer such words, confiding in their Lord, faith increases in their hearts many times over.

Thus, confessing our insufficiency to Allah (ﷻ) strengthens our faith. Allah (ﷻ) has informed us of our need for Him, saying:

---

[28] Requesting by humbling oneself before Allah (ﷻ) is among the lawful means of approaching Him through righteous deeds.

﴿ ۞ يَـٰٓأَيُّهَا ٱلنَّاسُ أَنتُمُ ٱلۡفُقَرَآءُ إِلَى ٱللَّهِ وَٱللَّهُ هُوَ ٱلۡغَنِيُّ ٱلۡحَمِيدُ ﴿١٥﴾ ﴾

(سورة فَاطِر: ١٥)

﴿O humankind, you are those in need of Allah, while Allah is the Free of need, the Praiseworthy.﴾ *(Qur'an 35: 15)*

13. Limiting the extent of long-term hope

This is very important for reviving faith.

Ibn al-Qayyim said: Among the greatest observations concerning it are these verses:

﴿أَفَرَءَيۡتَ إِن مَّتَّعۡنَـٰهُمۡ سِنِينَ ﴿٢٠٥﴾ ثُمَّ جَآءَهُم مَّا كَانُواْ يُوعَدُونَ ﴿٢٠٦﴾ مَآ أَغۡنَىٰ عَنۡهُم مَّا كَانُواْ يُمَتَّعُونَ ﴿٢٠٧﴾ ﴾

(سورة الشُّعَرَاء: ٢٠٥-٢٠٧)

﴿Then have you considered if We gave them enjoyment for years and then there came to them that which they were promised? They would not be availed by the enjoyment with which they were provided.﴾ *(Qur'an 26: 205-207)*

﴿ ... لَمۡ يَلۡبَثُوٓاْ إِلَّا سَاعَةً مِّن نَّهَارٍ بَلَـٰغٌ ... ﴿٣٥﴾ ﴾

(سورة الأحقاف: ٣٥)

﴿...as though they had not remained [in the world] except an hour of a day...﴾ *(Qur'an 46: 35)*

That is all there is to the world, so let a person not extend his expectation, thinking: I shall live on and on.

One of the righteous predecessors spoke to a man about leading them in the noon prayer. The man said: If I lead you in the noon prayer, I will not do so for the late afternoon prayer. The other said: It is almost as if you expect to live until the late

afternoon prayer. We seek refuge in Allah (ﷻ) from long-term hope.

14. Reflecting upon the insignificance of this world, which removes attachment to it from the servant's heart

Allah (ﷻ) said:

﴿ ... وَمَا ٱلْحَيَوٰةُ ٱلدُّنْيَآ إِلَّا مَتَٰعُ ٱلْغُرُورِ ۝ ﴾   (سورة الحديد: ٢٠)

❴...And what is the worldly life except the enjoyment of delusion?❵   *(Qur'an 57: 20)*

The Prophet (ﷺ) said: «The food of a son of Adam presents a comparison to this world. See how it emerges from the son of Adam; even though he has embellished and seasoned it, he knows what it will become.» (Recorded by aṭ-Ṭabarâni with a sound chain of narrators)

Abu Hurayrah (ﷺ) also reported: «I heard the Messenger of Allah (ﷺ) say: The world is cursed and what it contains is cursed, except for the mention of Allah and what is successive to it, or a scholar or a student.» (at-Tirmidhi; al-Albâni graded it as 'reliable but odd')

15. Honouring what Allah has made sacred

The Exalted has said:

﴿ ... وَمَن يُعَظِّمْ شَعَٰٓئِرَ ٱللَّهِ فَإِنَّهَا مِن تَقْوَى ٱلْقُلُوبِ ۝ ﴾   (سورة الحَجّ: ٣٢)

❴...And whoever honours the rites of Allah — it is indeed from the piety of hearts.❵   *(Qur'an 22: 32)*

This refers to the rites of Allah (ﷻ) that pertain to certain people, places and times. It would include, for example, observing

the rights of the Prophet (ﷺ) and honouring the sanctity of the Sacred Mosque in Makkah, or that of the month of Ramadan.

﴿ وَمَن يُعَظِّمْ حُرُمَٰتِ ٱللَّهِ فَهُوَ خَيْرٌ لَّهُۥ عِنـدَ رَبِّهِۦ ... ۝ ﴾

(سورة الحَجّ : ٣٠)

﴿...and whoever honours the sacred ordinances of Allah — it is best for him in the sight of his Lord...﴾   *(Qur'an 22: 30)*

This means also that one should not consider the lesser sins to be insignificant.

'Abdullâh ibn Mas'ood (ﷺ) reported that the Messenger of Allah (ﷺ) said: «Beware of trivial sins, for indeed they collect on a man until they destroy him, like people in an open land who prepared a meal. One man went and brought a stick and another brought a stick... until they collected a great mass and then kindled a fire and cooked whatever was thrown into it.» (Recorded by Ahmad with a sound chain of narrators)

Give up sins, both small and great, O righteous one
And do as one who walks a ground of thorns,
  cautious of what he sees
Never ignore a small sin, for indeed mountains
  are comprised of pebbles.

Ibn al-Jawzi said in *Sayd al-Khâtir*: Many people are careless about matters they think are unimportant, while they actually infringe upon the fundamental principles: such matters as looking at what is prohibited or a student's borrowing a portion [of the Qur'an] and failing to return it.

An early scholar said: "I indulged in a bite of food and partook of it, so today I am forty years behind." And this was said out of modesty, may Allah have mercy upon him.

16. Loyalty to the believers and disassociation from disbelievers

When a heart is attached to the enemies of Allah (ﷻ), it becomes extremely weak, and the creed declines therein. On the other hand, when loyalty is only for Allah (ﷻ), and one benefits and supports His believing servants, while opposing and detesting His enemies, it brings faith to life.

17. Modesty

This has an effective role in increasing faith and polishing the heart, ridding it of the rust of conceit. Modesty in one's speech, actions and appearance indicates the level of humility of the heart towards Allah (ﷻ).

The Prophet (ﷺ) said: «Being humble in dress is part of the faith.» (Abu Dâwood; al-Albâni graded it as sound)

He also said: «Whoever gives up [elegant] clothing out of humility to Allah while he is able to do otherwise, Allah will invite him on the Day of Resurrection before all of creation to choose from which ornaments of faith he would like to wear.» (A reliable hadith recorded by at-Tirmidhi)

Among those modest in appearance was 'Abdur-Raḥmân ibn 'Awf, who could not be distinguished from his slaves.

18. Deeds of the heart

Examples of these are: loving Allah (ﷻ), fearing Him, putting one's hope in Him, relying upon Him, accepting His decree, being grateful to Him, being honest with Him, believing in Him, trusting in Him, repenting to Him, and so on.

There are 'stations' or attributes that every servant should attain to complete the treatment, such as adherence to the straight path, continual return to Allah (ﷻ), retrospection and self-reminding, holding fast to the Qur'an and Sunnah, submissiveness to Allah, indifference to the world, piety, awareness, and so on — all of which Ibn al-Qayyim has discussed fully in his book *Madârij as-Sâlikeen*.

19. Taking account of the self

Allah (ﷻ) said:

﴿يَٰٓأَيُّهَا ٱلَّذِينَ ءَامَنُوا۟ ٱتَّقُوا۟ ٱللَّهَ وَلْتَنظُرْ نَفْسٌ مَّا قَدَّمَتْ لِغَدٍ ...﴾ (١٨)

(سورة الحَشر: ١٨)

◆O you who have believed, fear Allah. And let every soul look to what it has put forth for tomorrow...◗   *(Qur'an 59: 18)*

'Umar ibn al-Khaṭṭâb (ﷺ) advised: "Take account of yourselves before you are called to account."

Al-Ḥasan observed: "You will not meet a [true] believer who does not call himself to account."

Maymun ibn Maḥrân also remarked: "A pious person is stricter in taking account of himself than a greedy partner."

Ibn al-Qayyim said:

The soul's destruction is due to neglect in taking account of it, from giving in to it, and from following its inclinations. So a Muslim must take time to be alone and critically examine himself, call his soul to account, look into its condition, and consider what provision he has sent ahead for the Appointed Day.

20. Finally, supplication to Allah (ﷺ) is among the most powerful means that a servant can use to improve the strength of faith

The Prophet (ﷺ) said: «Faith becomes worn out inside one of you like a garment wears out, so ask Allah to renew the faith in your hearts.» (A reliable hadith recorded by al-Ḥâkim)

O Allah, we ask You by Your best names and exalted attributes to renew the faith in our hearts. O Allah, make us love faith and adorn it in our hearts, and make us hate disbelief, rebellion and disobedience. O Allah, make us of the rightly guided and of those with strong faith.

Exalted is the Lord of Might and Honour above what they describe, and peace be upon the messengers. Praise be to Allah, Lord of the worlds.

BIBLIOGRAPHY

al-Albâni, Muhammad Nâṣiruddin. *Aḥkâm al-Janâ'iz,* 4ᵗʰ ed. Beirut: al-Maktab al-Islâmi.

_____. *Arba' Masâ'il fil-Eemân.*

ad-Dhahabi, Muhammad ibn Aḥmad. *Siyar A'lam an-Nubalâ'.* Cairo: Dar El Hadith.

Ibn Ḥajar al-'Asqalâni, Aḥmad ibn 'Ali. *Fatḥ al-Bâri Sharḥ Ṣaḥeeḥ al-Bukhâri.* Riyadh: Darussalam.

_____. *Taghleeq at-Ta'leeq.* Beirut: al-Maktab al-Islâmi.

Ibn al-Jawzi, Abul-Faraj. *Manâqib 'Umar.*

_____. *Sayd al-Khâṭir.* Al-Maktabat-ul-Asriya, 2004.

Ibn Katheer, Abu al-Fidâ' 'Imâd ad-Deen Isma'eel ibn 'Umar. *Tafseer Ibn Katheer.* Dâr ash-Sha'b.

Ibn Taymiyah, Taqi ad-Deen. *Al-Kalim aṭ-Ṭayyib* (condensed and edited by Shaykh al-Albâni).

al-Jawziyah, Ibn Qayyim. *Ad-Dâ' wad-Dawâ'.* Beirut: Dar at-Tawzee wan-Nashr ul-Islamia.

_____. *Madârij as-Sâlikeen.* California: Dar al-Kitab al-Arabi, 2004.

_____. *Sharḥ al-Qaṣeedat an-Nooniyah.* Beirut: al-Maktab al-Islâmi, 1962.

_____. *Ṭareeq al-Hijratayn.* Beirut: Dâr al-Kutub al-'Ilmiya.

————. *Al-Wâbil as-Sayyib wa Râfi' al-Kalim aṭ-Ṭayyib.* Maktaba Dâr al-Bayyân.

al-Qurtubi, Abu 'Abdullâh. *At-Tadhkirah.* Egypt: Dâr al-Manârah.

Ṣaḥeeḥ International. *The Qur'an: Arabic Text with Corresponding English Meanings.* Jeddah: Abul Qasim - Publishing House, 1997.

GLOSSARY OF ISLAMIC TERMS*

ahl as-Sunnah wal-jamâ'ah	أهل السنّة والجماعة	'people of the Sunnah and the community'
Anṣâr	أنصار	'helpers': the Muslim citizens of Madinah who gave refuge to the Prophet (ﷺ) and the other Muslim emigrants from Makkah
dhikr Allâh	ذكر اللّه	remembrance of Allah; specifically, remembering Allah through praising and supplicating to Him
Eid ('eed)	عيد	*lit.* festival; the two celebrations: one at the end of Ramadan and the other at the culmination of the Hajj
Hadith (ḥadeeth)	حديث	the collected statements and actions of Prophet Muhammad (ﷺ) that with the Qur'an form the basis of Islamic law
hadith (ḥadeeth)	حديث	a statement or action of Prophet Muhammad (ﷺ) that was

---

* The Arabic words are transliterated according to the conventions of the Transliteration Chart found in this book. If a word has become part of the English language (i.e., is found in a dictionary of Standard English), that spelling is used in this book and appears first in this Glossary, with the transliterated form in brackets after it.

remembered and recorded by his Companions and followers

Hajj (ḥajj)   حج   the major pilgrimage to the Sacred Mosque, site of the Ka'bah at Makkah, to be undertaken by every able Muslim once in his/her lifetime

jihad (jihâd)   جهاد   struggle or striving (in Allah's cause)

jinn
(plural of jinni)   جن   non-human, rational beings created by Allah from fire, often referred to as 'demons' or 'devils'; They have free will like humans: some are Muslims, others disbelievers; some are obedient to Allah, others disobedient. Satan is a jinni. Some people try to 'foretell' the future by contacting a jinni. Some disobedient jinn mislead people into thinking that they can tell them what will happen in the future, near or far, or that the jinn can provide people with riches or some sort of power.

lâ ilâha   لا إله إلى الله   there is none worthy of worship
illâ Allâh   other than Allah

Quraysh   قريش   the dominant tribe in Makkah at the time of the Prophet's mission; their society was based on polytheism

raka'ah (pl. raka'ât)	ركعة	a unit of the formal prayer (ṣalât)
Ramadan (Ramaḍân)	رمضان	the ninth month in the Islamic calendar; the month of obligatory fasting; the month in which the first verses of the Qur'an were revealed
soorah or soorat	سورة	chapter of the Qur'an
subḥân Allâh	سبحان الله	glory be to Allah
Sunnah	سنَة	the practice and collected sayings of Prophet Muhammad (ﷺ) that together with the Qur'an forms the basis of Islamic law
sunnah	سنَة	acts that are recommended but not mandatory
Ummah	أمَة	community or nation: *usu.* used to refer to the entire global community of Muslims
'umrah	عمرة	a minor, non-obligatory pilgrimage to Makkah

Notes

Notes

Notes

....

....

....

....

....

....

....

....

....

....

....

Notes

Notes

....

....

....

....

....

....

....

....

....

....

....

Notes

....

....

....

....

....

....

....

....

....

....

Notes

....

....

....

....

....

....

....

....

....

....

....

TEACH YOURSELF

HEBREW

By

PROFESSOR R. K. HARRISON, PH.D.

THE ENGLISH UNIVERSITIES PRESS LTD
102 NEWGATE STREET
LONDON, E.C.1

First printed 1955
This impression 1962

Printed in Great Britain for the English Universities Press Limited
by Richard Clay and Company, Ltd., Bungay, Suffolk

AUTHOR'S PREFACE

HEBREW may seem to present a number of initial obstacles to the aspiring student. Its appearance is strange to those unfamiliar with Semitic languages, and it lacks almost all contact with the grammar and syntax of Classical or modern European languages. The alphabet is unfamiliar at first sight, and some of the letters are apt to be confused. Writing vocalised consonants from right to left is strange to the majority of people; the ring of Hebrew words and phrases, particularly when guttural letters are enunciated, is equally unfamiliar.

Another difficulty might appear to subsist in the triliteral nature of most Hebrew roots, so that to a beginner they not only sound alike, but would also seem to require a considerable amount of mental effort to fix them accurately in the memory. Furthermore, the virtual absence of compound forms demands a separate Hebrew word for verbs which to us may express the same root idea, a factor which again appears to make for excessive memory work.

Many such ideas arise through a beginner's unfamiliarity with the language, *but the student may be assured immediately that his efforts will bring a quicker dividend in the form of an ability to translate the original than would be the case with Classical and other languages generally.* A further merit is that previous experience in language-study is not essential; in fact, it may even be disadvantageous, and the majority of students grasp the principles of Hebrew grammar readily when only the mother-tongue is known. It is true, of course, that the study of any language requires enterprise, effort and perseverance, and in this respect Hebrew is no exception.

All students welcome the comparative smallness

of the Hebrew working vocabulary. Grammatical forms are quickly recognised as schematic, and once the primary rules have been mastered, they can be applied with almost mathematical regularity and precision to produce the required parts of speech. The verb paradigm is remarkably unelaborate, with its two themes expressing completeness or incompleteness, along with their characteristic modifications, and contrasts favourably with the complex verbs of Latin and Greek. There are two genders only, and no case-endings of the sort found in other languages. Hebrew syntax has rejected the elaborate formulation of subordinate clauses for a series of simple sentences coordinated by the copulative conjunction. This has given simplicity and vividness to the language, making it a powerful vehicle for conveying fundamental spiritual truths.

These factors largely compensate for the unfamiliarity of the language, and are always encouraging to the beginner. The author has endeavoured at every stage to introduce the various principles as clearly and attractively as possible, and has stated the main rules of articulation and grammar before attempts are made to translate phrases and sentences. In the writer's teaching experience this has worked most effectively with beginners, as it appeals to the rational processes of the mind.

Of a number of current systems of transliteration, what appears to be the least complex has been adopted. The mass of detail which characterises advanced Hebrew grammars has been avoided in the interests of presenting basic grammatical principles simply. This procedure imposes obvious limitations on the work, which nevertheless, as an introductory manual, may encourage the student to master what Ewald described as "the eternal mother-tongue of all true religion."

INTRODUCTION

A CERTAIN professor at an English University is said always to commence his initial lecture on the Hebrew language with the words, "Gentlemen, this is the language which God spoke". Since substantial portions of the Divine revelation were given through the medium of this language, it is disconcerting to encounter such a marked resistance amongst Christian students to the diligent study of Hebrew.

The present writer feels that one reason for this state of affairs is the complexity and obscurity of the bulk of grammars published in the last century, and the present book is an attempt to state the basic principles of what is, after all, a comparatively uncomplicated language, as simply as possible.

Since Hebrew is now the official language of the State of Israel, it has gained in importance during recent years, and this fact makes its study a matter of more than purely antiquarian or theological interest.

The student will have sufficient equipment to study the simpler prose passages of the Old Testament when he has mastered the contents of the book, and in addition he will derive greater benefit from subsequent perusal of such works as Gesenius–Kautzsch–Cowley, for the finer points of the language as met with in more advanced Hebrew prose and poetry.

This, then, is a book for beginners, and whilst the writer makes no claim whatever to originality of content or presentation, he trusts that the simplified arrangement of the material will be of assistance to students, and especially to those who are endeavouring to learn Hebrew through private study. The chapters follow the order observed by the majority of grammars, and for the first few chapters the Hebrew words are transliterated as they occur, to

enable the student to grasp their pronunciation and inflection. Proper names and technical terms are fully accented when they first occur, but subsequently they carry the minimum of accentuation, in order to simplify the format. The Divine Name is left unpointed throughout, and certain phrases are repeated in the exercises in a manner similar to the Biblical idiom.

A pocket lexicon suitable for beginners is the Hebrew–English lexicon published by S. Bagster and Sons, while for more advanced study the Oxford Hebrew Lexicon (Brown, Driver and Briggs), or the excellent two-volume work, Lexicon in Veteris Testamenti Libros, by Koehler and Baumgartner, will be found to satisfy all normal requirements.

I wish to acknowledge the kindness of a Canadian scholar, Rabbi David Kirshenbaum, of London, Ontario, in reading the manuscript and making suggestions for the improvement of this work. I am indebted to the Rev. J. M. Wilkie, M.A., B.D., formerly lecturer in Hebrew in the Universities of Durham and Cambridge, for his kindness and diligence in correcting the proofs.

A number of changes in the arrangement of the material have been suggested by scholars to whom the book was submitted in proof, and the majority of these modifications have been incorporated, so as to make the book as useful as possible within its obvious limitations. In this respect I am particularly indebted to the Rev. Robert Davidson, M.A., B.D., of Aberdeen. My final acknowledgment must be to Mr. Leonard Cutts, Editor of the Series, for his care and consideration in dealing with the book at all stages of its development.

R. K. Harrison.

CONTENTS

CHAPTER I

THE ALPHABET

Square form (Aramaic) — handwritten note

Archaic (Phoenician) — handwritten note

Form. Primary or Medial.	Final.	Name.	Transliteration.	Numerical Value.
א		'Aleph	'	1
בּ ב		Bêth	bh, b	2
גּ ג		Gîmel	gh, g	3
דּ ד		Dāleth	dh, d	4
ה		Hē	h	5
ו		Wāw	w	6
ז		Záyin	z	7
ח		Ḥêth	ḥ	8
ט		Ṭêth	ṭ	9
י		Yôdh	y	10
כּ כ	ך	Kaph	kh, k	20
ל		Lāmedh	l	30
מ	ם	Mêm	m	40
נ	ן	Nûn	n	50
ס		Ṣāmekh	ṣ	60
ע		'Ayin	'	70
פּ פ	ף	Pē	ph, p	80
צ	ץ	Çādhê	ç	90
ק		Qôph	q	100
ר		Rêš	r	200
שׁ שׂ		Sîn, Šîn	s, š	300
תּ ת		Tāw	th, t	400

The Hebrew alphabet comprises twenty-two letters, all of which are consonants, and whose shapes in the first instance were similar to the objects which they are supposed to have signified.

HEBREW is one of the north-west Semitic group of languages which also includes Phoenician, Punic, Moabitic and Aramaic. It has considerable affinity with Arabic as well. From a linguistic standpoint, Hebrew was probably at its best in the period which saw the composition of the historical books such as Samuel and Kings, and the pre-Exilic prophets. Aramaic increased in influence particularly after the Exile, and towards the start of the Christian era it supplanted Hebrew as the spoken language of the Israelites.

We will now look at the Hebrew alphabet in some detail, considering each letter separately, and noting the manner in which it is to be sounded in reading.

א must never be mistaken for the letter "a", since it is always a consonant. It is represented by a "smooth breathing" ('), and is similar in nature to the silent "h" in the word "honour".

ב is "bh" and is pronounced like a "v"; בּ is a hard "b" as in "bat".

ג is transliterated "gh", and is pronounced with a slight throaty sound; גּ is a hard "g", as in "get".

ד is "dh" and is pronounced like the "th" in the word "the"; דּ is a hard "d", as in "day".

ה is the letter for "h".

ו represents the letter "w".

ז is the letter "z".

ח is signified by "ḥ", the dot underneath helping to distinguish it from ה. It is pronounced like the

"ch" in the German "ach", or the Scottish "loch".

ט is transliterated "ṭ", the dot underneath the letter again serving to differentiate it from a subsequent "t". It is pronounced as a dull "t" by pressing the tongue to the palate.

י is the letter "y".

כ is transliterated "kh", and is very similar in sound, though somewhat lighter in tone, to the "ch" sound (ח) above ; כ is a hard "k" as in "kept".

ל represents "l".

מ is the letter "m".

נ is transliterated "n".

ס is represented by "ṣ", to distinguish it from a subsequent letter (שׁ), and has a dull "s" sound.

ע is transliterated by the "rough breathing" ('), and is pronounced with a harsh guttural sound from the back of the throat.

פ is "ph", pronounced like "f" ; פ is a hard "p" as in "peg".

צ is transliterated "ç", and has a sharp hissing sound of "s", like the "ç" in the French word "garçon".

ק is represented by the letter "q", and the sound is like a "k" or a "q" pronounced from the back of the throat.

ר is the letter "r".

שׁ with the dot over the right hand corner is transliterated "š", and is pronounced "sh" ; שׂ with the dot over the left hand corner is the letter "s".

ת is the equivalent of "th" as in "these" ; תּ is a hard "t" sound as in "tin".

It must be borne in mind that the sound for

'Aleph amounts to nothing more than the emission
of the breath in preparation for pronouncing the
word or syllable of which it is the commencing
consonant. When it occurs within a word its effect is
much the same as if we were to pronounce the word
"re-educate", by pausing slightly after the enunciation of the first syllable, and then stressing the second
"e" by a fresh emission of the breath. The sound for
'Ayin is as though one were clearing one's throat,
without, however, uttering a clear, deep grunt. Many
of these sounds are difficult to articulate, and this is
rendered more complicated by the fact that we cannot be absolutely certain of the original pronunciation. Furthermore, our Western articulation is
different from that in the Orient, so that each
experiences trouble in attempting to pronounce
certain words from the other's language. For
example, the Semites had a liberal sprinkling of
vowel sounds in their words, and seem to have been
almost unable to pronounce two or three consonants
together. Thus a word like "rhythm" would probably
have been broken up into three syllables by placing
a very short vowel sound between the "r" and the
"h", regarding the "y" as an "i" in sound, and
placing a further vowel between the last two letters
of the word.

However, our primary aim is not to secure a pronunciation as near as possible to what the original is
thought to have been, but to ensure the mastery of a
working pronunciation adequate for the articulation
of the language as printed. Careful attention to the
table of pronunciation will enable the student to
acquire a reasonable accuracy in representing the
original sounds. The letters with a guttural quality
should be enunciated most carefully, as this is not

always easy for Western people to master, to whom the majority of guttural sounds seem alike.

In writing Hebrew we shall use the printed "square" character, so that whilst we talk about "writing" Hebrew we are actually "printing" it. Care must be taken with letters which look alike but which in fact have some characteristic difference. Looking through the alphabet in order we notice that whilst the letters ב and כ exhibit some similarity, the ב (bh) has a small projection or "tittle" at the bottom right hand corner, whilst the כ is rounded off to make "kh". נ (gh) has a slightly angular projection to the left of its base, whilst נ (n) is square at the top and bottom, and thus is to be distinguished from כ, as well as being smaller in size.

ד (dh) and ך (kh, final form) are frequently confused at the start. The latter will be seen to come below the line of writing, whilst the former remains on it. Both must be distinguished from ר (r), which is rounded at the top, whereas both ד and ך have the "tittle".

The letter ה (h) is different from the guttural ח (ḥ) in that the top is closed in the latter, a fact which tends to be a source of confusion. The letter ת (th) is unlike both of these in that, whilst it is closed at the top, it has a "foot" at the bottom left hand corner.

Difficulty is sometimes experienced in distinguishing between ן (n) in its final form (which drops a little below the line of writing), and the letter ו (w), which has a slightly rounded projection at the top left, and also the letter ז (z) which carries a small angular bar on the top, extending to an equal distance on either side. Of the primary or medial

forms, qoph (ק) is the only one to drop below the line. The letter yodh (י) must always be written above the line, on a level with the top of the other letters except lamedh (ל), which is the only one to begin a little above the other letters. If the yodh is lengthened unduly it can be readily confused with reš (ר), and possibly with waw (ו).

Final ם (m) must be written as a square, and in this way will not be mistaken for samekh (ס), which is round, or for teth (ט), which, whilst also round, is open at the top. Primary or medial מ (m) is open at the bottom left hand corner. The letter ע (') has a different curvature from צ (ç), or from its final form (ץ), which drops below the line.

There are five letters which exhibit two distinct forms, which we have designated primary or medial, and final, in our table of the alphabet. These letters are כמנפצ, and when they occur as the initial letters (primary), or when they are found occurring within a word (medial), they are written as above, resting on the line. But when they constitute the last letter of a word, their forms are altered to ךמןףץ, coming below the line, with the exception of ם (m). This latter, as we have already observed, is written like a closed square when occurring in its final form.

Six of the consonants in the Hebrew alphabet have an alternative hardened form, which one may produce by inserting a point (·) inside the letters themselves. The consonants thus affected are בגדכפת, *i.e.*, "bh", "gh", "dh", "kh", "ph", "th", but when read with a point (*i.e.*, בגדכפת), they assume a hard sound and are transliterated "b", "g", "d", "k", "p" and "t".

We have seen that all the above letters are con-

sonantal in force. In ancient times the Hebrew words were written without vowels in what is called "unpointed" script, so that each word consisted of a group of consonants whose vowel sounds were supplied from memory by the reader. The Hebrews knew, from oral teaching and practice, which vowels were associated with the different words, and it was only after many centuries that a mechanical system of vowel "points" was devised, enabling the reader to pronounce any word without prior knowledge of its sound. Whilst a vowel-less text (*i.e.*, unpointed) might be thought to be fraught with difficulty for the student, it must be remembered that some systems of shorthand at the present time employ the same idea with excellent results in intelligibility. If we were to take, for example, the consonants BT, we should actually experience little practical difficulty in deciding from the context whether the word was BAT, BET, BIT or BUT, and the same would apply to more developed forms.

One of the stranger features of the Hebrew language in occidental eyes is the fact that, in common with many other Semitic languages, it is written across the page from right to left. It is frequently perplexing to beginners to have to commence writing the Hebrew characters from the right hand side of the page, but only a small degree of practice is necessary to become used to this procedure.

On the basis of the information which we now possess, we may begin to write some of the Hebrew equivalents of the English letters in our table of the alphabet. Let us take a number of English consonants, such as "d", "ph" and "l". To write this in Hebrew characters we commence at the right of

our paper and work in the direction of the left,
thus ←————— (l) ל (ph) פ (d) ד, making the word
דפל. What might appear to us to be the "last"
character (*i.e.*, ד) is actually the first one to be written
down, followed by the second, (פ) and third (ל) to the
left of it.

Now let us take a group of consonants and transliterate them into square Hebrew character :

1. nphš. 2. mwnʿ. 3. phʾrç. 4. ṭẓṣr. 5. šyrm.
This would be rendered as follows, beginning to
write at the top right hand side of the page :

1. נפש 2. מונע 3. פארץ 4. טזסר 5. שירם

A similar principle applies to the rendering of
Hebrew characters into English, except that in
transcribing them the student will begin writing at
the left hand side of the page and continue to the
right in the ordinary way. For example, a group of
consonants such as

1. הן 2. צדיק 3. חלמיסא 4. קארא 5. עלמות
will be rendered into English letters as follows :

1. hn. 2. çdhyq. 3. ḥlmyṣʾ. 4. qʾrʾ. 5. ʾlmwth.
Care must always be taken to form the
Hebrew letters correctly, and to avoid confusion in
transliterating those which are similar in sound or
appearance in English as well as in Hebrew.

Exercise 1

Practice in writing groups of consonants in English.

1. אתף 2. בלנו 3. קטלם 4. שלחיני 5. משלך 6. ערבינו
7. זפשלן 8. כלותי 9. צלעפא 10. זרגחם 11. תלטמעין
12. הוכלעים 13. חפעזיק 14. טיראש 15. שלקאלו 16. דפטאנין
17. עלישמו 18. סמטשב 19. כצפעיל 20. חזקהמש.

Practice in writing groups of consonants in Hebrew.

1. ḥṭšm. 2. lph'š. 3. çrmyw. 4. ṣnṭḥly. 5. t'ql'my.
6. sbhwy. 7. qphṣ'ṭç. 8. dh'rm'ly. 9. pmḥṭš'nwn.
10. krm'ṣphqy. 11. 'zw'ghn'. 12. ṭršdhmw. 13. bghlṣḥ'.
14. çhwghl'. 15. qmthwy. 16. 'nç'lyn. 17. ḥnbhṭs.
18. thç'nṣ'm. 19. 'myn'ṭw. 20. grql'myw.

CHAPTER TWO

VOCALISATION

Up to the first few centuries of the Christian era, the Old Testament was written in unpointed consonantal Hebrew, with the reader supplying the vowel sounds from memory. As Classical (*i.e.*, Biblical) Hebrew fell into disuse for conversational purposes, it became necessary to devise some system of vocalising the text so as to enable it to be read correctly without any necessary previous acquaintance on the part of the reader with the sound of the words.

This difficulty had been partly met in the unpointed text by the use of certain consonants to indicate the principal long vowels, the particular consonants being he, yodh and waw. In practice this was as follows :

ה signified â ; hence לה was read lâ.

י signified ê and î ; hence לי was read lê or lî.

ו signified ô and û ; hence לו was read lô or lû.

To show that these vowel-letters had a permanently long sound in their pronunciation, the English transliteration is accented by means of a circumflex (^). A knowledge of the context was necessary, of course, in deciding upon the correct word from the alternatives which these vowel-letters supplied.

When such letters are omitted in the spelling of words to avoid reduplication of consonants, the vowels are then said to be written " defectively," *e.g.*, עֵן for עֵוֹן. This is commonly found in the Hebrew Bible.

About the seventh century A.D. a vocalic system was introduced by the Massoretes, a group of people interested in preserving and vocalising the traditional Hebrew text, and who derived their name from the Hebrew word for "tradition". The system consisted of vowel points or signs which were written in and around the consonants so as not to interfere with their traditional sacredness. We will now study them in tabular form for convenience.

Table of Long Vowel Signs

Vowel	Name	Tran-scribed	Pronounced
◌ָ	Qāmēç	ā	As in calm.
◌ֵ ◌ֶ	Çērê	ē ê	As in obey.
◌ִ	Ḥîrĕq (long)	î	As in morphine

Table of Long Vowel Signs (*continued*)

Vowel	Name	Transcribed	Pronounced
ִ ְ } ֵ }	Ḥōlĕm	ô } ō }	As in tone.
וּ	Šûrĕq	û	As in mute.

Table of Short Vowel Signs

Vowel	Name	Transcribed	Pronounced
ַ	Páthăḥ	ă	As in mat.
ֶ	Şᵉghôl	ĕ	As in then.
ִ	Ḥîrĕq (short)	ĭ	As in hit.
ָ	Qāmĕç- Ḥaţûph	ŏ	As in top.
ֻ	Qïbbûç	ŭ	As in shut.

The line on which they would be written is indicated to show their relative positions as coming either above or below the line. To acquire the correct pronunciation of the various vowels it will be necessary

to practise saying them very carefully. One will notice from these tables that the vowel hireq has a long and a short form, and also that the same sign ($_{\tau}$) is used for a long "a" and a short "o". Whilst this latter may appear confusing, we shall shortly learn a means of differentiating between the two.

The three dots in qibbuç are written at a slight angle, whilst the yodh in full çere (˙.) and hireq (long) are written to the left of, and above the vowel point. Because the consonants yodh and waw are used with points to express the vowel sound, they are said to have homogeneous vowels, and in transliteration this is indicated by a circumflex accent placed over the corresponding English letter. Thus full holem (וֹ), defectively (ֹ), is written "ô" as distinct from the alternative rendering of holem as "ō". Exactly the same applies to çere. In pronouncing long hireq (˙.) and full çere (˙.) an attempt should be made to recognise the place of the quiescent yodh, analogous to the way in which the personal pronoun "I" is pronounced, when a faint "y" sound is enunciated at the end. The full form of these two vowels, i.e., including the quiescent consonant as well as the vowel itself, is said to be "permanently long", since the form of such vowels cannot be shortened under any circumstances, as opposed to the "tone long" vowels, which are only long in virtue of their relation

to the tone or accent, and which may become short in other forms of the same word.

All Hebrew words must start with a consonant, and when vowels are added, each one is placed in close association with the consonant with which it is to be pronounced, generally directly underneath the consonant. Thus, to write "bā" we would use ב with qameç directly under it, *i.e.*, בָּ. A more complex word "bārā'" would be בָּרָא, the consonant preceding the vowel in each case, so that it could not possibly be pronounced "bāār'", which would need to be spelled in a different way. When the vowel sign for holem is used, it is placed above the consonant, as in מֹר, mōr, or with full holem as in דּוֹר, dôr.

When holem precedes א, the point is placed on the upper right of the letter, as with יֹאמַר (yō'măr). When it follows the א, the point is placed on the upper left, as in אֹבֶד (ʾōbhēdh). When holem precedes שׁ, the points coincide, as with מֹשֵׁל (mōšēl). When holem follows שׁ, the points again coincide, as with שֹׁטֵן (sōṭēn). The letter שׁ will be "šō" to commence a syllable, *e.g.*, שֹׁמַע (šōmă'), and "ōs" in other places.

Exercise 2

(*a*) Transliterate into English as many renderings as possible of the following vowel-letter combinations :

7. חולי   6. מימו   5. יהלו   4. שה   3. כי   2. מה   1. לי

8. נהמי   9. סינו   10. לומי.

(b) Transliterate the following into Hebrew vowel-letters :

1. lâlâ. 2. lîlô. 3. lôlâ. 4. bhânâ. 5. môlû. 6. nêlû.
7. mûnê. 8. lêlê. 9. qînâ. 10. lînê.

(c) Write the vowels corresponding to the following vowel points :

. 9. וֹ 8. ִֽ 7. ֶ 6. ַ 5. ֹֽ 4. ֻ 3. ֳ 2. וּ 1.

ָ 12. ֵ 11. ֺ 10.

(d) Write the vowel points for the following vowels :

1. ā. 2. û. 3. ĕ. 4. ō. 5. ĭ. 6. ô. 7. ŭ. 8. ă.
9. ē. 10. ŏ. 11. ê. 12. î.

(e) Write the following practice words in pointed Hebrew :

1. bĕn. 2. bēn. 3. gôr. 4. mēm. 5. 'ākhăl. 6. çâphôn.
7. 'îš. 8. mēhĕn. 9. 'ĕmĕth. 10. qôṭēl. 11. ḥāšim.
12. ṣēphĕr. 13. gādhôl. 14. hû'. 15. šûrĕq. 16. mōlênû.
17. 'āphār. 18. hî'. 19. 'ênê. 20. 'ĕbhĕn.

(f) Write the following practice words in English, trans-literating (ָ) by qameç :

1. אָדָם 2. אֲרִית 3. שָׁלוֹם 4. מִימֵי 5. צָפוֹנָה 6. עִיר

7. בַּת 8. אֱלוֹמִי 9. לָנוּ 10. מַיִם 11. קָרָא 12. כּוֹכָבִים

13. יֶלֶת 14. גְּמְנוּ 15. אִלֵם 16. עָצוּם 17. יָרָא 18. כֹּפֶר

19. שׁוֹר 20. מְוָּה.

CHAPTER THREE

THE SYLLABLE AND THE ŠᵉWA

A SYLLABLE may be defined as a unit of pronunciation which in other than monosyllabic words forms part of a word, and which contains one vowel sound preceded—and often followed—by a consonant. Two types of syllable in Hebrew emerge as a result, and for convenience they are designated as "open" and "shut".

An open syllable is one ending in a vowel, whilst a shut syllable is one which has the vowel shut in between two consonants. An example of the first variety is בָּ, bā, which consists of one consonant and one vowel only, whilst the second kind is illustrated by the word בַּת, (băth,) containing two consonants with a vowel in between. So the word שָׁמַר (šāmăr) has the first syllable (שָׁ) open, whilst the second (מַר) is shut.

Words in Hebrew are generally accented or stressed on the final syllable, and in transcription this is denoted by a small arrow-head over the stressed syllable, *e.g.*, זָקֵן (zāqēn). When the accent falls on the last or ultimate syllable it is said to be Milraʿ (מִלְרַע means "from beneath"). But there are also a considerable number of words stressed on the

penultimate or next to the last syllable, *e.g.*, חֶסֶד
(ḥĕṣĕdh) and this accentuation is said to be Milʿel
(מִלְעֵיל means "from above", *i.e.*, above the end of
the word). The accent rarely if ever falls on the
ante-penultimate in a word of more than two
syllables.

The tone or accent is closely related to the vowel
properties of the syllable. An open syllable generally has a long vowel, but if it carries the accent it
can have a short vowel. The word for "heaven"
conveniently illustrates this point. The pretonic
syllable of שָׁמַיִם (šā-măyĭm), *i.e.*, שָׁ, is open and has
a long vowel, but the syllable carrying the tone or
accentuation (מַ) is short, although it too is open.

Similarly a shut syllable generally has a short
vowel, but it may have a long vowel if the accent
falls on it. So with דָּבָר (dābhār) the accentuation is
milraʿ, and whilst being a shut syllable it has a long
vowel.

Out of all this may be stated an important rule :

Any syllable which is shut and does not carry the
accent must have a short vowel.

In addition to the long and short vowels, there is
another variety of enunciation which is in effect a
very quick vocalic utterance, amounting in tonal
quantity to about half of an ordinary short vowel.

The ancient Hebrews called this hurried vowel-sound the "šᵉwa" (שְׁוָא, from a root meaning "nothingness") to show its lightness of sound.

Attempts to illustrate its function in English are not wholly satisfactory, but an analogy may be found in the pronunciation of the word "banana". When we enunciate it, we do not split it up into evenly balanced syllables and say "ba-na-na", as the word is spelled. Instead we practically obliterate the first vowel "a" and substitute for it a hurried, blurred "e" sound as we press on to pronounce the second and third syllables. If this were a Hebrew word, it would then be transliterated "bᵉnana", the small superscript "e" signifying that very short tonal quality characteristic of the hurriedly pronounced vowel. Similarly the word "police" is not uttered as "po-lice", but the "o" again undergoes a change of sound in the quickness of pronunciation, and would be transliterated "pᵉlice".

The šᵉwa may be simple or augmented in nature, and in addition to the quick, light vocal sound there is also a silent form of šᵉwa. The simple šᵉwa, vocal or silent, is represented by a colon-like sign (:) placed under a consonant, while an augmented or composite form (ḥāṭēph) has one of three short vowels added to the left of it. These may be compared as follows :

Table of Š^ewas

Sign	Name	Vocalised
ְ	Simple š^ewa	It may be silent ; or it may have a short " e " sound.
ֲ	Ḥāṭēph-Păthăḥ	Slight " a " sound, *e.g.*, חֲמוֹר ḥ^amôr.
ֱ	Ḥāṭēph-S^eghôl	Slight " e" sound, *e.g* , אֱלֹהִים '^elôhîm.
ֳ	Ḥāṭēph-Qāmĕç-Ḥăṭûph	Slight " o " sound, *e.g.*, חֳלִי ḥ^olî.

The difficulty which the Semites apparently experienced in pronouncing two or more consonants together perhaps explains the frequent occurrence of the š^ewa in its various forms, some of which may now be noted.

The š^ewa, simple or augmented, is placed under every consonant which does not have a full vowel of its own if the consonant is to be articulated, or if the consonant is not the last letter of a word. So the form נקטל (nĭqṭōl) would be incorrect as written, since the ק is pronounced, and thus needs a š^ewa under it to ensure its vocalisation, *e.g.*, נְקְטֹל.

The simple š^ewa is vocalic (or sounded) when it occurs under the first consonant of a syllable,

whether at the beginning (*e.g.*, קְטֹל qᵉṭol) or in the
middle (*e.g.*, קָטְלוּ qāṭᵉlû) of a word. When it closes
a syllable in the middle of a word it is silent, *e.g.*,
יִשְׁמְרוּ (yišmᵉrû), and is not represented by any
symbol in transliteration.

When two šᵉwas occur together, as in the previous
example, the šᵉwa which appears under the שׁ will be
silent, whilst that which is under the מ is vocalic.
A šᵉwa which follows a long vowel is generally
vocalic, *e.g.*, קָמְרוּ (qāmᵉrû), whilst that which comes
after a short vowel is normally silent, *e.g.*, יִכְבַּד
(yĭkhbădh).

Four letters א ה ח ע known as guttural letters,
from their throaty pronunciation, take a composite
or augmented šᵉwa instead of a simple one. The
shapes of these have already been given in the fore-
going table. Like the simple šᵉwas, these augmented
forms are placed under the consonants, and are given
the technical name of "ḥāṭēph", from a word חָטֵף
meaning "hurried". א prefers hateph sᵉghol (ֱ), but
the other letters within the guttural class do not
exercise any especial hateph preference.

A few rare words which terminate in two sounded
consonants have simple šᵉwa under each, *e.g.*, יֵשְׁק
(yăšq). A quiescent (*i.e.*, not sounded) letter does
not take šᵉwa, *e.g.*, בִּימֵי (bîmê), not בִּימֵי (bîᵉmê). The
final form of kaph (ך) takes simple šᵉwa inside rather
than beneath, *i.e.*, לָךְ (lākh).

An important function of the simple šᵉwa silent is that it indicates a shut syllable, and thus the existence of a short vowel within that syllable. This enables us to distinguish qameç (long "a") from qameç hatuph (short "o"), since if the vowel were long "a" the syllable could not then be regarded as shut. Thus יִקְטַל reads yŏqṭăl, not yāqᵉṭăl.

If two sounded simple šᵉwas come together at the beginning of a word in process of modifying its structure, or even appear to do so, the first becomes hireq (.) whilst the second is vocalised. This often happens with a preposition which attaches itself to another word, e.g., with בְּרָכָה (bᵉrākhâ), to which we might wish to add the inseparable preposition לְ ("to" or "for"). Ordinarily we would expect this to be לְבְּרָכָה, but since it is impossible for two sounded šᵉwas to come together, the לְ becomes לִ (lĭ), hence לִבְרָכָה, "for a blessing", the point being taken out of the letter בְּ in the process.

The existence of a vocal šᵉwa in words has been held by many scholars to mark the presence of a "half-open" syllable, neither completely open nor yet fully shut. In effect this makes a syllable out of each consonant with a vocal šᵉwa, so that קְטַלְתֶּם thus becomes not qᵉṭăl-tĕm but qᵉ-ṭăl-tĕm, and יְלִידֵי becomes not yᵉlî-dhê but yᵉ-lî-dhê. It must be observed at this point that the vocal šᵉwa not infrequently retains the force of what in other forms of

the word may be a full vowel, a fact which would be
obscured if it were regarded as a silent šᵉwa simply
marking a shut syllable, without any vocalic nature
at all. This may perhaps justify the term " half-
open syllable", which some authorities jettison.

Exercise 3

Transliterate and pronounce carefully the following
practice words :

(a) 1. אֲדֹנִי   2. מִשְׁפָּט   3. טוֹבִים   4. יִקְבְּרוּ   5. חָנַן

6. מַלְכְּךָ   7. חָלֵינוּ   8. עָמְדוּ   9. אֱמוֹר   10. גְּדוֹלַי   11. כֹּהֲנִים

12. יָדֶמֶר   13. לְבָבָם   14. שָׁאֲלוּ   15. אֲנָשִׁים   16. אֱלֹהִים

17. הֶחֱטִיא   18. תְּנָה   19. אֲשֶׁר   20. מַחֲנֶה.

(b) Transliterate into Hebrew :

1. šᵉlômî.   2. yĭqṭᵉlû.   3. dᵉbhăr.   4. bᵉnê.   5. 'ălêkhĕm.
6. kᵉnă'ăn.   7. yārᵉ'û.   8. yă'ᵃzōbh.   9. ḥazāqâ.
10. 'ăhᵃrōnî.   11. hăhᵃlôm.   12. 'ᵃnăḥnû.   13. mĭšmăr.
14. bᵉrākhăth.   15. ḥazāqôth.   16. bᵉ'ênê.   17. 'ēlāyw.
18. yă'ᵃsĕh.   19. 'ᵃdhăth.   20. bᵉkhôrê.

CHAPTER FOUR

THE DAGHEŠ

THE word "dagheš" is the designation applied to a dot placed in the middle of a letter, and means "piercing" (דָּגֵשׁ). There are two principal varieties, dagheš lene (or weak) and dagheš forte (or strong). We will first consider the principles underlying the behaviour of dagheš lene.

Acquaintance has already been made with six letters which take a point in their bosom to produce a hardened tonal quality. These letters, ב ג ד כ פ ת have this dot, called dagheš lene, placed inside them whenever they do not immediately follow a vowel sound. In order to remember the letters, a mnemonic word is made by pointing them thus : בְּגַדְכְּפַת (beghădhkephăth), and which at the same time illustrated the use of dagheš lene. The first letter ב has the dagheš because it is obviously isolated from any preceding vowel sound, since it begins the word. The šewa under it is vocal, and so ג does not take dagheš lene, since in this instance a vocal šewa, simple or augmented, has the same effect as an ordinary full vowel. ד again has no dagheš lene, since it follows the vowel sound pathah under ג.

We have seen that when two šewas occur together,

the first is silent and the second vocalic. Therefore, by our rule above, ‏כ‎ will of necessity have dagheš lene, since it does not immediately follow a vowel sound, the šᵉwa under ‏ד‎ being silent. ‏פ‎ and ‏ת‎ have no dagheš since they both follow a vocalic sound.

To summarise this we may say that dagheš lene is always found in the bᵉghadhkᵉphath letters at the beginning of a word if there is no vocalic connection with the previous word, and that it also occurs at the beginning of a syllable if the previous syllable of that word is shut.

Dagheš forte was perhaps so called because it hardens or sharpens the sound of the letters containing it, whilst dagheš lene indicated a softer or lighter degree of utterance. Dagheš forte has the effect of doubling the letter in which it appears, so that ‏קִטֵּל‎ would be equivalent to ‏קִטְטֵל‎. For this to take place it will be apparent that dagheš forte must follow immediately on a vowel sound. When the letters yodh and waw appear as consonants they may take dagheš forte, e.g., ‏צִיּוֹן‎ (çîyyôn). The guttural letters ‏א ה ח ע‎, along with ‏ר‎, cannot be doubled in enunciation very well, being throaty in sound, and so can never take a dagheš. An easy way of remembering the function of dagheš forte is to recall that in music the expression "forte forte" is shortened to "ff", i.e., the single letter is doubled.

When dagheš forte is found in the beghadhkephath letters, the doubled sound is of course hard. Thus כִּפֵּר is "kĭppēr" and not "kĭphphēr". There can never be any actual confusion between dagheš forte and dagheš lene, since the former is always preceded by a vowel whilst the latter never is.

Certain letters when written with a šewa frequently omit dagheš forte. These consonants are מ נ ק י ל ו (pointed מְנַקִּילוּ mĭnqîlû, for easy memorising). Examples of this are וַיְהִי (wăyehî), not וַיְּהִי (wăyyehî), and הַלֲלוּ (hălalû), not הַלְּלוּ (hăllalû).

Dagheš forte is commonly employed as a characteristic mark of certain grammatical forms ; for example, in the "intensive" form of the regular verb we would write קִטֵּל rather than קִטֵל or קְטֵל. Occasionally a dagheš is inserted in a consonant to give greater strength to the preceding vowel, as in לָמָּה (lāmâ), and less frequently in a consonant which has a vocal šewa, to ensure its more audible enunciation, e.g., עִקְּבוֹת for עִקְבוֹת ('ĭqqebhôth). This latter is called "dagheš forte dirimens" by some scholars and "dagheš forte disjunctive" by others.

Exercise 4

(a) Correct the following words :

1. בְּנֵי 2. יִשְׂכְּלוּ 3. קֶרֶב 4. שָׂרִים 5. יָדְגְתִּי 6. גָּדוֹל

7. אֲדֹנָם 8. כְּבַדְתֶּן 9. בְּתוֹרוּ 10. כָּלְפָּם.

(*b*) Write in Hebrew :

1. hăllê.   2. mĕlq^ekhăth.   3. mĕkhĕbh.   4. šĭggēr
5. mălk^ekhû.   6. b^ekhĕm.   7. lă'ărăth.   8. yĭbbām.
9. mĭdhb^erû.   10. kĭppēnî.

CHAPTER FIVE

THE GUTTURAL AND QUIESCENT LETTERS

WE have already observed that the letters ע ח ה א are styled "guttural," and to these may now be added the letter ר, which in certain respects may be regarded as coming within the same class. Their special characteristics are as follows :

None of these letters can take dagheš forte, and when the dagheš ought to be present, a short vowel preceding it is lengthened in compensation. For example, whereas a certain form of the regular verb קָטַל (qāṭăl) is קִטֵּל (qĭṭṭēl), the corresponding form of בָּרַךְ (bārăkh) is not בִּרֵךְ (bĭrrēkh) but בֵּרֵךְ (bērēkh), the hireq being lengthened to çere, since ר cannot be doubled. This procedure always happens before א and ר, and frequently before ע. With ה and ח, on the other hand, the compensatory lengthening is seldom needed, since their sounds are by nature almost as strong as a normally reduplicated consonant. In such cases the guttural is said to have an "implicit" dagheš, *i.e.*, not הָהוּא (hāhû') but הַהוּא (hăhû'), and is given the Latin name of "dagheš forte implicitum".

Gutturals never take a simple vocal šᵉwa, but always an augmented one, and often prefer a compound šᵉwa to a simple silent one. So we would write

אֱלֹהִים ('elōhîm) rather than אָלֹהִים, and יַחֲזִיק (yăḥᵃzîq) in place of יַחֲזִיק. Whilst, as we have already noticed, א prefers an "e" vowel (sᵉghol or hateph sᵉghol), the other gutturals generally have pathah under or preceding them. Thus, whilst we would write מֶלֶךְ (mĕlĕkh) with sᵉghol, the word מֶלַח (mĕlăḥ), ending in a guttural, takes pathah. Hireq under gutturals, however, is rare. Any short vowel occurring before a final guttural except א becomes pathah. If a guttural is preceded by a short vowel, the šᵉwa resulting under the guttural is the short-vowel augment of the hateph, e.g., בַּעֲלִי (bă'ᵃlî), יֶאֱמֹר (yĕ'ᵉmôr), לְחֳלִי (lŏḥᵒlî).

In practice we shall see that when a final guttural letter is preceded by any long vowel except qameç, it is not easy to articulate, and this difficulty was overcome by slipping in a pathah sound between the long vowel and the final guttural. The pathah in such a case is written under the guttural but is pronounced before it, e.g., רוּחַ is pronounced "rûăḥ" instead of being רוּח (rûḥ). This device is called "pathah furtive". When a word of this sort no longer terminates in a guttural the pathah disappears, e.g., רוּחִי (rûḥî).

Exercise 5

Correct and pronounce the following words:

1. רָאֶמֶת 2. חֲכָמִים 3. שָׂרִים 4. מִשְׁחָדוּ 5. רוּחוֹ 6. הַיֶּלֶךְ
7. מְאָדָם 8. זֶבַח 9. בַּעֲלִי 10. לְעָבִיר.

The Quiescent Letters are א ה ו י, and they frequently surrender their ordinary consonantal function in favour of coalescing or uniting with surrounding vowel sounds, and thus becoming silent or "quiescent". This, however, may happen only at the end of a syllable or word. When they occur at the beginning they are treated as full consonants. Final א is always silent, whilst yodh and waw are only silent when accompanied by a homogeneous vowel. The latter two consonants coalesce to form full hireq and çere, and full holem and šureq respectively, *i.e.*, ִי; ֵי; וֹ; וּ. Thus עֵינֵי is "'ênê", not "'êynêy", and הוּא is "hû'", not "hûw'". But when any other sort of vowel than those which are homogeneous to them, as above, is introduced, they retain their consonantal pronunciation. Thus חַו is "hăw" and גּוֹי is "gôy". Sometimes the consonants yodh and waw combine with vowels to produce sounds analogous to our diphthongs, as follows :

ַי or ָי is pronounced ai as in aisle, *e.g.*, סוּסַי (sûsāy).

וֹי is pronounced oi as in toil, *e.g.*, הוֹי (hôy).

ָיו is pronounced ou as in foul, *e.g.*, סוּסָיו (sûsâw).

When these consonants quiesce, they do not take the silent šᵉwa, *e.g.*, יֹאמֶר (yō'mēr), not יְאֹמֶר. When quiescent letters occur between a vowel and a

strongly enunciated consonant, they are not pronounced, e.g., רֹאשׁ (rô'š). Where a quiescent letter
terminates a word, the final vowel is generally long,
since otherwise the syllable would be virtually left
open, e.g., מָצָא (māçā') for מָצְא.

CHAPTER SIX

PRELIMINARY MARKS AND ACCENTS

SOME notice may now be taken of certain accents and their function in relation to words and sentences.

Măppîq (מַפִּיק, "extending") is the name given to the dagheš inserted in a final ה to ensure its pronunciation as a full consonant. Thus, whilst מָה would be "mâ", דָּמָה is "dāmāh", with the ה audibly enunciated. Similarly, גָּבַה is "gābhăh".

Rāphĕ (רָפֶה "soft") is a short horizontal line written above the letter to call attention to the absence or omission of a dagheš forte or mappiq in the interests of smoother enunciation, *e.g.*, וּלְמִקְצֵה (ûleˈmĭqçēh) for וּלְמִקְצֵה.

Măqqēph (מַקֵּף, "binding"), is a small horizontal stroke written at the top of the line, between two or more words, to connect them in such a way that they become one for purposes of tonal stress and accentuation. Thus, whereas the words כֹּל (kōl) and אָדָם ('ādhām) would each have their own accents, when joined by maqqeph the accent for the phrase thus formed becomes milra', *i.e.*, כָּל־אָדָם, and because of this the holem of כֹּל becomes the short vowel qameç hatuph, since it is now in a shut unaccented syllable. The same happens with the accusative

particle אֵת, which, when joined to another word, loses its own accentuation and thus has a short vowel, *e.g.*, אֶת־כָּל־עֵשֶׂב ('ĕth-kŏl-'ēsĕbh). When זֶה (zĕh) and מָה (mâ) are joined to the next word by maqqeph, a "conjunctive" dagheš forte is always inserted in the initial letter following maqqeph, *e.g.*, זֶה־סּוּסִי (zĕh-ṣûṣî) or מַה־לָּךְ (măh-lāk).

Mĕthĕg (מֶתֶג "bridle") is a small perpendicular stroke placed to the left of a vowel in close proximity to the tone, to make sure that the vowel is properly pronounced and not neglected in favour of accenting the tone vowel. Metheg is placed by the second full open syllable from the tone, whether it is long, *e.g.*, הָאָדָם (hā-'ā-dhām), or short, *e.g.*, הֶהָרִים (hĕ-hā-rîm). Metheg also stands by the vowel which precedes a simple or augmented šᵉwa, *e.g.*, קָטְלָה (qāṭᵉlâ), פֶּעֳלוֹ (pŏ‘ᵒlô), and thus indicates that the šᵉwa is vocal. Again, this helps to distinguish between long "a" and short "o", as in אָכְלָה ('ŏkhlâ) and אָכְלָה ('ākhᵉlâ). In the latter word the šᵉwa with its consonant does duty as a syllable.

Hebrew, as we have noted, is a strongly accented language, and the purpose of the accent-symbols is generally twofold. Firstly, they show the relation of the particular word to the rest of the sentence by acting as punctuation marks, and secondly they serve to mark the tone syllable. For our present

purposes only two major punctuation marks need be mentioned, as follows :

The sign (ְ) or 'Ăthnāḥ (אֶתְנָח) is placed under the tone syllable of the word which constitutes the most important logical pause within the sentence, which in English would probably be marked by a colon or semicolon.

Ṣĭllûq (סִלּוּק) is a perpendicular line identical in form with metheg, and is always placed under the tone syllable of the last word of a verse, which is then always followed by the Hebrew "period" or "full stop" (:), the Ṣôph pāṣûq (סוֹף פָּסוּק), *e.g.,*: הָאָרֶץ.

Though the same sign does duty for metheg and silluq, and though they can both occur in the same word, *e.g.*, מֵהָאָדָם (mēhā'ādhām), there need be no real confusion. If the perpendicular stroke comes under the accented syllable at the end of a verse it must be silluq ; if it is found under a word in the middle of a verse it is metheg. If it is under the tone it is silluq ; if it is under the second full syllable from the tone and that syllable is open, it is metheg.

A word is said to be "in pause" when it has 'athnah or silluq as its accentuation, and any short vowel thus accented becomes long. Thus, מַיִם (măyĭm) in pause becomes : מָיִם with silluq or מָיִם with 'athnah. Most sentences in the Hebrew Bible

will be seen to illustrate the position of these two major stops.

When perusing a Hebrew Bible the reader will notice in the margin at the bottom of the page a number of variant readings, consisting of consonants which are to be preferred to their counterparts in the text. Because the ancient Hebrew text was regarded as sacred, the consonants therein could not be modified or disturbed at all, hence the variants were assigned to the foot of the page in the printed text. The original consonantal text was called the Keᵗhîbh (כְּתִיב, "written"), whilst the variants were named Qeᵉrê (קְרִי "to be read"). Generally an asterisk or small circle calls attention in the text to the presence of a variant. The procedure then is to read the consonants of the Qeᵉre in conjunction with the vowels already under the particular word in the Keᵗhibh. Thus, in Psalm ix. 13, the Keᵗhibh is עֲנִיִּים whilst the marginal consonantal variant reads עניים קרי, i.e., "עניים is to be read". Thus the correct word combines the vowels of the Keᵗhibh with the consonants of the Qeᵉre, which is עֲנָיִּם.

In instances of such frequent occurrence that it would be tedious to print the Qeᵉre each time the Keᵗhibh requires such modification, a permanent Qeᵉre or "Qeᵉre perpetuum" has been devised, which the student retains in his memory. In this, the

vowels for the variant reading are placed in the text as usual, but the consonants are omitted from the margin, and the reader substitutes the reading for the Kᵉthibh without being warned to do so by an asterisk or circle appearing over the word in question.

The Divine Name illustrates this adequately. יהוה, the name of the God of Israel, is generally pointed יְהֹוָה, from which by transliteration comes our hybrid English form "Jehovah". It was regarded as too sacred to pronounce in its original form (which may have sounded something like "Yahweh"), so another sound was supplied by the word אֲדֹנָי ('adhonāy), and the consonants יהוה were given the pointing of אֲדֹנָי, making the impossible form יְהֹוָה (the hateph under א becoming a simple šᵉwa under י).

The consonantal form of the third singular personal pronoun "she" appears frequently in the Pentateuch as הוא. At some time confusion has arisen between the masculine הוא (hû') and the feminine היא (hî'), and this is obvious from the Kᵉthibh (הוא). Again, the Qᵉre for the feminine is not given because it occurs so often.

CHAPTER SEVEN

THE DEFINITE ARTICLE

THERE is no indefinite article in Hebrew. Thus מַיִם (măyĭm) means "water" or "waters", and יוֹם (yôm) means "a day", representing the noun in its simplest form. When we wish to say "the waters" or "the day", it is necessary to employ a prefix, the consonant ה, with various vowels accompanying it. Originally the definite article may have been הַל (like the Arabic article "al" as in "algebra"), with the ל being assimilated to the next consonant, and this may be the reason why dagheš forte is used frequently with the article.

Generally the article is ה, pointed with pathah and followed by dagheš forte in the first consonant of the word to which it is prefixed. When such a word begins with א ה ח ע or ר, the dagheš forte cannot be inserted, since these letters are guttural in force, and the pathah of the article in such cases is lengthened to qameç in compensation, except with ה and ח. When ע and ה as initial letters have the tone or accent, and are written with qameç, the pointing of the article is again qameç, but when they occur with qameç and do not take the tone, the pointing of the article then becomes seghol. Before חָ and הָ the article always takes seghol.

These rules may be conveniently illustrated in tabular form as follows :

Before Consonants	Article Pointing	Examples
Ordinary	הַ	הַקּוֹל, הַמַּיִם
א ע ר	הָ	הָאוֹר, הָעַיִן, הָראֹשׁ
ה ח	הַ	הַהוּא, הַחשֶׁךְ
עֲ הָ	הָ	הָעָם, הָהָר
עָ הָ	הֶ	הֶעָפָר, הֶהָרִים
חָ חֱ	הֶ	הֶחָכָם, הֶחֱלִי

In a few common nouns the vowel of the initial consonant is lengthened to qameç when the article is prefixed. These words include אֶרֶץ ('ĕrĕç), הַר (hăr), עַם ('ăm), and רַע (ră'), which become הָאָרֶץ (hā'ārĕç), הָהָר (hāhār), הָעָם (hā'ām) and הָרָע (hārā').

The article in Hebrew may be used demonstratively, e.g., הַיּוֹם means "this day" or "to-day". The vocative is also expressed by the article on occasions, as הַבַּעַל "O Baal", and is sometimes used generically to designate the member of a class where English

usage would lead us to expect an indefinite article, *e.g.*, "an enemy" in Hebrew is הָאֹיֵב (hā'ōyēbh). The article is also attached to an attributive adjective qualifying a definite noun. So "the good man" would be "the man, the good one". A further distinctive use of the article is with proper names, to show that the individual is supreme in his class, *e.g.*, "God" is הָאֱלֹהִים (hā'elōhîm).

From this point we shall abandon the practice of transliterating each Hebrew word, except in special cases where the modification of the word affects the pronunciation, and which would not be recognisable by other means. We shall also introduce a vocabulary before each subsequent exercise, which the student is expected to learn carefully. In these vocabularies all nouns will be considered to be masculine unless otherwise marked.

VOCABULARY

אֶרֶץ	earth (*f*).	שָׁמַיִם	heavens.	טוֹב	good.
יוֹם	day.	עַם	people.	רַע	bad.
אִישׁ	man.	אֱלֹהִים	God (*pl.*).	עַיִן	eye (*f*).
קוֹל	voice.	בֹּקֶר	morning.	עָפָר	dust.
מֶלֶךְ	king.	מַיִם	water(s) (*pl.*)	רָקִיעַ	firmament.
אִשָּׁה	woman (*f*).	עִיר	city (*f*).	גָּדוֹל	great.
רָם	high.	חֹשֶׁךְ	darkness.	אוֹר	light.

Exercise 6

Write out the following :

The man, the people, the waters, to-day, the king, the firmament, the voice, the darkness, the eye, the morning, a woman, a day, the dust, the light.

CHAPTER EIGHT

THE CONJUNCTION : ADJECTIVES

THE usual form of the conjunction "and" in Hebrew is waw with simple vocal šᵉwa, but there are variations of this as follows :

Under ordinary circumstances it is וְ, e.g., אִישׁ וְאִשָּׁה, (man and woman.) Because it is a labial it cannot have a šᵉwa before another labial sound, and so it becomes וּ before מ ו ב and פ, e.g., וּפָרָה, (and a cow). This is the only exception to the rule which we learned earlier, that no Hebrew word begins with a vowel, but even here the consonantal waw, in one sense, still begins the spelling of the word, and only becomes a vowel (šureq) by the addition of dagheš in its bosom.

If the conjunction comes immediately before the accent, however, the waw may have qameç instead of being šureq, e.g., לֶחֶם וָמַיִם, bread and water. Before another šᵉwa it also becomes šureq, e.g., וּדְבָרִים, (and words), but before a hateph it takes the corresponding short vowel, שׁוֹר וַחֲמוֹר, ox and ass.

When occurring before yodh with šᵉwa, the yodh quiesces and the conjunction then takes hireq, e.g., וִיהוּדָה and Judah, not וְיְהוּדָה. Before יהוה the con-

junction takes pathah, *i.e.*, וַיִּהְיֶה, but when written
to אֱלֹהִים it takes çere, which is then assimilated into
the vowel sound under the 'aleph to become וֵאלֹהִים,
and God, for וֵאלֹהִים. When a word is written with
the article, the conjunction does not displace the ה of
the article, *e.g.*, וְהָאִישׁ, and the man.

Adjectives

When an adjective qualifies a noun in Hebrew, it
follows it in the order of words. Thus, "a good man"
would be "a man, a good one", *i.e.*, אִישׁ טוֹב. The
adjective always agrees in gender and number with
its noun, as in other languages. Until we have
learned the inflections of the noun we will confine
ourselves to the masculine singular form as above.
When the adjective is used predicatively, *e.g.*, "the
man is good", it does not take the article and
generally precedes the noun.

The present tense of the verb "to be" is not
normally expressed in Hebrew. Thus the sentence
"the man is good" would be rendered "the man (is)
good" (הָאִישׁ טוֹב), or more frequently "good (is) the
man" (טוֹב הָאִישׁ). When an attributive adjective
qualifies a definite noun, it has the article attached.
So, "the good man" would be הָאִישׁ הַטּוֹב, *i.e.*, "the
man, the good one". If there is more than one
adjective, the article is repeated with each, *e.g.*, "the
great and good day" becomes הַיּוֹם הַגָּדוֹל וְהַטּוֹב.

VOCABULARY

הַר	mountain.	זָהָב	gold.	כֶּסֶף	silver.
רֹאשׁ	head.	קָצֵר	short.	יָד	hand (f).
דָּבָר	word.	אֶבֶן	stone (f).	בַּת	daughter (f).
עֶרֶב	evening.	חֲלִי	disease.	נָבִיא	prophet.
לַיְלָה	night.	הֵיכָל	temple, palace.	חֶרֶב	sword (f).
יַרְכָה	side (f).	קָרָא	to call.	רָאָה	to see.

Exercise 7

Translate the following :

‏(a) ‏1. ‏טוֹב הַנָּבִיא ‏2. ‏הַנָּבִיא הַטּוֹב ‏3. ‏הַבֹּקֶר הַגָּדוֹל וְהַטּוֹב
‏4. ‏רָם הָהָר ‏5. ‏הָאִישׁ וְהַנָּבִיא ‏6. ‏הַהֵיכָל גָּדוֹל וְטוֹב
‏7. ‏הַלַּיְלָה וְהַיּוֹם ‏8. ‏הַבַּת וְהָאִשָּׁה ‏9. ‏הָאִישׁ הַמֶּלֶךְ ‏10. ‏טוֹב
‏הַזָּהָב.

(b) 1. The great man. 2. To-day. 3. The evening and the morning. 4. Gold and silver. 5. The king is great and good. 6. The hand and the eye. 7. The woman and the man. 8. The people is great. 9. The disease and the prophet. 10. The great day and the bad night.

CHAPTER IX

THE NOUN AND ITS INFLECTION

THERE are only two genders in Hebrew, masculine and feminine, and three numbers, singular, plural and dual. The dual is used with nouns only, chiefly with objects coming in pairs.

The masculine nouns in the singular have scarcely any termination to indicate their gender, whereas in the feminine there are several distinctive terminations.

Masculine nouns may be classified thus :

(a) Names of members of the male sex, with their office, e.g.., דָּוִד David, סוּס horse, שֹׁפֵט judge.

(b) Names of kingdoms and peoples, e.g., אַשּׁוּר, people of Assyria, יִשְׂרָאֵל, Israel.

(c) Names of mountains, rivers, metals ; months of the year, e.g., לְבָנוֹן Lebanon, פְּרָת Euphrates, כֶּסֶף silver, אָבִיב Abib.

The plural ending of masculine nouns is ־ִים, or written defectively, ־ִם, and is generally attached to the singular form, e.g., סוּסִים, horses. The ending ־ֶה modifies to ־ִים in plural forms, e.g., רֹעֶה becomes רֹעִים, shepherds. Not all masculine nouns have the normal plural ending, however ; אָב

father, is אָבוֹת in the plural, whilst others have an irregular form, *e.g.*, אִישׁ in the plural is אֲנָשִׁים.

Nouns ending in הָ‍ are generally feminine, and this form was an original תָ‍ or ‍תְ‍, the former of which is preserved in some names, *e.g.*, אֵילַת Elath, נַחַת rest. A great number of forms are construed as feminine, however, which do not possess the feminine ending.

Feminine nouns may be classified as follows :

(*a*) Names of females, with their functions, *e.g.*, מִרְיָם Miriam, אֵם mother, כַּלָּה bride.

(*b*) Names of the elements, *e.g.*, אֵשׁ fire, אֶרֶץ earth, אֶבֶן stone.

(*c*) Countries regarded as mothers of their peoples : פָּרַס Persia, צִיּוֹן Zion.

(*d*) Organs of the body coming in pairs : יָד hand, רֶגֶל foot, קֶרֶן horn.

(*e*) Things abstract : נֶפֶשׁ soul, life, בְּכוֹרָה birthright, טוֹבָה goodness.

(*f*) Names of instruments and utensils : כּוֹס cup, חֶרֶב sword, מִשְׁכָּב couch.

The plural ending of feminine nouns is וֹת‍, or written defectively ‍ת‍. When the singular form has no feminine ending, the plural termination is joined immediately to it, *e.g.*, בְּאֵר well, בְּאֵרוֹת. The ordinary feminine singular ending is replaced by the

plural termination, *e.g.*, שָׂרָה princess, becomes שָׂרוֹת
princesses.

The above inflections may be clarified by means of
a table :

Masculine Singular	Feminine Singular	Masculine Plural	Feminine Plural
סוּס	סוּסָה	סוּסִים	סוּסוֹת
נָבִיא	נְבִיאָה	נְבִיאִים	נְבִיאוֹת
דָּג	דָּגָה	דָּגִים	דָּגוֹת

The dual masculine and feminine of סוּס would be
סוּסַיִם and סוּסָתַיִם respectively.

The dual ending ־ַיִם used above is found with
both masculine and feminine nouns. It is employed
for substantives and pairs of objects as follows :

(*a*) Bodily organs : אָזְנַיִם ears, רַגְלַיִם two feet.

(*b*) Objects comprising two parts : מֶלְקָחַיִם tongs,
דְּלָתַיִם double-door.

(*c*) Double and quantitative numbers : שְׁנַיִם two,
שִׁבְעָתַיִם sevenfold.

Adjectives, as we have seen, agree in gender and
number with the nouns which they qualify, *e.g.*, the
good woman, הָאִשָּׁה הַטּוֹבָה, good years, שָׁנִים טוֹבוֹת.

Some nouns are found only in plural form, the most common being שָׁמַיִם heaven, מַיִם water, פָּנִים face, חַיִּים life, עֲלוּמִים youth, זְקֻנִים old age.

Some common nouns of masculine gender with the plural form in ־וֹת are :

אָב father.	מִזְבֵּחַ altar.	עוֹר skin.
חֲלוֹם dream.	מָקוֹם place.	קוֹל voice.
לֵב, לֵבָב heart.	בְּאֵר well, cistern.	שֻׁלְחָן table.
לַיְלָה night.	אוֹת sign.	שֵׁם name.
שׁוֹפָר trumpet.	מַקֵּל staff.	כִּסֵּא throne.

Some common feminine nouns with the plural form in ־ים are :

אֶבֶן stone.	עִיר city.	שְׂעוֹרָה barley.
אִשָּׁה woman.	חִטָּה wheat.	מִלָּה word.
יוֹנָה dove.	אֵלָה terebinth.	תְּאֵנָה fig tree.

VOCABULARY

אֹזֶן ear (f).	כּוֹכָב star.	רֶגֶל foot (f).
פַּר ox.	מִדְבָּר desert.	נַעַל sandal (f).
שָׁמַע to hear.	עֵץ tree.	דָּג fish.
יֶלֶד boy.	שָׂפָה lip (f).	לָקַח to take.
־עַל over, upon	קָדוֹשׁ holy.	יָשַׁב to sit.
־אֶל unto.	צַדִּיק righteous.	שַׁבָּת sabbath.
אֵשׁ fire.	קֶרֶן horn (f).	הֲלֹם hither.

Exercise 8

(a) Translate :

1. דְּבָרִים 2. סוּסִים 3. אָבוֹת 4. הַיָּדַיִם 5. הַיַּרְכָתַיִם
6. זְקֵנִים 7. לְבָבוֹת 8. בְּאֵרוֹת 9. עָרִים 10. רַגְלַיִם

(b) 1. Tables. 2. Stones. 3. Two-years. 4. Trumpets.
5. The horse and the mare. 6. Good fathers. 7. The
princess is great. 8. Two eyes and two ears. 9. Good
men and good women. 10. Sons and daughters.

CHAPTER X

PRONOUNS AND PARTICLES

PRONOUNS do duty for nouns, and may be separable or inseparable. The Personal pronoun is used only to express the nominative case, but in fragmentary form it is attached to other words to represent the oblique cases.

The Personal pronoun is as follows :

Singular	Plural
אֲנִי I אָנֹכִי I	אֲנַחְנוּ we.
אַתָּה thou (m.)	אַתֶּם you (m.)
אַתְּ thou (f.)	אַתֶּן, אַתֵּנָה you (f.)
הוּא he	הֵם, הֵמָּה they (m.)
הִיא she	הֵנָּה (הֵן) they (f.)

Modifications occur in pause, e.g., first singular אָנִי, אָנֹכִי, second singular masculine אָתָּה, second singular feminine אָתְּ, first plural אֲנָחְנוּ. Both second plural feminine forms are rare.

The third person of the pronoun is sometimes used

as a copulative in the appropriate gender and number in sentences where the verb "to be" occurs :

The woman is good.   הָאִשָּׁה הִיא טוֹבָה

The mountains are lofty.   הֶהָרִים הֵם רָמִים

Jehovah is (the) God.   יהוה הוּא הָאֱלֹהִים

Sometimes the third person pronoun is used with a subject of the second person, *e.g.*, Thou (he) art the God, אַתָּה הוּא הָאֱלֹהִים.

Demonstrative Pronouns

The pronouns used to indicate relative objects are :

	Masculine	Feminine
this	זֶה	זֹאת
these	אֵלֶּה	אֵלֶּה
that	הוּא	הִיא
those	הֵם, הֵמָּה	(הֵן) הֵנָּה

When a demonstrative is used adjectivally it follows the noun, which is definite, and so it too takes the article, *e.g.*, "that day" becomes הַיּוֹם הַהוּא. When used predicatively they do not take the article, and the order of the Hebrew follows that of the English. So "this is the good man" is זֶה הָאִישׁ הַטּוֹב.   The

demonstrative of the near object when repeated acquires a correlative significance, "the one . . . the other" (זֶה . . . זֶה or זֹאת . . . זֹאת) ; and "some . . . others" (אֵלֶּה . . . אֵלֶּה).

Interrogative Pronoun

The absence of a question mark in Hebrew makes it necessary for simple questions to have some characteristic interrogative prefix. One of these is the particle הֲ, which is pointed as follows :

(a) With ordinary consonants it is הֲ, *e.g.*, הֲזֶה is this ?

(b) With simple šᵉwa as the first vowel it is הַ, *e.g.*, הַמְאֹד, is it much ? This is sometimes followed by dagheš forte.

(c) Before gutturals without qameç it is הַ, *e.g.*, הַאַתָּה art thou ?

(d) Before any guttural with qameç the הֲ takes sᵉghol, *e.g.*, הֶחָזָק is it strong ?

Two other interrogative pronouns are also used : מִי "who ?" which is invariable in form, and מָה "what ?" Both of these are indeclinable, and usually come first in a sentence. The pointing of מָה is exactly like that of the article, and it is joined by maqqeph to the next word, with the insertion of dagheš forte in non-guttural letters, *e.g.*, מַה־זֶּה what is this ?, מָה־אֲנִי what am I ?

מָה may also be used as an exclamatory expression with another word, *e.g.*, מַה־נּוֹרָא הַמָּקוֹם הַזֶּה, how dreadful is this place ! (Genesis xxviii. 17). Before verbs and adverbs it frequently does duty as an adverb, *e.g.*, מַה־טּוֹב how good. מִי and מָה may be used in an indefinite sense to mean "whoever" and "whatever".

Relative Pronouns

The word אֲשֶׁר is indeclinable and is a general term of relation which is made specific by some other word in the context. Thus whilst we would say in English, "the house where he dwelt" (שָׁכַן), the Hebrew idiom would render it "the house which he dwelt there", the last word of the phrase defining the exact nature of the relation, *i.e.*, הַבַּיִת אֲשֶׁר שָׁכַן שָׁם. Similarly, "the house whence he came (בָּא)" would be הַבַּיִת אֲשֶׁר בָּא מִשָּׁם, *i.e.*, "the house that he came from there".

Notice should be taken of the following combinations :

שָׁם there,	אֲשֶׁר . . . שָׁם where.
שָׁמָּה thither,	אֲשֶׁר . . . שָׁמָּה whither.
מִשָּׁם thence,	אֲשֶׁר . . . מִשָּׁם whence.

Other pronominal expressions are :

שָׁם . . . שָׁם	here . . there.
לֹא . . . אִישׁ	nobody ("not a man").

or	לֹא . . . כֹּל	none ("not any").
	כֹּל . . . לֹא	
	אִישׁ . . . אִישׁ	one . . . another.
	אֵלֶּה . . . אֵלֶּה	some . . . others.

VOCABULARY

עָשָׂה	to do.	תּוֹרָה	law (f).	גִּבּוֹר	mighty man,
שֶׁמֶשׁ	sun.	פֶּה	mouth.		hero.
נֶפֶשׁ	soul (f).	נָתַן	to give, set.	שִׁיר	song.
בַּיִת	house.	זָכַר	to remember.	רוּחַ	wind,
בֵּן	son.	שָׁכַח	to forget.		spirit (f).
יָרַד	to go down.	דָּם	blood.	שָׁמַר	to keep.
סוּס	horse.	אָסַף	to gather.	יָם	sea.
מִצְוָה	command (f).	לֹא	not.	מַלְכָּה	queen (f).
אֲהָהּ	alas!	בְּרָכָה	blessing.	דֶּרֶךְ	way.

Exercise 9

Translate:

‏1. אֲנִי הָאִישׁ.   2. הַחֹשֶׁךְ הַגָּדוֹל הוּא הַלַּיְלָה.   3. אַתְּ הַבַּת הַטּוֹבָה   4. הוּא אִישׁ טוֹב.   5. מַה־הִיא.   6. הַגִּבּוֹרִים הָאֵלֶּה   7. מַה־זֹּאת אֲשֶׁר עָשָׂה.   8. הַבַּת הַטּוֹבָה הַהִיא   9. מַה־רָם הַמָּקוֹם הַזֶּה.   10. הֶעָצוּם מְאֹד הוּא.

1. These are the wise men.   2. Those heavens.   3. This woman is good.   4. This good man. 5. This is the good and powerful man.   6. What a city!   7. What a palace! 8. He is the man who was over the house.   9. I am the powerful king who is over the great land.   10. These are the heavens and the earth and the sea.

CHAPTER XI

THE INSEPARABLE PREPOSITIONS

ORIGINALLY the prepositions with which we are now concerned were nouns, but have become fragmentary in process of time and are always prefixed to the word which they govern. They are :

בְּ, in, on, by, with (perhaps from an original בַּיִת).

כְּ, like, about, as, according to (from a possible original כֵּן).

לְ, at, to, for (perhaps from אֶל־ or אַל־).

The rules for pointing are as follows :

(a) The general pointing is šᵉwa, e.g., בְּעִיר in a city כְּאֶבֶן like a stone.

(b) Before another šᵉwa they take hireq in the ordinary way, e.g., לִבְרָכָה,, for a blessing, not לְבְרָכָה.

(c) Before gutturals with a hateph the šᵉwa is replaced by the corresponding short vowel of the augment, e.g., כַּאֲרִי like a lion. The only exceptions to this are words like אֱלֹהִים which are frequently found in the text, where the א becomes quiescent, the hateph sᵉghol is removed, and the preposition takes çere, i.e., לֵאלֹהִים. The Divine Name יהוה, taking its pointing from אֲדֹנָי, has pathah under the preposition in the same way, e.g., לַאדֹנָי for לַאֲדֹנָי, and so לַיהוָה.

63

(*d*) If the preposition falls in the pretone, the vowel under it is frequently qameç, *e.g.*, בְּמַ֫יִם in water, לָבֶ֫טַח securely.

(*e*) A word which has the article prefixed also generally surrenders the ה, and the preposition then assumes its vowel, *e.g.*, לְהָאִישׁ to the man, becomes לָאִישׁ ; בְּהַסֵּ֫פֶר becomes בַּסֵּ֫פֶר.

The preposition לְ frequently indicates a dative of possession, as in the phrase "the man has a daughter", which becomes בַּת לָאִישׁ, "there is a daughter to the man". The inseparable prepositions are frequently joined with מה to form adverbs, thus לָ֫מָּה why? ; בַּמֶּה or בַּמָּה, wherein? ; כַּמָּה, כַּמֶּה, how much? ; עַד־מָה, עַד־מֶה, how long? ; עַל־מֶה, עַל־מָה, wherefore, whereupon.

The preposition מִן is partly separable and partly not. When followed by the article it may remain separable, and is followed by maqqeph, *e.g.*, מִן־הָעִיר, from the city, though the final נ may be dropped and the hireq lengthened to çere as a compensation, *e.g.*, מֵהָעִיר. מִן does not displace the consonant of the article like the inseparable prepositions.

Before non-gutturals the weak terminal נ is generally assimilated to the following consonant, which being in effect doubled takes a compensative dagheš forte, *e.g.*, מִמֶּ֫לֶךְ from a king, instead of מִנְמֶ֫לֶךְ. The dagheš may be omitted from a letter

pointed with šᵉwa, e.g., מִמְּלִילֹת for מִמְּלִילוֹת. When the initial consonant is yodh with šᵉwa, the dagheš is omitted whilst the yodh drops the šᵉwa and coalesces to form long hireq, e.g., מִירִיחוֹ, from Jericho, for מִיְרִיחוֹ. Before gutturals or ר the full form may be used, מִן־עִיר from a city, or the final ן may be dropped and the hireq lengthened to çere, e.g., מֵעֵץ, from a tree, for מִן־עֵץ, making the preposition inseparable.

VOCABULARY

אֲרִי lion.	בְּהֵמָה beast, cattle. (f)	בְּרִית covenant. (f).
חֲמוֹר ass.	שָׁבַת to rest.	עַד־עוֹלָם for ever.
מְאֹד very.	שָׁפַךְ to shed.	מָשַׁל (בְּ) to rule (over).
אָדָם mankind.	שָׁאַל to ask.	פָּעַל to do.
אֲדָמָה ground (f).	תְּפִלָּה prayer (f).	שְׁמוּאֵל Samuel.
כָּתַב to write.	עַד־ until, unto.	יוֹסֵף Joseph.
כָּרַת to cut.	רַב much (pl. רַבִּים).	אָח brother.
יְהוֹשֻׁעַ Joshua.	אֹכֶל food.	חָדַל to leave off, cease.
מִצְרַיִם Egypt.	מֵעוֹלָם from of old.	
עוֹלָם age, duration.		

Exercise 10

Translate :

‎1. בְּשָׁלוֹם ‎2. כַּיהוָה ‎3. לְחָלִי ‎4. לִשְׁמוּאֵל ‎5. יוֹם וָלַיְלָה ‎6. בֶּן לַמֶּלֶךְ ‎7. לֶחֶם וָמַיִם הֵם טוֹבִים מְאֹד הֵם בַּשָּׁמַיִם ‎8. מַחְשָׁךְ עַד־הַיּוֹם ‎9. עָפָר מִן־הָאֲדָמָה אֲנַחְנוּ ‎10. הָאֱלֹהִים הוּא בַּהֵיכָל הַזֶּה.

C

1. In God.　2. As a lion.　3. To Joshua.　4. Jehovah is in the heavens.　5. From the mountain.　6. The son is like the king.　7. On the lofty mountain in the morning. 8. The palace is for the king.　9. The wise people are in the temple in the evening.　10. The prophet has a daughter and a son.

CHAPTER XII

THE VERB : ORDER OF WORDS

IN earlier chapters we have considered two important
groups of words which comprise the sentence,
namely nouns and particles, and on this basis we
have been able to build up small synthetic Hebrew
sentences. Now we have to begin consideration of
an important component of all sentences, and that is
the verb. In Hebrew there are a number of inflections and tenses which express developed meanings
of the simple verb stem, but we shall leave the bulk
of these to later sections, and concentrate on the
parts necessary for simple expression.

The verb generally stands first in order at the
beginning of a sentence, and elsewhere precedes its
subject. This structure emphasises the importance
of the verb as the "action-word" of the sentence.
The presence of a direct object of a verb is indicated
by means of a particle, אֵת, which is the sign of the
accusative case, and is regularly used in prose before
the direct object. If a noun is indefinite, or if it is
the indirect object of a verb, the particle is not
employed, nor is it used very much in poetic
writings. אֵת is largely joined to its noun by maqqeph,
and since it then becomes a shut syllable, the çere
becomes sᵉghol, i.e., אֶת־. If there are more than

one of such nouns, the accusative particle is repeated
with each of them. Whereas in English and some
other languages the root or simplest form of the verb
is the infinitive, in Hebrew the third person singular
of the perfect active is used instead. Thus, קָרָא does
not really mean "to call", as is generally written in
vocabularies and lexicons, but "he called".

The inflection of the verb is made by adding the
endings of the personal pronoun to the root, observing the usual modifications in pointing with respect
to the position of the tone. The verb קָטַל is used as
a model for the paradigm, since it illustrates these
inflections well, although it is a rare word found only
in poetry. The perfect tense is as follows :

קָטַל	he killed, he has killed	(3rd sing. masc.)
קָטְלָה	she killed, has killed	(3rd sing. fem.)
קָטַלְתָּ	thou hast killed	(2nd sing. masc.)
קָטַלְתְּ	thou (f.) hast killed	(2nd sing. fem.)
קָטַלְתִּי	I killed, have killed	(1st sing. common)
קָטְלוּ	they killed, did kill	(3rd plur. common)
קְטַלְתֶּם	ye killed, have killed	(2nd plur. masc.)
קְטַלְתֶּן	ye (f) killed, have killed	(2nd plur. fem.)
קָטַלְנוּ	we killed, have killed	(1st plur. common)

To be strictly accurate we should speak of "forms"
rather than "tenses" of the verb, since it is the completeness or otherwise of an action which is being
expressed and not the time factor, as in English.
Thus the perfect expresses completed action and

includes all perfect tenses such as future perfect and
pluperfect. The imperfect is concerned with un-
finished activity, and thus includes the future and
present alike. The various shades of the subjunctive
are also part of the category of the imperfect.

The inflection of the imperfect follows a similar
pattern to that of the perfect, as follows :

יִקְטֹל he will kill, may kill, was killing, etc.
                              (3rd sing. masc.)

תִּקְטֹל she will kill, may kill, was killing, etc.
                              (3rd sing. fem.)

תִּקְטֹל thou wilt kill, mayest kill, etc.
                              (2nd sing. masc.)

תִּקְטְלִי thou (f.) wilt kill, mayest kill, etc.
                              (2nd sing. fem.)

אֶקְטֹל I will kill, may kill, was killing, etc.
                              (1st sing. common)

יִקְטְלוּ they will kill, may kill, were killing, etc.
                              (3rd plur. masc.)

תִּקְטֹלְנָה they (f.) will kill, may kill, etc.
                              (3rd plur. fem.)

תִּקְטְלוּ ye will kill, may kill, were killing, etc.
                              (2nd plur. masc.)

תִּקְטֹלְנָה ye (f.) will kill, may kill, etc.
                              (2nd plur. fem.)

נִקְטֹל we will kill, may kill, were killing, etc.
                              (1st plur. common)

When the negative form of a verb is required, the

particle לֹא is used, and immediately precedes the verb. Thus the sentence "the man did not call the boy" would be לֹא קָרָא הָאִישׁ אֶת־הַיֶּלֶד.

VOCABULARY

שָׁכַן	to dwell.	נַעַר	lad.	הָלַךְ	to go.
בָּרָא	to create.	נַעֲרָה	girl (f).	הָרַג	to slay.
אָמַר	to say.	עוֹף	fowl.	אֹיֵב	enemy.
הָיָה	to be.	אָכַל	to eat.	הֵן, הִנֵּה	behold.
סֵפֶר	book.	שָׂרָף	seraph.	יִצְחָק	Isaac.
חָכָם	wise.	מָחָר	to-morrow.	מִדְבָּר	desert.
צָפוֹן	north.	עָצוּם	powerful.	מָחָה	to destroy.

Exercise 11

Translate :

1. שָׁמַעְתִּי אֶת־הַנָּבִיא 2. לֹא שָׁמְעָה הָאִשָּׁה אֶת־הַקּוֹל בַּן הַגָּדוֹל 3. זָכַרְתִּי אֵת הָאִישׁ אֲשֶׁר שָׁפַךְ אֶת־הַדָּם בַּמִּדְבָּר 4. כָּתַבְתִּי בַּסֵּפֶר בַּיּוֹם הַזֶּה 5. אֵלֶּה הַסּוּסוֹת הָרָעוֹת אֲשֶׁר הָרְגוּ בָאֲדָמָה 6. יִשְׁמֹר אֵת הַמַּלְכָּה הַטּוֹבָה בַּהֵיכָל 7. וְהִנֵּה לָקַח הָאִישׁ אֶת־הָאִשָּׁה הַזֹּאת לְאִשָּׁה 8. וְהָאִישׁ יִצְחָק גָּדוֹל מְאֹד בָּאָרֶץ 9. תִּשְׁמְרוּ אֶת־הַמִּצְוֹת אֲשֶׁר נָתַן הָאֱלֹהִים 10. הָאִישׁ אֲשֶׁר בָּרָא הָאֱלֹהִים הוּא טוֹב.

1. I will write in a book. 2. Who are these mighty men and these prophets ? 3. One called to another and said, Great is Jehovah. 4. Thou(f) hast eaten from the tree. 5. Jehovah will hear the man who does not shed blood. 6. Did not God give a son and a daughter to the prophet ? 7. Ye (f) shall keep the words which are in the book. 8. God has created good and evil and day and night. 9. I remembered what I heard in the temple. 10. He will not keep the words which the prophet gave to the people in the desert.

CHAPTER XIII

THE CASES

CASE endings as such have not survived in Hebrew, any more than they have in modern Arabic. Indeed, it is difficult to think of cases at all in Hebrew in the strictest sense. At an earlier stage of the language there may have been three : nominative, accusative and genitive. The first of these has no distinctive indication, being recognisable either by its position in relation to the verb, or by the general sense of the passage in which it occurs.

The accusative is somewhat more clearly marked, since it frequently has the particle אֵת, which we discussed in the last chapter, and which is the usual sign of the accusative. A possible survival of an ancient accusative case-ending is seen in the un-accented הָ֫, the so-called "hē locale", which generally indicates "motion towards", e.g., towards the north, is צָפ֫וֹנָה ; towards Babylon, is בָּבֶ֫לָה.

The genitive relation has no case-endings, but is characterised by an intimate connection of nouns, and is known as the construct state. This may be illustrated by saying that, whereas in English we would say "the-word of-the-man," making "the word" absolute, and expressing "the man" in the

dependent genitive case, Hebrew reverses the process by recognising that "the word" would be dependent upon "the man" for its expression. Thus Hebrew would say "the-word-of the-man", or more accurately "word-of the-man", thus putting "word-of" in construction with the absolute "man". Similarly, in the phrase "the horse of the king", the noun in the absolute would be "king", whilst "horse-of" would be in this dependent relation called the construct state.

Whereas the absolute is never modified in its form, the construct is shortened as much as the language will allow, so as to be uttered quickly, with the principal stress in pronunciation falling on the absolute noun. As a result the construct has certain modifications in form, which may be seen in the masculine word דָּבָר thus :

absolute sing. דָּבָר (word) ; construct sing. דְּבַר (word of).

absolute plur. דְּבָרִים (words) ; construct plur. דִּבְרֵי (words of).

The construct singular shortens the absolute as much as possible, whilst the construct plural elides the terminal "m" of the absolute plural and changes the full hireq to full çere. A feminine noun inflects as follows :

absolute sing. סוּסָה (mare) ; construct sing. סוּסַת (mare of).

absolute plur. סוּסוֹת (mares) ;   construct plur. סוּסוֹת (mares of).

Whilst the feminine construct plural ends like the absolute, it must be shortened as much as possible. Thus the absolute plural of צְדָקָה, righteousness, is צְדָקוֹת but the construct is צִדְקוֹת, formed by rule from צְדָקוֹת. A dual construct from the absolute סוּסָתַיִם would be סוּסְתֵי, the šᵉwa being vocal to represent an original full vowel.

A table of examples may assist in learning the modifications of the construct state :

	horse	mare	son	star	upright	queen
Ab. sing.	סוּס	סוּסָה	בֵּן	כּוֹכָב	יָשָׁר	מַלְכָּה
Ab. pl.	סוּסִים	סוּסוֹת	בָּנִים	כּוֹכָבִים	יְשָׁרִים	מְלָכוֹת
Cst. sing.	סוּס	סוּסַת	בֶּן	כּוֹכַב	יְשַׁר	מַלְכַּת
Cst. pl.	סוּסֵי	סוּסוֹת	בְּנֵי	כּוֹכְבֵי	יִשְׁרֵי	מַלְכוֹת
Ab. dual.	סוּסַיִם	סוּסָתַיִם				
Cst. dual.	סוּסֵי	סוּסְתֵי				

Since the construct is as short as possible, it is axiomatic that it never takes the article.   This latter is put with the absolute noun if it is definite, and in this way suffices for both.   For example, סוּס הַמֶּלֶךְ means "the horse of the king" (literally, "horse-of

the-king''), and אִישׁ הַמִּלְחָמָה "the man of war"
(literally, ''man-of the war''). Because of the close
relationship between construct and absolute, any
adjectives qualifying the construct will naturally
follow the absolute, and will agree in gender and
number. Thus, ''the good mares of the king'' would
be rendered סוּסוֹת הַמֶּלֶךְ הַטּוֹבוֹת, *i.e.*, mares-of the
king, the good ones (*f*).

When two absolutes occur, the construct is
repeated with each, as with ''the sons of the king and
queen'', בְּנֵי הַמֶּלֶךְ וּבְנֵי הַמַּלְכָּה. Adjectives and participles may be placed in the construct before a noun,
thus showing that the construct is not a true genitive,
e.g., ''the poor people'' is אֶבְיוֹנֵי הָעָם, *i.e.*, the poor
of the people.

The deficiency which exists in the development of
the Hebrew adjective is frequently overcome by the
use of a noun in the construct state. Thus the phrase
''a holy mountain'' would be rendered ''a mountain
of holiness'', *i.e.*, הַר־קֹדֶשׁ, and ''a godly man'' as ''a
man of God'', אִישׁ־אֱלֹהִים.

The preposition לְ resolves the apparent confusion
which might arise in rendering the expressions ''a
horse of the king'' and ''the horse of a king'', for if
the article were attached to the second noun, both
words would become definite. Furthermore, according to our rule above, the construct cannot take the

article. Thus these phrases would be translated סוּס לְמֶלֶךְ, "a horse belonging to the king", and הַסוּס לְמֶלֶךְ, "the horse belonging to a king".

VOCABULARY

שָׁלוֹם	peace.	דָּוִד	David.	עֶבֶד	servant.
פַּרְעֹה	Pharaoh.	שָׁנָה	year.	יַעֲקֹב	Jacob.
עַל־	upon, over.	שָׁאוּל	Saul.	יָשָׁר	upright.
חַיִּים	life (pl.).	תָּמִים	perfect.	בָּשָׂר	flesh.
אַבְרָהָם	Abraham.	קָדוֹשׁ	holy.	קָבַץ	to gather.

Exercise 12

Translate :

‪1. סוּסוֹת הַמֶּלֶךְ הַטּוֹבוֹת‬   ‪2. לָקַח הַנָּבִיא סוּס אֲשֶׁר לַמֶּלֶךְ‬
‪3. אֵלֶּה יְמֵי שְׁנֵי חַיֵּי הַמֶּלֶךְ הָרָע‬   ‪4. נָתַן אֱלֹהִים אֶת־הַשֶּׁמֶשׁ‬
בִּרְקִיעַ הַשָּׁמָיִם   ‪5. אָמַר עֶבֶד אַבְרָהָם אָנֹכִי‬   ‪6. וְעַל־פְּנֵי כָל־‬
הַנְּבִיאִים יִשְׁפֹּן   ‪7. שָׁמַרְתָּ אֶת־לְבַב הַמֶּלֶךְ הַגָּדוֹל מֵרַע‬
‪8. לֹא שָׁמַע הָעָם אֶת־דִּבְרֵי נְבִיאֵי הָאֱלֹהִים‬   ‪9. חֶרֶב הַזָּהָב בְּיַד‬
הַגִּבּוֹר   ‪10. לֹא זְכַרְתֶּם אֵת הַדְּבָרִים אֲשֶׁר אָמְרוּ בְּנֵי נְבִיאֵי‬
הָאֱלֹהִים.

1. The God of heaven and earth. 2. The voice of God is in the city of David. 3. The eyes of the man are upon the horses of Pharaoh. 4. The words of the people are very bad in the ears of the prophet. 5. The horse which belongs to the good king is in the desert. 6. The mighty man of Saul slew the prophets of Jehovah in the place where David dwelt. 7. I am no prophet, neither am I a prophet's son. 8. And he said, I am the God of Abraham, the God of Isaac and the God of Jacob. 9. The law of Jehovah is good in the eyes of the people. 10. Hast thou(f) eaten from the tree which is in the garden of Jehovah ?

CHAPTER XIV

PRONOMINAL SUFFIXES

THE same closeness of relation observed in the
construct state marks the connection between nouns
and possessive pronouns. Hebrew does not say "my
word", but "word-of me", so that in effect we have
the noun in the construct and the pronoun in the
absolute. To this end, fragments of the personal
pronoun are attached in suffixal form to the noun
concerned. There are both singular and plural
suffixes, which may be added to singular or plural
words. Suffixes may be classed as "light" when they
contain one consonant, and "heavy" when two consonants are involved. Suffixal forms are derived as
follows :

Masculine Nouns

Singular.	סוּס (horse)	פָּקִיד (overseer)	דָּבָר (word)
Suffix 1 c. my	סוּסִי	פְּקִידִי	דְּבָרִי
sing. 2 m. thy	סוּסְךָ	פְּקִידְךָ	דְּבָרְךָ
2 f. thy	סוּסֵךְ	פְּקִידֵךְ	דְּבָרֵךְ
3 m. his	סוּסוֹ	פְּקִידוֹ	דְּבָרוֹ
3 f. her	סוּסָהּ	פְּקִידָהּ	דְּבָרָהּ
Suffix 1 c. our	סוּסֵנוּ	פְּקִידֵנוּ	דְּבָרֵנוּ
plur. 2 m. your	סוּסְכֶם	פְּקִידְכֶם	דְּבַרְכֶם

2 f. your	סוּסְכֶן	פְּקִידְכֶן	דִּבְרְכֶן
3 m. their	סוּסָם	פְּקִידָם	דִּבְרָם
3 f. their	סוּסָן	פְּקִידָן	דִּבְרָן

Plural. סוּסִים (horses) פְּקִידִים (overseers) דְּבָרִים (words)

Suffix	1. c. my	סוּסַי	פְּקִידַי	דְּבָרַי
sing.	2 m. thy	סוּסֶיךָ	פְּקִידֶיךָ	דְּבָרֶיךָ
	2 f. thy	סוּסַיִךְ	פְּקִידַיִךְ	דְּבָרַיִךְ
	3 m. his	סוּסָיו	פְּקִידָיו	דְּבָרָיו
	3 f. her	סוּסֶיהָ	פְּקִידֶיהָ	דְּבָרֶיהָ
Suffix	1 c. our	סוּסֵינוּ	פְּקִידֵינוּ	דְּבָרֵינוּ
plur.	2 m. your	סוּסֵיכֶם	פְּקִידֵיכֶם	דְּבְרֵיכֶם
	2 f. your	סוּסֵיכֶן	פְּקִידֵיכֶן	דְּבְרֵיכֶן
	3 m. their	סוּסֵיהֶם	פְּקִידֵיהֶם	דְּבְרֵיהֶם
	3 f. their	סוּסֵיהֶן	פְּקִידֵיהֶן	דְּבְרֵיהֶן

Feminine Nouns

Singular. סוּסָה (mare) שָׁנָה (year) צְדָקָה (righteousness)

Suffix	1.c. my	סוּסָתִי	שְׁנָתִי	צִדְקָתִי
sing.	2 m. thy	סוּסָתְךָ	שְׁנָתְךָ	צִדְקָתְךָ
	2 f. thy	סוּסָתֵךְ	שְׁנָתֵךְ	צִדְקָתֵךְ
	3 m. his	סוּסָתוֹ	שְׁנָתוֹ	צִדְקָתוֹ
	3 f. her	סוּסָתָה	שְׁנָתָה	צִדְקָתָה
Suffix	1 c. our	סוּסָתֵנוּ	שְׁנָתֵנוּ	צִדְקָתֵנוּ
plur.	2 m. your	סוּסַתְכֶם	שְׁנַתְכֶם	צִדְקַתְכֶם
	2 f. your	סוּסַתְכֶן	שְׁנַתְכֶן	צִדְקַתְכֶן
	3 m. their	סוּסָתָם	שְׁנָתָם	צִדְקָתָם
	3 f. their	סוּסָתָן	שְׁנָתָן	צִדְקָתָן

Plural.			סוּסוֹת (mares)	שָׁנוֹת (years)	(righteous- צִדְקוֹת nesses)
Suffix	1 c.	my	סוּסוֹתַי	שְׁנוֹתַי	צִדְקוֹתַי
sing.	2 m.	thy	סוּסוֹתֶיךָ	שְׁנוֹתֶיךָ	צִדְקוֹתֶיךָ
	2 f.	thy	סוּסוֹתַיִךְ	שְׁנוֹתַיִךְ	צִדְקוֹתַיִךְ
	3 m.	his	סוּסוֹתָיו	שְׁנוֹתָיו	צִדְקוֹתָיו
	3 f.	her	סוּסוֹתֶיהָ	שְׁנוֹתֶיהָ	צִדְקוֹתֶיהָ
Suffix	1 c.	our	סוּסוֹתֵינוּ	שְׁנוֹתֵינוּ	צִדְקוֹתֵינוּ
plur.	2 m.	your	סוּסוֹתֵיכֶם	שְׁנוֹתֵיכֶם	צִדְקוֹתֵיכֶם
	2 f.	your	סוּסוֹתֵיכֶן	שְׁנוֹתֵיכֶן	צִדְקוֹתֵיכֶן
	3 m.	their	סוּסוֹתֵיהֶם	שְׁנוֹתֵיהֶם	צִדְקוֹתֵיהֶם
	3 f.	their	סוּסוֹתֵיהֶן	שְׁנוֹתֵיהֶן	צִדְקוֹתֵיהֶן

It will be noticed that the šᵉwa in the second masculine singular and second masculine and feminine plural of the singular noun is vocal, and thus bᵉghadhkᵉphath letters will not have dagheš lene. The letter yodh persists in every suffixal form of the plural words. Suffixes for the dual are exactly the same as those of the plural, *i.e.*, שְׂפָתַי, my lips, שְׂפָתֶיךָ, thy (*m.*) lips, etc.

Prepositions may take suffixes in exactly the same way, though feminine forms are sometimes wanting. The following table indicates the inflections of some of the more commonly used prepositions:

Singular	מִן	לְ	עַל	בֵּין	אֶת־	אַחֲרֵי	אֶת (with)
1 c.	כִּמֹּנִי	לִי	עָלַי	בֵּינִי	אֹתִי	אַחֲרַי	אִתִּי
2 m.	מִמְּךָ	לְךָ	עָלֶ֫יךָ	בֵּינְךָ	אֹתְךָ	אַחֲרֶיךָ	אִתְּךָ
2 f.	מִמֵּךְ	לָךְ	עָלַיִךְ		אֹתָךְ	אַחֲרַ֫יִךְ	אִתָּךְ

3 m.	מִמֶּ֫נּוּ	לוֹ	עָלָיו	בֵּינוֹ	אֹתוֹ	אַחֲרָיו	אִתּוֹ
3 f.	מִמֶּ֫נָּה	לָהּ	עָלֶ֫יהָ		אֹתָהּ	אַחֲרֶ֫יהָ	אִתָּהּ
Plural							
1 c.	מִמֶּ֫נּוּ	לָ֫נוּ	עָלֵ֫ינוּ	בֵּינֵ֫ינוּ	אֹתָ֫נוּ	אַחֲרֵ֫ינוּ	אִתָּ֫נוּ
2 m.	מִכֶּם	לָכֶם	עֲלֵיכֶם	בֵּינֵיכֶם	אֶתְכֶם	אַחֲרֵיכֶם	אִתְּכֶם
2 f.		לָכֶן			אֶתְכֶן	אַחֲרֵיכֶן	אִתְּכֶן
3 m.	מֵהֶם	לָהֶם	עֲלֵיהֶם	בֵּינֵיהֶם	אֹתָם	אַחֲרֵיהֶם	אִתָּם
3 f.		לָהֶן			אֹתָן	אַחֲרֵיהֶן	אִתָּן

VOCABULARY

אֵת	with	תַּחַת	under	חָדָשׁ	new
אַחֲרֵי	after	רָדַף	to pursue	יֶלֶד	boy
לִפְנֵי	before	מָכַר	to sell	יָשַׁב	to sit
דָּג	fish	שׁוֹר	ox	בֵּין	between
אֶל־	towards	כֹּהֵן	priest	לֶחֶם	bread

Exercise 13

Translate :

‎1. מִכֶּם‏ ‎2. מִמֶּ֫נּוּ‏ ‎3. אַחֲרֶ֫יךָ‏ ‎4. אַתָּה‏ ‎5. לִפְנֵי הָאִישׁ‏ ‎6. סוּסֵיהֶן‏
‎7. סוּסוֹתֶ֫יהָ‏ ‎8. צִדְקוֹתֵיכֶן‏ ‎9. שָׁמַ֫עְתִּי אֶת־דִּבְרֵיכֶם‏ ‎10. יְדֵיכֶם‏
‎11. לָהֶם‏ ‎12. דִּבְרֵיהֶם הֵם רָעִים בְּעֵינֵי יהוה‏ ‎13. שָׁלַח הַנָּבִיא
אֶת־בָּנָיו וְאֶת־בְּנוֹתָיו אֶל־הַמִּדְבָּר‏ ‎14. שָׁמַ֫עְנוּ אֶת־קוֹלְךָ
בְּהֵיכַל הָאֱלֹהִים‏ ‎15. בֵּינִי וּבֵינֶ֫ךָ‏ ‎16. וְלֹא רָדַ֫פְתִּי אַחֲרֵי בְּנֵי
יַעֲקֹב‏ ‎17. כִּי שָׁמַ֫רְתִּי אֶת־דַּרְכֵי יהוה אֱלֹהֵי יִשְׂרָאֵל‏ ‎18. בְּסֵ֫פֶר
מַלְכֵי יִשְׂרָאֵל וִיהוּדָה‏ ‎19. לֹא שָׁמְרוּ אֶת־מִצְוֹת יהוה אֲשֶׁר
נָתַן לָהֶם בָּהָר‏ ‎20. וְכָל־מִשְׁפָּטָיו לְפָנֶ֫יךָ.‏

1. Before me. 2. After them(*f*). 3. Upon him. 4.
From thee(*f*). 5. Towards you (*m. pl.*). 6. Before you
(*m. pl.*). 7. Before thee(*m*). 8. My face. 9. Our hands.
10. Thy(*f*) lips. 11. Their(*f*) righteousnesses. 12. Our
words. 13. Their(*m*) horse. 14. Your(*f*) horses. 15.
Your(*f*) mares. 16. Between us. 17. Under him. 18.
Behold me. 19. Their(*m*) lips. 20. Thy strong hand is
with the people.

CHAPTER XV

THE VERB: OTHER FORMS

In an earlier chapter we examined briefly two of the most important forms of the regular verb, where we recognised that Hebrew has no "tenses" in the normal sense of that word. Instead there are two "states": the perfect, which expresses any kind of completed action, and the imperfect, which denotes any incomplete action, past, present or future. Thus, the perfect would be used to translate such phrases as "he ate", "he would have eaten", "he had eaten", whilst the imperfect state is reflected in such expressions as "he will eat", "he eats", "he was eating," "he might eat", and so on. To express a development of the basic verbal idea there are in all seven "themes", including active and passive, intensive and causative themes, and a reflexive.

Verbs are spoken of as "strong" where the three radicals do not change, or where one of them is a guttural, and "weak" where either one radical is assimilated or where a verb ends in a weak consonant, e.g., ה. The "stative" verbs are so called because they generally describe the state, physical or mental, of the subject, e.g., to be heavy, to be old. Usually they are intransitive, but not wholly so, and the

term "stative" must not be taken as synonymous with "intransitive". We can now study some special forms of the verb in subsequent sections.

The Imperative

When the preformatives are dropped, the imperative Qal is identical with the imperfect. It is important to notice that the šᵉwa in the first syllable is sounded, making the syllable open in each case. The imperative is never used with the negative to express a prohibition, being employed exclusively for positive commands, e.g., מִשְׁלוּ, rule ye.

The Jussive

This is in speech a shortened form of the imperfect to express the quick reaction of the mind to a situation, generally in terms of a wish or a command. It coincides with the imperfect in form in all parts of the regular verb except the hiph'il (or causative) but is used only in the second and third persons. Its negative is אַל, not לֹא. It is used mainly :

(a) To express a positive command in the third person, e.g., יְהִי אוֹר, let there be light.

(b) As a request or entreaty, e.g., אַל תִּקְטֹל, do not thou (m.) kill.

(c) As a prohibition, e.g., אַל־תִּקְטְלוּ, do not kill. When Divine prohibitions are recorded, the

negative לֹא is used in the sense of "thou shalt not", often with the simple imperfect, *e.g.*, לֹא תִּרְצַח (Deut. v. 17), "thou shalt not kill", as a permanent prohibition.

The Cohortative

This form is generally confined to the first person singular and plural, and in speech tends to lessen the abruptness of a command, to exhort, or to express the resolution of the speaker. It is marked by the ending הָ‍ָ added to the imperfect, *e.g.*, נִשְׁמְרָה let us keep, we would keep. An emphatic imperative particle, נָא, is frequently added to the Cohortative, Jussive and Imperative, as well as to particles such as הִנֵּה (behold!), to introduce an additional supplicatory note, or to strengthen the exhortation, *e.g.*, בֹּא־נָא, go, I pray.

Waw Consecutive

The comparative scarcity of subordinate clauses in Hebrew, combined with the limited modifications of the verb, made it necessary to employ a special device for denoting sequence of events in connected clauses or sentences. The effect is to introduce a subordinating quality into the initial verb of the sentence or phrase, so that what happens as a result is in direct sequence to the general tenor of the preceding verb.

In this construction, a consecutive narrative of past events which commences with a perfect tense is continued by a succession of imperfects coupled with waw, which is pointed like the article under such conditions. Conversely, when such a sentence begins with a simple imperfect, successive events are expressed by means of waw with the perfect, when the pointing for waw is exactly the same as for the conjunction וְ.

Thus, in the sentence "he went out and pursued and captured", the initial verb is in the perfect, but since the succession of events depends so intimately upon it, they are expressed by the waw consecutive form, יָצָא וַיִּרְדֹּף וַיִּלְכֹּד. Where, however, the sequence is disrupted, the tense reverts to the perfect, as may be seen from a continuation of the above sentence, "he went out and pursued and captured, and did not rest in the city", which would now become יָצָא וַיִּרְדֹּף וַיִּלְכֹּד וְלֹא שָׁבַת בָּעִיר. Here the negative intervenes between waw and the verb "rest", which according to our rule necessitates a reversion to the perfect form.

Similarly, in a sentence commencing with an imperfect, subsequent verbs are perfect if immediately preceded by waw, e.g., "he will remember the prophets, and will go out and hear them in the temple", which is rendered יִזְכֹּר אֶת־הַנְּבִיאִים וְיָצָא

וְשָׁמַע אֹתָם בַּהֵיכָל. Again, if a word intervenes between waw and the verb, the latter reverts to the tense of the first verb in the series.

It is important to grasp these principles clearly, as the waw consecutive is found very widely in the Hebrew of the Old Testament. We may summarise the matter as follows :

(a) After a simple perfect, connected successive verbs have waw with the imperfect.

(b) After a simple imperfect, verbs consequent upon it have waw with the perfect.

In Hebrew narrative, the verb הָיָה, to be or become, is usually followed by waw consecutive when other words occur between the two verbs. The imperfect of הָיָה (יִהְיֶה) has a shortened form, יְהִי, used with waw consecutive, i.e., וַיְהִי, the dagheš forte usually being omitted with יְ. In such a usage the verb "to be" is generally rendered "and it came to pass", e.g., . . . וַיְהִי אַחֲרֵי הַדְּבָרִים הָאֵלֶּה וַיָּקָם, "and it came to pass after these words that he arose . . ."

In the imperfect with waw consecutive, the accentuation is generally mil'el when the penultimate is open, e.g., וַיֵּשֶׁב, and he dwelt. Conversely, the perfect with waw consecutive has a milra' accentuation wherever possible, e.g., וְשָׁמַרְתָּ, and thou wilt keep. Sometimes waw consecutive marks the consequent

clause in a conditional sentence, *e.g.*, . . . אִם עָבַרְתָּ אִתִּי
וְהָיִיתָ עָלַי, "if thou passest on with me, then thou
shalt be to me . . . " (2 Sam. xv. 33).

A "weak" waw, or one which does not influence
the form of the verb, is normally only found in the
third person of the Jussive (וְיִקְטֹל, and let him kill)
and with the Cohortative (וְאֶקְטְלָה, and let me kill).

The Infinitive

There are two infinitives in Hebrew, known as the
absolute and construct, of which the latter is the
more common. The infinitive absolute stands entirely alone, having neither prefix nor suffix, and
serves principally to emphasise the verb. Thus the
sentence "he hath indeed kept my commandments"
would be rendered in Hebrew "in-the-act-of-keeping
he has kept my commandments", *i.e.*, שָׁמוֹר שָׁמַר אֶת
מִצְוֹתַי. It has thus an adverbial force, like "truly",
"certainly", "surely", and as such generally stands
in order before the verb. On the occasions when it
occurs after the finite verb it expresses continuity,
e.g., שִׁמְעוּ שָׁמוֹעַ, "hear ye continually". Infrequently
it expresses the imperative sense, as in the injunction
"keep the sabbath day", שָׁמוֹר אֶת־יוֹם הַשַּׁבָּת.

Unlike the absolute form, the construct may have
a preposition prefixed, as well as pronominal suffixes.
Most frequently the infinitive construct takes the

preposition לְ as a prefix, *e.g.*, לִשְׁפֹּט, to judge, expressing the English infinitive "to". The daghéš lene is inserted in the second radical only with לְ, and with other prepositions the first syllable remains open, *e.g.*, בִּשְׁפֹט. The construct is negatived by removing לְ and prefixing it to בִּלְתִּי ("so as not to"), which then precedes the infinitive, *i.e.*, לְבִלְתִּי שְׁמֹעַ, (so as) not to listen. Often the infinitive is connected by maqqeph to its object, *e.g.*, לִכְרָת־עֵצִים, to cut down trees. In form it is generally the same as the second singular of the imperative. The suffixes of the infinitive construct may be illustrated by the use of the verb כָּתַב to write :

	Singular	Plural
1 c.	{ כָּתְבִי { כָּתְבֵנִי	כָּתְבֵנוּ
2 m.	{ כָּתְבְּךָ { כָּתְבְךָ	{ כָּתְבְּכֶם { כְּתָבְכֶם
2 f.	כָּתְבֵךְ	{ כָּתְבְּכֶן { כָּתְבְכֶן
3 m.	כָּתְבוֹ	כָּתְבָם
3 f.	כָּתְבָהּ	כָּתְבָן

Hebrew idiom would say "in-the-writing-of-me" for "when I wrote", hence the value of the suffixal form for showing the gerund-like nature of the infinitive construct.

The Participle

In the regular verb there are two forms of the participle, the active (קֹטֵל, killing) and the passive (קָטוּל, killed). For their inflections in gender and number they are regarded as nouns, thus:

| | Singular | | Plural | |
	Absol.	Cstr.	Absol.	Cstr.
Active m.	קֹטֵל	קֹטֵל	קֹטְלִים	קֹטְלֵי
f.	קֹטְלָה, קֹטֶלֶת	קֹטֶלֶת	קֹטְלוֹת	קֹטְלוֹת
Passive m.	קָטוּל	קְטוּל	קְטוּלִים	קְטוּלֵי
f.	קְטוּלָה	קְטוּלַת	קְטוּלוֹת	קְטוּלוֹת

The holem in these forms is invariably long.

They are frequently used as ordinary substantives, and as such belong to distinct groups of nouns whose changes will be noted in a later chapter. The participles imply continuous activity, and this is especially true of the active form. In meaning they are like gerundives or verbal adjectives, and may agree in gender and number with a noun or pronoun, *e.g.*, אֲנַחְנוּ מֹשְׁלִים, we are ruling. When the third radical of a verb is a guttural, a furtive pathah appears with the passive participle, *e.g.*, יָדוּעַ, known. On occasions the passive participle may have a future connotation, *e.g.*, שָׁדוּד, that which ought to be destroyed. The negative אֵין is generally used with participles instead of לֹא.

VOCABULARY

כִּי אִם	except.	נָהָר	river.	פָּקַד	to visit.
יָצָא	to go out.	כָּבוֹד	glory.	נָפַל	to fall.
קָצַף	to be angry.	גָּנַב	to steal.	מֵת	dead.
קוּם	to arise, stand.	נָשָׂא	to lift up.	אֶבְיוֹן	poor.
עָבַר	to pass over, cross.	פֶּן־	lest.	זָכָר	male.

Exercise 14

Translate :

1. אַל תִּקְצֹפוּ 2. לֹא תִגְנֹב 3. אִמְרִי־נָא 4. וַלֹּאמֶר אֱלֹהִים נֹפֹל לְפָנַי וְלֹא אֶקְצֹף בְּךָ עַד־עוֹלָם 5. רָדְפוּ אַחֲרָיו 6. אַל יִכָּתֵב בְּסֵפֶר תּוֹרַת יהוה אֱלֹהֵי יִשְׂרָאֵל 7. הָלַכְתִּי וָאֶמְכֹּר אֶת־הַיֶּלֶד 8. שָׁכַח הָאִישׁ אֶת־דִּבְרֵי הַנָּבִיא וְלֹא שָׁמַר אֶת־תּוֹרַת יהוה 9. וַיִּתֵּן אֹתוֹ עַל־כָּל־אֶרֶץ מִצְרַיִם 10. שָׁמוֹר יִשְׁמֹר אֶת־תּוֹרַת אֱלֹהִים 11. וְכָזְכֹּר הַנָּבִיא אֶת־הַדְּבָרִים הָאֵלֶּה וַיֹּאמֶר רָדַף אַחֲרֵיהֶם צָפוֹנָה 12. אַתֶּם זֹכְרִים אֶת־דִּבְרֵי הָאֱלֹהִים אֲשֶׁר אָמַרְתִּי בַּיּוֹם הַזֶּה 13. הִנְנִי שֹׁלֵחַ אֶת־הַנָּבִיא הָעִירָה.

1. Thou shalt keep my commandments. 2. May he keep thee from all evil in the land. 3. Let me go, I pray, to the house of the prophet. 4. And God made the firmament between the waters which were under the firmament, and between the waters which were above the firmament. 5. Let me keep thy commandments. 6. He kept on walking towards the house of Joseph. 7. I will

keep thy commandments continually. 8. They left off counting the stars of heaven. 9. They went down to Egypt to buy food in that place. 10. And behold, he sent the boy to watch the city of the mighty men. 11. Jehovah is thy keeper in the day of evil. 12. The prophets are keeping the law of Jehovah, the God of Israel. 13. The king rules over the people in the land.

CHAPTER XVI

PARADIGM OF THE REGULAR VERB

In the last chapter we noted that there are a number of "themes" which serve to convey a developed idea of the simple verb, and these must now be given somewhat closer scrutiny. Their names are a reminder of the time when פָּעַל was used to illustrate the paradigm of the regular verb, since the "themes" are named according to the corresponding inflection of פָּעַל in the third singular masculine of the perfect. Thus the simple passive of פָּעַל would be נִפְעַל, and so the passive voice in the regular verb is called the Niph'al. קָטַל has replaced פָּעַל as the standard form for the verb paradigm because פָּעַל, having the second radical a guttural, is thus unable to take dagheš forte in three important forms of the strong or regular verb. The various forms, whose full inflections will be found in the paradigm section at the end of the book, are as follows :

Simple active or Qal.	קָטַל
Simple passive or Niph'al.	נִקְטַל
Intensive active or Pi'el.	קִטֵּל
Intensive passive or Pu'al.	קֻטַּל
Causative active or Hiph'il.	הִקְטִיל
Causative passive or Hoph'al.	הָקְטַל
Reflexive or Hithpa'el.	הִתְקַטֵּל

These forms are derived by internal changes of the root and other modifications. The second radical of the Pi'el, Pu'al and Hithpa'el has dagheš forte to intensify the form. The Pu'al and Hoph'al lack an imperative and infinitive construct, and with the exception of the Niph'al, all participles have a prefixed מ.

Niph'al.

In the perfect, the letter נ is prefixed to the stem and pointed with hireq, whilst the imperfect has a prefixed יִ with the nun becoming assimilated to the first radical, which then takes a compensating dagheš forte, *i.e.*, יִקָּטֵל. The imperative is marked by a prefix הִן, which by assimilation becomes הִקָּטֵל. Before a vowel suffix the çere under the second radical becomes vocal šᵉwa, except in pause, *i.e.*, הִקָּטְלִי but in the second feminine plural it changes to pathah, *i.e.*, הִקָּטַלְנָה. This latter becomes qameç in pause. The infinitive construct is like the imperative, but in the absolute the çere is replaced by holem, הִקָּטֹל, with an alternative form נִקְטֹל. The Niph'al participle may have gerundive force, and as such is often used for phrases with a passive meaning, *e.g.*, the broken of heart, would be נִשְׁבְּרֵי־לֵב, *i.e.*, the broken ones of heart, with "heart" appearing normally in such an expression in the shorter form in preference to לֵבָב. The Niph'al is inflected like the Qal.

The primary force of the Niph‘al is reflexive, *e.g.*,
נִסְתַּר he hid himself, though it is found in a reciprocal
or "middle" sense, *e.g.*, נִלְחֲמוּ, they fought (one another), and predominantly as the simple passive of
the Qal.   מִן, בְּ and לְ are used as the agent when the
Niph‘al, has a passive force. Some verbs are used
only in the Niph‘al *e.g.*, נִלְחַם, he fought, without
any reflexive or passive meaning.

Pi‘el

A dagheš forte in the middle radical is characteristic of this form.   In the first syllable the vowel is
generally hireq, whilst the second syllable may have
pathah or çere. In three verbs, כִּבֵּס, he washed, כִּפֶּר,
he atoned, and דִּבֶּר, he spoke, sᵉghol replaces çere.
The imperfect יְקַטֵּל is inflected regularly, whilst of
the infinitives, the absolute קַטֹּל is less frequently used
than the form קַטֵּל, which is the same as that of the
construct.   The participle has a prefixed מ, pointed
with šᵉwa.   The Pi‘el is inflected like the Qal.

The Pi‘el is an intensive form of the Qal, *e.g.*, רָדַף,
to follow, רִדֵּף, to pursue. Where intensity becomes
iteration, a causative force may be evident, *e.g.*, גָּדַל,
to be great, גִּדֵּל, to cause to be great, make great ;
קָדַשׁ, to be holy, קִדֵּשׁ, to hallow.

Pu‘al

This form is marked by dull vocalic sounds, but
like the Pi‘el has regular inflections.   In the perfect,

qibbuç is found under the first radical, whilst the pathah of the second radical becomes vocal šᵉwa before vowel afformatives. In this latter respect the imperfect is similar. There is no imperative form of the Puʻal, since it is properly the passive of the Piʻel in meaning.

VOCABULARY

לחם	to fight (Niph.).	זֶבַח	sacrifice.	יְאֹר	river.
אֱמֹרִי	Amorites.	חָבַשׁ	to bind, gird.	בְּכוֹר	firstborn.
נחם	to repent (Niph.).	אָרַר	to curse.	כֹּה	thus.
קָטֹן	small, little.	בקשׁ	to seek (Pi.).	זָקֵן	old, elder.
כסה	to conceal (Pi.).	סתר	to hide (Pi.).	זָבַח	to sacrifice.
צֶלֶם	image, likeness.	יָכֹל	to be able.	אַהֲרֹן	Aaron.
זְרוֹעַ	arm.	שָׁתָה	to drink.	כָּבֵד	to be heavy; (Pi.) to harden.

Exercise 15

Translate :

2. וְשָׁבַתְנוּ   1. וַיֹּאמֶר יהוה אֵלַי אֱמֹר לָהֶם לֹא תִלָּחֵמוּ

3. וַיִּנָּחֶם יהוה כִּי עָשָׂה אֶת־הָאָדָם   בַּמָּקוֹם הַהוּא יָמִים רַבִּים

4. וַיְכַסּוּ כָל־הֶהָרִים הַגְּדֹלִים אֲשֶׁר־תַּחַת כָּל־הַשָּׁמַיִם   בָּאָרֶץ

6. תִּשְׁלַח לְעַבְדְּךָ לֵב שֹׁמֵעַ לִשְׁפֹּט   5. זִבְחֵי אֱלֹהִים רוּחַ נִשְׁבָּרָה

אֶת־עַמְּךָ הַזֶּה 7. בֵּן־אָדָם שָׁבַרְתִּי אֶת־זְרוֹעַ פַּרְעֹה מֶלֶךְ

מִצְרַיִם וְהִנֵּה לֹא־הֻבְּשָׁה 8. אָמַרְתָּ בַּקְּשׁוּ פָנָי אֶת־פָּנֶיךָ

אֲבַקֵּשׁ 9. וְעַתָּה אָרוּר אָתָּה מִן־הָאֲדָמָה אֲשֶׁר בָּרָא הָאֱלֹהִים

10. וַיְכַבֵּד פַּרְעֹה אֶת־לִבּוֹ וְלֹא שִׁלַּח אֶת־הָעָם.

1. And the Amorites which dwelt in that mountain sent
and pursued you. 2. Do not fight (*pl.*) with small or great,
but only (except) with the king of Israel. 3. And God
said, Shall I conceal (*part.*) from Abraham that which I
have done ? 4. The one shedding man's blood, by man
shall his blood be shed, for in the image of God he made
man. 5. And in the books of the house of Israel they shall
not be written. 6. Behold thou hast sent me this day
from upon the face of the ground, and from thy face shall
I be hidden. 7. They were not able to drink of the waters
of the river. 8. And thou shalt say unto Pharaoh, thus
said the Lord, My son, even my firstborn, is Israel. 9.
And they will hear thy voice, and thou shalt come, thou
and the elders of Israel, to the king of Egypt, and ye shall
say unto him, Let us go, we pray, unto the desert that
we may sacrifice to the Lord our God. 10. And Aaron
spoke all the words which Jehovah said unto Moses.

CHAPTER XVII

PARADIGM OF THE REGULAR VERB
(*continued*)

Hiph'il

This is the active causative form, and in the perfect consists of the verb stem prefixed by ה and the vowel hireq (which occasionally becomes s^eghol), with the insertion of a full hireq between the second and third radicals, *i.e.*, הִקְטִיל.

The Imperfect has the same final syllable, but takes pathah under the initial letter, thus, יַקְטִיל. It should be noticed that in the Hiph'il only there exists a difference between the ordinary imperfect and the jussive (יַקְטֵל). The çere may be shortened to s^eghol in the jussive if the tone alters in position, *e.g.*, from יַקְטֵל to יַקְטֶל־. The inflection of the Hiph'il is regular.

Its typical meaning is the causative of the Qal, *e.g.*, קָדַשׁ, to be holy, הִקְדִּישׁ, to cause to be holy, to sanctify. It may also have a declaratory meaning, as with הִצְדִּיק, he pronounced righteous. Stative verbs frequently appear in the Hiph'il, *e.g.*, הִשְׁמִין, to become fat. If the Qal of the verb is transitive, the Hiph'il may govern two accusatives in a sentence, *e.g.*, הִנְחִיל אֹתָם אֶת־הָאָרֶץ, he caused them to inherit the land.

Hophʿal

The first syllable of this form is always closed, as with the Hiphʿil, though sometimes the qameç hatuph may be replaced by qibbuç, and this is especially the case with the participle, *e.g.*, מָקְטָל for מֻקְטָל.

The Hophʿal is inflected in the normal manner, and since it is passive in meaning it has no regular imperative form.

Hithpaʿel

This is formed by prefixing הִת to the Piʿel, with pathah under the first radical, *e.g.*, הִתְקַטֵּל. When a sibilant follows the prefix, the sibilant and the taw of the prefix exchange places thus, הִשְׁתַּמֵּר, for הִתְשַׁמֵּר, he was on his guard. With צ and ז the taw is replaced by the appropriate hard or soft lingual, *e.g.*, הִצְטַדֵּק for הִתְצַדֵּק, and הִזְדַּמֵּן for הִתְזַמֵּן.

In meaning it is primarily the reflexive of the Piʿel, *e.g.*, נָקַם, he avenged, הִתְנַקֵּם, he showed himself revengeful. It may also express reciprocal action, *e.g.*, הִתְרָאוּ, they looked at each other, and infrequently may be intransitive and similar in force to the Qal, *e.g.*, הִתְאַבֵּל, to mourn. Another connotation is that of "playing the part of" something, *e.g.*, הִתְחַכֵּם, he pretended to be a wise man ; הִתְנַבֵּא, he behaved like a prophet.

At this juncture it may be advisable to notice the structure of some rare intensive and causative formations of the verb. Occasionally full holem is inserted in the intensives between the first and second radical to form the Poʻel (קוֹטֵל), the Poʻal (קוֹטַל) and the Hithpoʻel (הִתְקוֹטֵל). Some intensive formations have the third radical doubled, and these are the Piʻlel (קִטְלֵל), the Puʻlal (קֻטְלַל) and the Hithpaʻlel (הִתְקַטְלֵל). Where the last two stem letters are repeated, the form is called the Peʻalʻal (קְטַלְטַל). The Pilpel repeats the first and third radicals (קִלְקֵל). These forms are comparatively rare in their incidence, and there are one or two others connected with the Hiphʻil which are even less frequently found.

VOCABULARY

שׁחת destroy (Hiph.).	כָּשַׁל to stumble.	רָשָׁע wicked, guilty.
בּוֹא to enter.	אָדוֹן lord, master.	קָבַר to bury.
עֵץ tree, twig.	קֶבֶר grave.	כֵּן so, thus.
כֶּתַח opening, gate.	(יֵשׁ), יֵשׁ there is.	חבא (Hith.) to hide oneself.
קָשַׁשׁ to gather, collect.	שׁלך (Hiph.) to cast.	תָּוֶךְ middle.
מות to kill, put to death.	בְּתוֹךְ among, within.	אַיִן no, none.

D

מָלַךְ to be king ;　　קָדֵשׁ to be holy ;　　חָזַק to be strong ;
　(Hiph.) to　　　　　(Pi.) to　　　　　　(Hith.) to
　make king.　　　　　hallow,　　　　　　take courage.
　　　　　　　　　　　sanctify.

Exercise 16

Translate :

1. וַיֹּאמֶר יהוה אֶל־שְׁמוּאֵל שְׁמַע בְּקוֹלָם וְהִמְלַכְתָּ לָהֶם מֶלֶךְ
2. וַיָּבֹא אֶל־פֶּתַח הָעִיר וְהִנֵּה שָׁם אִשָּׁה מְקֹשֶׁשֶׁת עֵצִים .3 וְאַתֶּם
הִכְשַׁלְתֶּם רַבִּים בְּתוֹרַת יהוה .4 וְהִנֵּה אֲדֹנֵיהֶם נֹפֵל אַרְצָה מֵת
5. וְאַתָּה הָשְׁלַכְתָּ מִן־הַשָּׁמַיִם בְּכָל־אֲשֶׁר עָשָׂה אֵת הָרָע .6 וַיֹּאמֶר
יַעֲקֹב לְבָנָיו לָמָּה תִּתְרָאוּ הִנֵּה שָׁמַעְתִּי כִּי יֶשׁ־לֶחֶם בְּמִצְרָיִם
7. וַיֹּאמְרוּ הִתְהַלַּכְנוּ בָאָרֶץ וְהִנֵּה כָל־הָאָרֶץ יֹשֶׁבֶת .8 הִיא הָעִיר
הַפְּקֻדָה בְּיַד יהוה אֱלֹהֵי יִשְׂרָאֵל .9 וְכִשְׁמֹעַ הַנָּבִיא אֵת הַדְּבָרִים
הָאֵלֶּה הִתְחַזַּק .10 רָאִיתִי אֶת־הָרְשָׁעִים קְבֻרִים וַיִּשְׁתַּכְּחוּ בָעִיר
אֲשֶׁר־כֵּן־עָשׂוּ שָׁם.

1. There entered a man of the people to destroy the
king.　2. Thou art come to me to bring to remembrance
my sin and to slay my son.　3. These are the luminaries
in the firmament of heaven to divide between the day
and the night.　4. And he shall be laid (Hoph.) in his
grave in the place which the king has given him.　5. And
Joshua said to the people, Sanctify yourselves, for Jehovah
is in this place.　6. His head was cast upon the ground
by the hand of the mighty man.　7. And they heard the
voice of Jehovah walking about in the garden.　8. And the
man and his wife hid themselves from before the Lord God
amongst the trees of the garden.　9. And Pharaoh said,
Behold, the people of the land are many, and you make
them rest themselves in this place.　10. And they
prophesied unto the evening, and there was no voice.

CHAPTER XVIII

DECLENSIONS OF NOUNS

It is generally found convenient to classify nouns in declensions, according to the changes which take place in the vowels when the tone is altered. The first declension, which we have already noticed, deals principally with nouns having qameç in the tone, the pretone, or both. Such nouns are similar to the perfect of the verb.

The second declension, which has affinity to the imperfect, consists of words formed from stems which originally terminated in two consonants but to which an auxiliary vowel, usually sᵉghol, has been added. For this reason they are called "sᵉgholates", and fall into three principal classes, governed by the original vowel. The "a" class is like יֶלֶד, formed from יַלְד ; the "e" class is illustrated by סֵפֶר, from an original סִפְר ; whilst the "o" class is represented by חֹדֶשׁ, formed from חָדְשׁ.

In inflection the singular construct is the same as the absolute. For the singular of the noun, the suffixes are added to the stem, and the dual is formed in exactly the same way. But the plural absolute

has qameç under the second radical, and the first vowel then becomes šᵉwa to accord with the tone.

The following table will illustrate these changes :

	" a " class	" e " class	" o " class
Singular abs. cstr.	יֶ֫לֶד	סֵ֫פֶר	חֹ֫דֶשׁ
light suff.	יַלְדִּי	סִפְרִי	חׇדְשִׁי
heavy suff.	יַלְדְּכֶם	סִפְרְכֶם	חׇדְשְׁכֶם
Plural abs.	יְלָדִים	סְפָרִים	חֳדָשִׁים
cstr.	יַלְדֵי	סִפְרֵי	חׇדְשֵׁי
light suff.	יְלָדַי	סְפָרַי	חֳדָשַׁי
heavy suff.	יַלְדֵיכֶם	סִפְרֵיכֶם	חׇדְשֵׁיכֶם
Dual absol.	רַגְלַיִם	בִּרְכַּיִם	אׇזְנַיִם
cstr.	רַגְלֵי	בִּרְכֵּי	אׇזְנֵי
light suff.	רַגְלַי	בִּרְכַּי	אׇזְנַי
heavy suff.	רַגְלֵיכֶם	בִּרְכֵּיכֶם	אׇזְנֵיכֶם

These nouns are inflected regularly, but care should be taken to ensure the proper recognition of the šᵉwa, whether silent or vocal. When the terminal letter is a guttural, the preference for pathah is noticed throughout, e.g., זֶ֫רַע, seed, זַרְעִי, my seed, זַרְעֲךָ, thy seed, etc. The absence of an auxiliary sᵉghol in this type of noun indicates something of the inadequacy of the term "sᵉgholates" as a class designation.

Feminine segholates are formed by adding הָ֫ to the original or primitive stem, e.g., מַלְכָּה, queen, and in the singular are formed regularly. The plural has וֹת— added to the masculine singular, e.g., מְלָכוֹת, and the construct is inflected normally, i.e., מַלְכוֹת. Some feminines have a primitive ת as the final letter attached to the stem, e.g., מִשְׁמֶ֫רֶת, which takes suffixes in the normal manner, e.g., מִשְׁמַרְתִּי, etc. A group of feminine nouns, mostly prefixed by מ, have an ending הָָ֫, e.g., מַמְלָכָה, kingdom. The construct singular becomes segholate, i.e., מַמְלֶ֫כֶת, with suffix, מַמְלַכְתִּי, whilst the plural is מַמְלָכוֹת.

A third declension may be made up of words similar in form to the active participles. Such nouns generally have an unchangeable vowel in the pen-ultimate, and a tone long çere in the ultimate syllable. They are declined like participles, whose form has already been noted in Chapter XV. Some nouns are not participial in form, and generally relinquish the çere in declensions, e.g., מִזְבֵּ֫חַ, altar, cstr. sing. מִזְבַּח, suffix מִזְבְּחִי, plur. מִזְבְּחוֹת, with suffix מִזְבְּחוֹתַי, etc.

We may now notice the inflections of some irregular nouns which belong to the various declensions. Where relevant, the particular one is indicated by number.

SINGULAR

	father	son (3)	daugh-ter (2)	bro-ther	name	house (2)
Sing. abs.	אָב	בֵּן	בַּת	אָח	שֵׁם	בַּיִת
constr.	אֲבִי	בֶּן־	בַּת	אֲחִי	שֶׁם, שֶׁם־	בֵּית
suffix	אֲבִי	בְּנִי	בִּתִּי	אָחִי	שְׁמִי	בֵּיתִי
	אָבִיךָ	בִּנְךָ	בִּתְּךָ	אָחִיךָ	שִׁמְךָ	בֵּיתְךָ
	אָבִיו	בְּנוֹ	בִּתּוֹ	אָחִיו	שְׁמוֹ	בֵּיתוֹ

PLURAL

	father	son	daugh-ter	brother	name	house
Plur. abs.	אָבוֹת	בָּנִים	בָּנוֹת	אַחִים	שֵׁמוֹת	בָּתִּים
cstr.	אֲבוֹת	בְּנֵי	בְּנוֹת	אֲחֵי	שְׁמוֹת	בָּתֵּי
suffix.	אֲבוֹתַי	בָּנַי	בְּנוֹתַי	אַחַי	שְׁמוֹתַי	בָּתַּי

SINGULAR

	wife	sister	mouth	man	day (2)	city(2)
Sing. abs.	אִשָּׁה	אָחוֹת	פֶּה	אִישׁ	יוֹם	עִיר
cstr.	אֵשֶׁת	אֲחוֹת	פִּי	אִישׁ	יוֹם	עִיר
suffix	אִשְׁתִּי	אֲחוֹתִי	פִּי	אִישִׁי	יוֹמִי	עִירִי
	אִשְׁתְּךָ		פִּיךָ		יוֹמְךָ	עִירְךָ

PLURAL

	wife	sister	mouth	man	day (2)	city(2)
Plur. abs	נָשִׁים	(אֲחָיוֹת)	פִּיּוֹת	אֲנָשִׁים	יָמִים	עָרִים
cstr.	נְשֵׁי	אַחְיוֹת	פִּיפִיּוֹת	אַנְשֵׁי	יְמֵי	עָרֵי
suffix	נָשַׁי	אַחְיוֹתַי		אַנְשֵׁי	יָמַי	עָרַי

VOCABULARY

צֶדֶק righteous-ness.　גֹּדֶל greatness.　מַלְאָךְ messenger.

קֶשֶׁת bow (f).　חָכְמָה wisdom (f).　חַיִל force, army.

כֶּרֶם vineyard.　עֵצָה counsel (f).　עֵגֶל calf.

רֶגֶל foot (f).　נְקָמָה vengeance (f).　שִׁפְחָה handmaid (f).

שָׂפָה lip (f).　עַתָּה now, shortly.　בֶּרֶךְ knee (f).

Exercise 17

Translate :

‏1. רַגְלַיִם　2. מַלְאָכָיו　3. שְׁנֵיהֶם　4. מְקוֹמוֹתֵיכֶם　5. בִּלְבָבוֹ

‏6. עֶגְלֵךְ　7. עֲצוֹתֵינוּ　8. נְשֵׁיהֶם　9. מֵימֵיהֶם　10. שׁוֹרֵיהֶן

‏11 שִׁפְחוֹתֶיךָ　12. פִּיכֶם　13. עָרֵיהֶן　14. כַּרְמִי　15. בִּרְכַּיִם

1. Two eyes. 2. Two ears. 3. Their(m) hands. 4. Your(m) blessing. 5. Their(m) words. 6. Your(m) brother. 7. Their(f) houses. 8. Their(m) daughters. 9. My(m) brothers. 10. Their(m) heads. 11. His righteousness. 12. Their(m) calves. 13. My greatness. 14. Your(m) king. 15. Our armies.

CHAPTER XIX

DEGREES OF COMPARISON : NUMERALS

IN a relatively primitive and simple language such as
Hebrew it would be out of place to expect special
forms to indicate degrees of comparison. It is possible, however, to express such ideas, though a
certain amount of circumlocution is involved.

The comparative degree of superiority or inferior-
ity is expressed by attaching the preposition מִן after
the positive adjective to the word with which the
noun is being compared, *e.g.*, גָּדוֹל מִן־דָּוִד, greater
than David ; טוֹב מֵאַבְרָהָם, better than Abraham,
where מִן ("from") has the force of "in comparison
with".

The superlative degree may be indicated in a
number of ways, as follows :

(*a*) By prefixing the article to the positive adjective
coming after a definite noun, *e.g.*, הַבֵּן הַגָּדוֹל, the
eldest son (*i.e.*, the great one amongst those sons
mentioned).

(*b*) By placing the adjective in the construct before
a definite noun, *e.g.*, קְטֹן בָּנָיו, his youngest son
(*i.e.*, the young one of his sons).

(c) By using the preposition בְּ, "amongst", e.g., הָאִישׁ הֶחָזָק בָּאָרֶץ, the strongest man in the earth ; or the comparative with כֹּל, e.g., גָּדוֹל מִכֹּל הָעָם, the greatest of all the people ; or by using a pronominal suffix with an adjective, e.g., גְּדוֹלָם, their greatest (i.e., the great of them).

(d) Absolute superlatives use adverbs like מְאֹד after the adjective, e.g., גָּדוֹל עַד־מְאֹד, very great ; or nouns in the construct, e.g., שִׁיר הַשִּׁירִים, the most excellent song (i.e., the song of songs).

Numerals

The numbers one to nineteen have masculine and feminine forms, whilst numbers one to ten have a construct as well as an absolute state. Numbers may be described as "cardinals" (answering the question "how many ?") and "ordinals" (answering the question "in what order ?"). The cardinal numbers are as follows :

	With masculine nouns		With feminine nouns	
	Abs.	Cstr.	Abs.	Cstr.
I	אֶחָד	אַחַד	אַחַת	אַחַת
2	שְׁנַיִם	שְׁנֵי	שְׁתַּיִם	שְׁתֵּי
3	שְׁלֹשָׁה	שְׁלֹשֶׁת	שָׁלֹשׁ	שְׁלֹשׁ
4	אַרְבָּעָה	אַרְבַּעַת	אַרְבַּע	אַרְבַּע
5	חֲמִשָּׁה	חֲמֵשֶׁת	חָמֵשׁ	חֲמֵשׁ
6	שִׁשָּׁה	שֵׁשֶׁת	שֵׁשׁ	שֵׁשׁ

7	שִׁבְעָה	שִׁבְעַת	שֶׁבַע	שֶׁבַע
8	שְׁמֹנָה	שְׁמֹנַת	שְׁמֹנֶה	שְׁמֹנֶה
9	תִּשְׁעָה	תִּשְׁעַת	תֵּשַׁע	תֵּשַׁע
10	עֲשָׂרָה	עֲשֶׂרֶת	עֶשֶׂר	עֶשֶׂר

11	אַחַד עָשָׂר / עַשְׁתֵּי עָשָׂר	אַחַת עֶשְׂרֵה / עַשְׁתֵּי עֶשְׂרֵה
12	שְׁנֵים עָשָׂר / שְׁנֵי עָשָׂר	שְׁתֵּים עֶשְׂרֵה / שְׁתֵּי עֶשְׂרֵה
13	שְׁלֹשָׁה עָשָׂר	שְׁלֹשׁ עֶשְׂרֵה
14	אַרְבָּעָה עָשָׂר	אַרְבַּע עֶשְׂרֵה

etc.   etc.

20	עֶשְׂרִים	60	שִׁשִּׁים
30	שְׁלֹשִׁים	70	שִׁבְעִים
40	אַרְבָּעִים	80	שְׁמֹנִים
50	חֲמִשִּׁים	90	תִּשְׁעִים

100   מֵאָה (*f.*), cstr. מְאַת, plur. מֵאוֹת, hundreds.

200   מָאתַיִם (dual for מְאָתַיִם).

300 חְמֵשׁ מֵאוֹת 500   אַרְבַּע מֵאוֹת 400   שְׁלֹשׁ מֵאוֹת etc.

1000 אֶלֶף (*m.*) 2000 אַלְפַּיִם (dual). 3000 שְׁלֹשֶׁת אֲלָפִים

4000 אַרְבַּעַת אֲלָפִים 20,000 רִבּוֹתַיִם 10,000 רְבָבָה (dual).

The numeral "one" is an adjective, and generally follows its noun, agreeing with it in gender, *e.g.*, שָׁנָה אַחַת, one year. The number "two" is a dual form, and agrees in gender with its noun, *e.g.*, שְׁתֵּי נָשִׁים, two women. As a construct it precedes the word numbered, but as an absolute it follows it in apposition.

The cardinals from three to ten are nouns which disagree with the noun in gender, the masculine form standing with the feminine noun, and *vice versa*, e.g., שְׁלֹשֶׁת בָּנִים, three sons ; שָׁלֹשׁ בָּנוֹת, three daughters. The numerals from eleven to nineteen have the unit before the ten, and the noun is generally in the plural, though after common substantives such as day, year, man, the singular is used. The tens from thirty to ninety are expressed by the plural of the corresponding units, whilst twenty represents the plural of ten. Tens and units are usually joined by the conjunction waw, *e.g.*, שִׁבְעִים וְשִׁבְעָה, seventy-seven (*i.e.*, seventy and seven). The numerals occasionally have suffixes, as with שְׁלָשְׁתָּם, they three.

The ordinals have distinctive forms for the numbers one to ten only, as follows :

	Masculine	Feminine
first	רִאשׁוֹן	רִאשׁוֹנָה
second	שֵׁנִי	שֵׁנִית
third	שְׁלִישִׁי	שְׁלִישִׁית
fourth	רְבִיעִי	רְבִיעִית
fifth	חֲמִשִׁי	חֲמִישִׁית
sixth	שִׁשִּׁי	שִׁשִּׁית
seventh	שְׁבִיעִי	שְׁבִיעִית
eighth	שְׁמִינִי	שְׁמִינִית
ninth	תְּשִׁיעִי	תְּשִׁיעִית
tenth	עֲשִׂירִי	עֲשִׂירִית

These ordinals are adjectives, agreeing with the substantive in number and gender, and coming generally after the noun. After ten, the ordinals have no distinct form, and the corresponding cardinals are then employed. The age of people is normally expressed by בֶּן־, "son of" or בַּת, "daughter of", e.g., אִישׁ בֶּן־שְׁלֹשִׁים שָׁנָה, a man of thirty. In dates, the cardinals frequently replace ordinals in usage, e.g., בְּאֶחָד לַחֹדֶשׁ, on the first of the month.

About the Maccabean period the consonants of the alphabet came to be used as numerical signs, with the values assigned to them which we have already included in our table of the alphabet. From this it will be seen that the letters א to ט comprise the first nine numerals, the letters י to צ the tens, whilst the hundreds are signified by the letters from ק to ת. In combinations of numbers the greater symbol generally precedes the lesser, e.g., יב equals 12, i.e., 2 plus 10, the latter number being written first. Thus לג equals 3 plus 30, ריא equals 1 plus 10 plus 200, תר equals 200 plus 400, and so on. Exceptions to this are numbers 15 and 16, which are not symbolised by יה and יו respectively, since these combinations are fragments of the Divine Name. This difficulty was avoided by using טו (6 plus 9) for fifteen, and טז (7 plus 9) for sixteen.

VOCABULARY

גָּבֹהַּ tall.	אָהֵב to love.	פֶּקַח Pekah.
רָחֵל Rachel.	שֵׁבֶט tribe, sceptre.	בָּבֶל Babylon.
לֵאָה Leah.	שְׁלֹמֹה Solomon.	יָדַע to know.
חֶסֶד kindness.	חֹדֶשׁ month.	בָּטַח to trust.
גָּדַל to grow, become great.	בַּעַל lord, master, husband.	מִלְחָמָה battle, war (f).

Exercise 18

Translate :

‎1. קָטֹן מִן־אָחִיו ‎2. דָּוִד הַגָּדוֹל מֵאֶחָיו ‎3. בְּנוֹ הַקָּטֹן
‎4. עֶבֶד עֲבָדִים ‎5. אֶגְדַּל מִמְּךָ ‎6. גָּבֹהַ אָנֹכִי מִמֶּנּוּ ‎7. אַחַד
שְׁבָטֶיךָ ‎8. שְׁלֹשֶׁת בָּנָיו ‎9. בַּחֲמִשָּׁה עָשָׂר יוֹם ‎10. שְׁנַת שְׁמֹנֶה
עֶשְׂרֵה לִשְׁלֹמֹה ‎11. בִּשְׁנַת שְׁתַּיִם לְפֶקַח ‎12. בְּחֹדֶשׁ שְׁנֵים
עָשָׂר בַּשָּׁנָה הַשְּׁלִישִׁית ‎13. בִּשְׁנַת שְׁמֹנֶה עֶשְׂרֵה לְמֶלֶךְ יִשְׂרָאֵל
‎14. שְׁנֵיהֶם ‎15. שְׁנַיִם שָׁנִים.

1. Better than gold. 2. His youngest daughter. 3. He is taller than his wife. 4. From the greatest of them to the least of them. 5. Jacob loved Rachel more than Leah. 6. I am not better than my fathers. 7. The two mountains. 8. Her three daughters. 9. Fifteen sons. 10. Sixty-two years. 11. Twenty-seven. 12. Eleven years. 13. The first earth. 14. The tenth month. 15. In the second year.

Translate from the Hebrew Bible, using a lexicon where necessary : Jeremiah 52, verses 28-32.

CHAPTER XX

VERBAL SUFFIXES

THE pronominal accusative of a verb may be expressed by את with the appropriate suffix, or by a pronominal suffix attached to the verb. Normally only a direct object is implied by the use of a verbal suffix.

The form of the suffix itself is similar to those attached to nouns, except that in the first singular נִי is preferred, whilst in the third plural we find ם and ו more often than הֶם— and הֶן—. The addition of a suffix naturally affects the tone or accent, which tends to move in the direction of the suffix, and which modifies the pointing accordingly.

The inflections will be seen from the following tables :

Regular Verb

PERFECT QAL SINGULAR

	3 m.	3 f.	2 m.	2 f.	1 c.
Sing.					
1 c.	קְטָלַנִי	קְטָלַתְנִי	קְטַלְתַּנִי	קְטַלְתִּינִי	–
2 m.	קְטָלְךָ	קְטָלַתְךָ	–	–	קְטַלְתִּיךָ
2 f.	קְטָלֵךְ	קְטָלָתֶךְ	–	–	קְטַלְתִּיךְ

	3 m.	3 f.	2 m.	2 f.	I c.
3 m.	{ קְטָלוֹ קְטָלָהוּ }	קְטָלַתּוֹ קְטָלַתְהוּ	קְטַלְתּוֹ קְטַלְתָּהוּ	(קְטַלְתִּיו) קְטַלְתִּיהוּ	קְטַלְתִּיו קְטַלְתִּיהוּ
3 f.	קְטָלָה	קְטָלַתָּה	קְטַלְתָּה	קְטַלְתִּיהָ	קְטַלְתִּיהָ
Plur.					
I c.	קְטַלְנוּ	קְטַלְתְנוּ	קְטַלְתָּנוּ	קְטַלְתִּינוּ	—
2 m.	קְטַלְכֶם	(קְטַלַתְכֶם)	—	—	קְטַלְתִּיכֶם
2 f.	קְטַלְכֶן	(קְטַלְתְכֶן)	—	—	קְטַלְתִּיכֶן
3 m.	קְטָלָם	קְטָלַתָם	קְטַלְתָּם	קְטַלְתִּים	קְטַלְתִּים
3 f.	קְטָלָן	קְטָלַתָן	קְטַלְתָּן	קְטַלְתִּין	קְטַלְתִּין

PERFECT QAL PLURAL

	3 c.	2 c.	I c.
I c.	קְטָלוּנִי	קְטַלְתּוּנִי	—
2 m.	קְטָלוּךָ	—	קְטַלְנוּךָ
2 f.	קְטָלוּךְ	—	קְטַלְנוּךְ
3 m.	קְטָלוּהוּ	קְטַלְתּוּהוּ	קְטַלְנוּהוּ
3 f.	קְטָלוּהָ	קְטַלְתּוּהָ	קְטַלְנוּהָ
I c.	קְטָלוּנוּ	קְטַלְתּוּנוּ	—
2 m.	(קְטָלוּכֶם)	—	קְטַלְנוּכֶם
2 f.	(קְטָלוּכֶן)	—	קְטַלְנוּכֶן
3 m.	קְטָלוּם	קְטַלְתּוּם	קְטַלְנוּם
3 f.	קְטָלוּן	קְטַלְתּוּן	קְטַלְנוּן

The student will not encounter undue difficulty in learning these forms, as they inflect quite regularly. In the ordinary way only active verbs take suffixal

forms, since the reflexives and passives cannot govern an object. Where forms are exactly alike, as with the second singular feminine and the first singular common with the third masculine suffixes, the context determines the meaning.

The Pi'el and Hiph'il follow the same general scheme, as the following two examples will indicate :

	Pi'el		Hiph'il	
	3 sg. m.	3 pl. c.	3 sg. m.	3 pl. m.
I c.	קְטָלַ֫נִי	קְטָל֫וּנִי	הִקְטִילַ֫נִי	הִקְטִיל֫וּנִי
2 m.	קְטָלְךָ	קְטָל֫וּךָ	הִקְטִילְךָ	הִקְטִיל֫וּךָ
2 f.	קְטָלֵךְ	קְטָל֫וּךְ	הִקְטִילֵךְ	הִקְטִיל֫וּךְ
3 m.	קְטָלוֹ	קְטָל֫וּהוּ	הִקְטִילוֹ (‑הוּ)	הִקְטִיל֫וּהוּ
3 f.	קְטָלָהּ	קְטָל֫וּהָ	הִקְטִילָהּ	הִקְטִיל֫וּהָ
I c.	קְטָלָ֫נוּ	קְטָל֫וּנוּ	הִקְטִילָ֫נוּ	הִקְטִיל֫וּנוּ
2 m.	קְטָלְכֶם	קְטָל֫וּכֶם	הִקְטִילְכֶם	הִיקְטִיל֫וּכֶם
2 f.	קְטָלְכֶן	קְטָל֫וּכֶן	הִקְטִילְכֶן	הִקְטִיל֫וּכֶן
3 m.	קְטָלָם	קְטָלוּם	הִקְטִילָם	הִקְטִילוּם
3 f.	קְטָלָן	קְטָלוּן	הִקְטִילָן	הִקְטִילוּן

The suffix of the imperfect generally prefers an ''e'' vowel where the perfect has an ''a'' vowel. The imperfect has regular suffixal endings because the change of persons occurs with the commencing syllable. The imperfect and imperatives often have an assimilated נ, called ''nun energicum'' before the

suffix, with dagheš forte, *e.g.*, יִשְׁמְרֶךָ for יִשְׁמְרֶנְךָ. This is common in pause.

The following tables indicate the suffixal forms found in the imperfect and imperative :

	Imperfect Qal			Imperative		
	3 sg. m.	3 sg. m. with nun energicum	3 pl.	2 sg. m.	2 sg. m. with nun energicum	2 pl. m.
1 c.	יִקְטְלֵ֫נִי	יִקְטְלֶ֫נִּי	יִקְטְל֫וּנִי	קָטְלֵ֫נִי	קָטְלֶ֫נִּי	קָטְל֫וּנִי
2 m.	יִקְטָלְךָ	יִקְטָלֶ֫ךָּ	יִקְטְל֫וּךָ	–	–	–
2 f.	יִקְטְלֵךְ	–	יִקְטְל֫וּךְ	–	–	–
3 m.	יִקְטְלֵ֫הוּ	יִקְטְלֶ֫נּוּ	יִקְטְל֫וּהוּ	קָטְלֵ֫הוּ	קָטְלֶ֫נּוּ	קְטָל֫וּהוּ
3 f.	(יִקְטְלֶ֫הָ)	יִקְטְלֶ֫נָּה	יִקְטְל֫וּהָ	(קָטְלָהּ)	קָטְלֶ֫נָּה	קְטָל֫וּהָ
1 c.	יִקְטְלֵ֫נוּ	יִקְטְלֶ֫נּוּ	יִקְטְל֫וּנוּ	קָטְלֵ֫נוּ	קָטְלֶ֫נּוּ	קָטְל֫וּנוּ
2 m.	יִקְטָלְכֶם	–	יִקְטְלוּכֶם	–	–	–
2 f.	יִקְטָלְכֶן		יִקְטְלוּכֶן	–	–	–
3 m.	יִקְטְלֵם	–	יִקְטְל֫וּם	קָטְלֵם	–	קְטָל֫וּם
3 f.	יִקְטְלֵן		יִקְטְל֫וּן	קָטְלֵן		קְטָל֫וּן

	Infinitive constr.	Pi'el 3 sg. m.	Hiph'il 3 sg. m.
1 c.	קָטְלִי (קָטְלֵ֫נִי)	יְקַטְּלֵ֫נִי	יַקְטִילֵ֫נִי
2 m.	קָטְלְךָ (קָטְלֶ֫ךָ)	יְקַטֶּלְךָ	יַקְטִילְךָ
2 f.	קָטְלֵךְ	יְקַטְּלֵךְ	יַקְטִילֵךְ
3 m.	קָטְלוֹ	יְקַטְּלֵ֫הוּ	יַקְטִילֵ֫הוּ
3 f.	קָטְלָהּ	יְקַטְּלָהּ	יַקְטִילֶ֫הָ (יַקְטִילָהּ)

1 c.	קָטְלֵנוּ	יַקְטְלֵנוּ	יַקְטִילֵנוּ
2 m.	קְטָלְכֶם	יַקְטֶלְכֶם	יַקְטִילְכֶם
2 f.	קְטָלְכֶן	יַקְטֶלְכֶן	יַקְטִילְכֶן
3 m.	קְטָלָם	יַקְטְלֵם	יַקְטִילֵם
3 f.	קְטָלָן	יַקְטְלֵן	יַקְטִילֵן

The student should notice that the vowel under the second masculine singular and plural of the imperfect Qal is qameç hatuph, as also in the shut syllables of the infinitive construct. The participle generally has the suffixes of the noun rather than the verb, *e.g.*, מְבַקְשָׁיו, rather than מְבַקְשֵׁהוּ, "those who seek him".

The infinitive construct has the force of a gerund, and can govern an object. Thus the phrase "when he kept the man" may be rendered בְּשָׁמְרוֹ אֶת־הָאִישׁ, with בְּ prefixed to the infinitive. If the object is a pronoun, אֵת in suffixal form is employed.

The suffixes to the verb might at first glance appear confusing and highly intricate, but with even the slightest degree of familiarity they become apparent as an ingenious method of expression involving a direct relation between subject, verb and object, and the economy of language which results is in many ways typical of the Hebrew idiom. Thus one word, שְׁמָרַתַם, means "she has kept them (*m*)", just as יַמְלִיכוּנִי does duty for the expression "they (*m*.) will make me (*c*) king". A glance at the suffix

is sufficient to indicate the person of the object, whilst the state of the subject and verb is readily deduced from the remainder of the word.

VOCABULARY

בקשׁ	(Piʻel.) to seek.	קֶדֶם	east.	מֹשֶׁה	Moses.
שׁמד	(Hiph.) to destroy.	לְמַעַן	in order that.	עוֹלָה	burnt-offering.
מָצָא	to find.	אַיֵּה	where ?	זֶרַע	seed.
רָעָב	famine.	אֵיךְ	how ?	לָשׁוֹן	tongue (f).
שָׂרַף	to burn.	רֹעֶה	shepherd.	מִנְחָה	meal-offering.

אֱמֶת	truth (f).	שָׁפַט	to judge.	בָּנָה	to build.
יָרֵא	to fear.	בָּחַר	to choose.	אַף	also, moreover.
כָּרַת בְּרִית	to make a covenant.	מָאַס	to reject, despite.	רֵעַ	friend, companion.

Exercise 19

Translate :

1. יְבַקְשֵׁנִי‎ 2. שְׁמָרֵנוּ‎ 3. יַמְלִיכֵנִי‎ 4. יִשְׁמְרוּכֶן‎ 5. שְׁמַרְתּוּנִי

6. שְׁמַרְתִּינִי‎ 7. שְׁמָרָן‎ 8. אַחֲרֵי כָּרְתָם בְּרִית‎ 9. בְּקָשְׁנוּךְ

10. בַּהֵיכָל‎ 11. בְּשָׁמְרוֹ אֵת דְּבָרֶיךָ

12. הַמְלִיכוּהוּ עַל־הָעָם הַזֶּה‎ 13. מַצְדִּיקִי הוּא אֱלֹהִים

14. יַשְׁמִידֵנִי בַּיּוֹם הַהוּא‎ 15. כִּי־מְכַבְּדַי אֲכַבֵּד.

1. She has made me king (Hiph.).   2. I have kept thee.
3. They have kept them.   4. Make me king.   5. They(*m*)
will seek me.   6. Ye(*f*) have sought me.   7. We have kept
thee(*m*).   8. In thy(*f*) keeping.   9. When the man
remembered thy law.   10. In the day when I visit them.
11. He will honour me in that city.   12. I will judge thee(*f*)
according to thy ways.   13. God has sent me before you.
14. They sought him with their whole heart.   15. Hast
thou found me, O my enemy ?

Translate : Isaiah 41, verses 8-12.

CHAPTER XXI

WEAK VERBS : PE NUN, PE GUTTURAL, PE 'ALEPH

WEAK verbs are normally classified in terms of the old paradigm verb פָּעַל, which earlier grammarians regarded as the typical regular or strong verb, later being displaced in favour of קְטַל because of its guttural content, as we have seen. Thus, the first radical of any verb is designated the פ" letter ; the second is styled the ע" letter, whilst the third is called the ל" letter. On this basis פ"ן verbs are those which have נ as the first letter, and ע"ו are those which have waw as the second radical. Since א and ה are gutturals at the beginning, and quiescent letters at the end of a word, they have a twofold designation, e.g., בָּכָה is a ל"ה verb, but הָלַךְ is a פ" guttural. Where a verb has the second and third radicals identical it is called a Double 'Ayin verb, e.g., סָבַב.

These verbs are styled "weak" because of the necessary modification of certain forms in the paradigm where the radicals are normally doubled. Since many of these radicals are gutturals, dagheš forte cannot be inserted, as in the strong or regular verb. The student should avoid the term "irregular" as far

as possible in this connection, since the form which
ensues is fully consonant with the normal procedure
governing guttural letters, already familiar to us.

Pe Nun Verbs

This type is marked by the ready assimilation of
the radical נ at the end of a syllable, since in this
position it does not carry a full vowel. This assimilation occurs in the imperfect Qal, the Niph'al perfect
and participle, and throughout the Hiph'il and
Hoph'al. Thus יִנְגַּשׁ becomes יִגַּשׁ ; נִנְגַּשׁ becomes נִגַּשׁ,
and so on. In this type of verb, qibbuç replaces
qameç hatuph in the Hoph'al.

The nun is dropped in the imperative by stative
verbs and those with pathah under the second
radical, e.g., גַּשׁ for נְגַשׁ, draw near. If a verb has
holem with the second radical, the nun is generally
retained, e.g., נְפֹל, fall thou. The infinite construct
relinquishes the nun, but assumes the feminine termination to form a segholate noun, e.g., גֶּשֶׁת. With
ל as a prefix it is pointed with qameç, e.g., לָגֶשֶׁת, to
draw near. With a suffix this becomes לְגִשְׁתִּי, "for
my drawing near". But verbs which have holem in
the imperative form the infinitive construct in the
usual manner, retaining the nun, e.g., לִנְפֹּל to fall.

The verb לָקַח, to take, is treated as a Pe Nun verb
in the Qal and Hoph'al. Thus the Qal imperfect is

יִקַּח, and the Hoph'al imperfect is יֻקַּח. In other formations, however, the ל is not assimilated, e.g., Niph'al, נִלְקַח. In the verb נָתַן, to give, set, the final nun is assimilated where pointed with silent šᵉwa, e.g., נָתַנְתָּ becomes נָתַתָּ. The initial nun is also assimilated in the imperfect Qal and takes çere under the second radical, e.g., יִתֵּן. The imperative likewise has çere, but before maqqeph it becomes sᵉghol, i.e., תֶּן־. The emphatic form of this is תְּנָה and with suffix is תְּנֵהוּ. The infinitive construct is תֵּת, from תֶּנְת, and with a suffix is תִּתִּי, etc. With ל the infinitive construct is לָתֵת. Fuller forms will be found in the paradigm at the end of the book.

Pe Guttural Verbs

These verbs are modified because of the peculiarities of the guttural letters. As we have seen, these letters cannot be doubled by a dagheš forte, and also they prefer a hateph to a simple vocal sᵉwa. In the imperfect Niph'al and related forms the initial radical has the hireq lengthened to çere in compensation, e.g., יֵעָמֵד. In the perfect Qal, the second plural masculine and feminine have hateph pathah as the guttural vowel, i.e., עֲזַבְתֶּם and עֲזַבְתֶּן, where the regular verb would have simple šᵉwa. In the imperfect the hateph occurs consistently under the guttural, and corresponds with the vowel of the prefix, e.g., אֶעֱזֹב. Normally the vowel preferred by

the guttural is of a different class from that of the
last syllable. So in the imperfect Qal, with a final
holem the guttural vowel is generally pathah, e.g.,
יַעֲמֹד, and with a terminal pathah the vowel chosen
is usually sᵉghol, e.g., יֶחֱזַק. However, sᵉghol is
regularly found with the first person singular of the
imperfect Qal, אֶעֱמֹד, whilst in the imperative the
hateph is usually hateph pathah, e.g., עֲמֹד. Where
forms end with a vowel letter, the hateph becomes a
full vowel before a šᵉwa. Thus whilst the third
singular masculine imperfect Qal of עָמַד is יַעֲמֹד, the
third plural is יַעַמְדוּ, with the šᵉwa under the mem
being vocal. Obviously a form יַעֲמְדוּ would be impossible, since two vocal šᵉwas cannot occur together.

Pe 'Aleph Verbs

Because א is a quiescent letter as well as a guttural,
it relinquishes its consonantal force in the case of five
verbs, and these then form a subdivision of the Pe
guttural class. They are אָבַד, to perish ; אָמַר, to
say ; אָכַל, to eat ; אָפָה, to bake, and אָבָה, to be
willing. The last two are ל״ה verbs also. One or
two verbs have both Pe guttural and Pe 'Aleph forms,
e.g., אָחַז, to seize, and אָסַף, to gather.

In the perfect Qal they are like the Pe gutturals,
but in the imperfect א quiesces to the vowel holem,
e.g., יֹאכַל for יֶאֱכַל. In the infin. const. either hateph
pathah or hateph sᵉghol are found under the א, e.g.,

אֱמֹר, אָכֹל. Whilst the infinitive construct when governed or preceded by לְ normally has hateph seghol, one verb only, אָמַר has a contracted form, לֵאמֹר for לֶאֱמֹר. In the imperfect with waw consecutive, אָמַר has seghol, וַיֹּאמֶר and he said, but in the first singular pathah is found, e.g., וָאֹמַר.

VOCABULARY

נגשׁ (Niph.) to draw near.	נצל (Hiph.) to deliver.	חֲצִי half.
נָקַם to avenge.	נבא (Niph.) to prophesy.	עָמַד to stand.
נָשַׁק to kiss.	חָטָא to sin.	שָׁכַב to sleep.
חָלַק to divide.	חָלַם to dream.	קֹדֶשׁ holiness.
דבר (Pi.) to speak.	עָנָה to answer.	יְהוֹנָתָן Jonathan.
חָכַם to be wise.	עֲנָתוֹת Anathoth.	נָגַע to touch, reach.
נַחֲלָה possession, inheritance (f).	נכה (Hiph.) to strike, kill.	עָבַד to serve, till ground.
רָחַק to be distant, withdraw.	נָטַשׁ to leave, allow.	סָפַר to count, write ; (Pi.) to recount.

Exercise 20

Translate :

וַיֹּאמֶר אֵלַי בֶּן־אָדָם עֲמֹד עַל־רַגְלֶיךָ וַאֲדַבֵּר אֹתָךְ 1.
אֶעֱבָדְךָ שֶׁבַע שָׁנִים בְּרָחֵל בִּתְּךָ הַקְּטַנָּה 2. וְשִׁלְחוּ זִקְנֵי 3.
עִירוֹ וְלָקְחוּ אֹתוֹ מִשָּׁם וְנָתְנוּ אֹתוֹ בְּיַד־הַמֶּלֶךְ 4. כֹּה אָמַר

יהוה לְאַנְשֵׁי עֲנָתוֹת הַמְבַקְשִׁים אֶת־נַפְשֶׁךָ לֵאמֹר לֹא תִנָּבֵא
בְּשֵׁם יהוה 5. וּפַרְעֹה חֹלֵם וְהִנֵּה עֹמֵד עַל־הַיְאֹר 6. וַיְדַבֵּר
יְהוֹנָתָן בְּדָוִד טוֹב אֶל־שָׁאוּל אָבִיו וַיֹּאמֶר אֵלָיו אַל־יֶחֱטָא
הַמֶּלֶךְ בְּעַבְדּוֹ 7. וְעָבַדְתָּ אֶת־אֹיְבֶיךָ אֲשֶׁר יְשַׁלְּחֶם בְּךָ יהוה
8. בְּיוֹם הָרָע אֶקְרָאֶךָ כִּי תַעֲנֵנִי 9. לֹא נְטַשְׁתַּנִי לְנַשֵּׁק לְבָנַי
וְלִבְנֹתָי 10. וַיַּחֲלֵק עֲלֵיהֶם לַיְלָה הוּא וַעֲבָדָיו.

1. Ye(m) shall serve God upon this mountain. 2. And
thou, son of man, prophesy unto the mountains of Israel.
3. And they dreamed a dream in one night. 4. And he
said, Draw ye near hither, all the people. 5. For the place
on which you are standing (*part.*) is holy ground (ground
of holiness). 6. And thou shalt not cause the land to sin,
which the Lord thy God has given thee for an inheritance.
7. Thus saith Jehovah, send out (Pi'el) my people, that
they may serve me. 8. And Jehovah will answer and say
to his people, Behold I am sending(*part.*) bread in the desert.
9. In all these words he did not sin with his lips. 10. And
his father said unto him, draw near, I pray thee, and kiss
me, my son.

Translate : Genesis 28, verses 11-15.

CHAPTER XXII

'AYIN GUTTURAL, LAMEDH GUTTURAL AND LAMEDH 'ALEPH VERBS

'Ayin Guttural

BECAUSE the second radical in this type of verb is a guttural, certain modifications associated with gutturals take place. Thus a vocal šᵉwa under a guttural becomes a hateph, and because of the preference for "a" sounds it is usually hateph pathah, e.g., בָּחֲרוּ for בָּחְרוּ. The perfect Qal follows the normal pattern except for the third feminine singular and third plural, which have the hateph under the guttural. This occurs also in the second feminine singular, third masculine plural and second masculine plural of the imperfect, and also in the cohortative. In the feminine singular and masculine plural of the imperative the first radical takes the short vowel corresponding to the hateph, e.g., שַׁחֲטוּ instead of שְׁחֲטוּ. In both the imperfect and imperative Qal, pathah may replace holem, e.g., יִשְׁחַט rather than יִשְׁחֹט.

The Pi'el, Pu'al and Hithpa'el naturally omit dagheš forte from the middle radical, being a guttural. The preceding vowel is lengthened in com-

pensation before ר (בְּרֵךְ for בְּרַךְ), and often before א
(מְאֵן for מְאַן). ה, ח and ע generally require no such
compensation.

Lamedh Guttural

This is a type of verb whose third radical is a
guttural, and includes final ה with mappiq. Final א
and ה simple are quiescent, and fall into different
classes to be considered later. Verbs of this general
class are peculiar because of the rule that all final
gutturals must have an "a" sound connected with
them. The imperfect and imperative Qal and
Niph'al have pathah before the guttural, whilst
pathah furtive occurs after a fully accented vowel in
the infinitives Qal and in the active participle. When
the guttural is final and preceded by a permanently
long vowel, pathah furtive is employed in the normal
manner, e.g., הִשְׁלִיחַ. An auxiliary pathah is placed
under the guttural of the second feminine singular in
the perfect Qal and elsewhere without altering the
pointing of the taw, e.g., שָׁלַחַתְּ, not שָׁלַחְתְּ.

Lamedh 'Aleph

In this class it is important to bear in mind the
quiescent nature of the final guttural, as we mentioned above. Apart from the third and second
person feminine plural of the imperfect, the preceding vowel is always long when the א quiesces, for
the syllable thus has the effect of being open.

In the perfect Qal, qameç is retained throughout, except in the stative verbs, which have çere, *i.e.*, מָצָאתָ, but מָלֵאתָ. The infinitive construct Qal may be regular, *e.g.*, חֲטֹא, but may be formed by adding ת, *e.g.*, מְלֹאת. The imperfect Qal has qameç as the second vowel, but an accented sᵉghol precedes the א in the third and second persons femininc plural, *e.g.*, תִּמְצֶאנָה.

There is a tendency to confuse forms from this class with corresponding forms of the ל"ה class of verbs, as in I Samuel xiv, 33, where we find הֹטְאִים for הֹטְאִים. א may relinquish a vowel in contraction, *e.g.*, מֹצֵאת for מֹצֵאת, or it may drop out itself entirely in writing, *e.g.*, מָצָתִי for מָצָאתִי.

VOCABULARY

בַּרֵךְ (Pi.) to bless.	מָלֵא to be full, (Pi.) to fill.	חֲנִית spear.
שָׁעַן (Niph.) to lean.	שָׁלַח to send, let go.	חָמָס violence.
שָׁבַע (Niph.) to swear.	נָתַץ to break down.	שָׁחַת to be corrupt.
שָׂנֵא to hate.	מָשַׁח to anoint.	אָדוֹן lord, master.
מָאַן (Pi.) to refuse, be unwilling.	יָצַק to pour out.	רָעָה evil (*f*).
אִם if, whether.	מִשְׁחָה unction (*f*).	נָבַט to look (Hiph.)

Exercise 21

Translate :

١. וַיֹּאמֶר יהוה אֶל־מֹשֶׁה כָּבֵד־לֵב פַּרְעֹה מֵאֵן לְשַׁלַּח אֶת הָעָם

٢. וַתִּשָּׁחֵת הָאָרֶץ לִפְנֵי אֱלֹהִים וַתִּמָּלֵא הָאָרֶץ חָמָס   ٣. וְאַתָּה

תְּדַבֵּר אֶל־כָּל־חַכְמֵי־לֵב אֲשֶׁר מִלֵּאתִיו רוּחַ חָכְמָה   ٤. וַיִּמָּאֵן

וַיֹּאמֶר אֶל־אֵשֶׁת אֲדֹנָיו הֵן לֹא־יָדַע אֲדֹנִי וְכֹל אֲשֶׁר־יֶשׁ־לוֹ

נָתַן בְּיָדִי   ٥. וְאֵיךְ אֶעֱשֶׂה אֶת הָרָעָה הַגְּדוֹלָה וְחָטָאתִי לֵאלֹהִים

٦. וַאֲנִי שְׂנֵאתִיו כִּי לֹא יִתְנַבֵּא עָלַי טוֹב   ٧. וְאִם רַע בְּעֵינֵיכֶם

לַעֲבֹד אֶת־יהוה בַּחֲרוּ לָכֶם הַיּוֹם אֶת־מִי תַעֲבֹדוּן   ٨. וּזְעַקְתֶּם

בַּיּוֹם הַהוּא מִלִּפְנֵי מַלְכְּכֶם אֲשֶׁר בְּחַרְתֶּם לָכֶם   ٩. לֹא

יַשְׁחִיתְךָ וְלֹא יִשְׁכַּח אֶת־בְּרִית אֲבֹתֶיךָ אֲשֶׁר נִשְׁבַּע לָהֶם

١٠. וּמָשַׁחְתָּ לִי אֵת אֲשֶׁר־אֹמַר אֵלֶיךָ.

1. And God blessed the seventh day and sanctified it.
2. He will not repent, for he is not a man, to repent. 3. He
will send his messenger before thee. 4. And he sware
to him concerning (עַל) these words. 5. And behold,
Saul leaned upon his spear. 6. And the blood of thy
sacrifices shall be poured upon the altar of the Lord thy
God, and thou shalt eat the flesh. 7. Her poor will I
satisfy with bread. 8. And he said unto Jacob, I find
her not. 9. Thou shalt not hate thy brother in thine
heart. 10. And thou shalt take the oil of unction and
pour it upon his head and anoint him.

Translate : Genesis 6, verses 5-8.

CHAPTER XXIII

PE YODH, PE WAW; 'AYIN YODH AND 'AYIN WAW VERBS

Pe Yodh and Pe Waw Verbs

THE majority of the Hebrew Pe Yodh verbs originally had waw as the first root letter, but since few words ordinarily begin with waw, and in those in which it would appear as a radical it becomes yodh, the true difference between these types is less apparent in the Qal than in the Niᵱh'al and the Hiph'il. Thus the verb יָטַב, to be good, is a genuine Pe Yodh, whilst יָשַׁב, to sit, comes from an original וְשַׁב, and is thus a Pe Waw. In the Hiph'il these become הֵיטִיב, retaining the original ' after the ה, and הוֹשִׁיב, with the original ו, now quiescent, following the ה.

The original פ״י verbs are few in number, the most important being יָנַק, to suck, יָלַל, to howl (Hiph.), יָטַב, to be good, and יָקַץ, to awake.

The imperfect Qal is regular, with the yodh quiescing in the long hireq and pathah as the final vowel, *e.g.*, יִיטַב. The infinitive construct Qal is also regular, יְטַב, whilst all Hiph'il forms have çere under the preformative ה, followed by quiescent ', *e.g.* הֵיטִיב.

A number of verbs with ‫ צ‬as their second radical
are like ‫ פ״י‬verbs in the Qal, but in other forms are
like ‫ פ״ן‬verbs in assimilating the first and second root
letters, and using dagheš forte. These verbs are ‫יָצַג‬,
to place, ‫יָצַב‬, to stand, ‫יָצַת‬, to burn, and ‫יָצַק‬, to pour.
Assimilation takes place chiefly in the perfect
Niph'al, and all forms of the Hiph'il and Hoph'al.
Thus the Niph'al of ‫ יָצַת‬is ‫נִצַּת‬, the Hiph'il is ‫הִצִּית‬,
and the Hoph'al is ‫יֻצַּת‬. The verbs ‫יָצַר‬, to fashion,
and ‫יָצָא‬, to go out, are exceptions to this
procedure.

Many original ‫ פ״ו‬verbs surrender the consonantal
force of the quiescents with many preformatives, but
the Hiph'il and Hoph'al retain them to a certain
extent. Thus the perfect Hiph'il of ‫ יָשַׁב‬is ‫הוֹשִׁיב‬, and
the imperfect is ‫יוֹשִׁיב‬. The waw also reappears in the
Niph'al, ‫נוֹשַׁב‬. The imperfect Niph'al has waw with
consonantal force, i.e., ‫יִוָּשֵׁב‬. The first person imperfect singular has hireq rather than s[e]ghol under
the ‫א‬. The Hoph'al ‫ הָוְשַׁב‬becomes ‫הוּשַׁב‬.

The imperfect Qal varies somewhat in formation.
In certain verbs it follows the pattern of the ‫פ״י‬
class, e.g., ‫יִירָא‬, from ‫יָרֵא‬, to fear. These include ‫יָרַשׁ‬,
to inherit, ‫יָעַץ‬, to take counsel, ‫יָעֵף‬, to be weary, and
‫יָשֵׁן‬, to fall asleep. It will be seen that such verbs
change waw to yodh in the imperfect, forming it like
that of the strong stative verbs.

In other verbs the initial yodh is dropped, and a permanently long çere appears under the first consonant, with either çere as the last vowel, or pathah before a guttural. Thus יָשַׁב becomes יֵשֵׁב in the imperfect Qal, and יָדַע becomes יֵדַע. The most important of these verbs are יָשַׁב, to sit, dwell, יָרַד, to go down, יָלַד, to bear, beget, יָדַע, to know, and יָצָא, to go out. הָלַךְ, to go, is regarded also as one of these, except for the perfect and infinitive absolute Qal, and the Hithpa'el.

Adverbs

These are less developed in Hebrew than in other languages, and in addition to their derivation from nouns and pronouns may be rendered idiomatically by Hebrew verbs. Thus the perfect Hiph'il of יָטַב is employed for the adverb "well", *e.g.*, הֵיטִיבוּ לְדַבֵּר, they have spoken well, is literally "they have 'made good' in speaking"; the phrase "and she bore again" becomes "she added and bore", *i.e.*, וַתּוֹסֶף לְלֶדֶת, or וַתּוֹסֶף וַתֵּלֶד (and she added to bear).

'Ayin Yodh and Waw Verbs

These classes have a quiescent yodh or waw as the middle radical, which does not appear in the perfect Qal. Thus an original קָוַם becomes קָם, and שָׁיַם becomes שָׂם. Though עׁו verbs are more common, both types are identical in conjugation except for the imperative, imperfect and infinitive Qal, where the

E

original medial root letter is found as a vowel, *i.e.*,
יָשִׂים, יָקוּם. In the perfect, waw is omitted throughout, whether the vowel is "a", "e", or "o", *e.g.*, בּוֹשׁ,
מֵת, בָּן. The Jussives of שָׂם and קָם are יָשֵׂם and יָקֵם
respectively, and when waw consecutive is added to
the shortened form of the imperfect, the accent falls
on the yodh, making the last syllable shut and the
vowel short, *i.e.*, וַיָּקָם, wayyaqom, וַיָּשֶׂם, wayyasem.

A number of statives are included in this class but
do not conform to any particular set pattern. Thus
מוּת has a Qal perfect מֵת, מֵתָה etc., whilst בּוֹשׁ has
holem instead of šureq in the Qal, בֹּשְׁתָּ, בֹּשְׁתְּ etc. In
the imperfect full holem reappears, יֵבוֹשׁ, etc., as in
the infinitive and active participle, בּוֹשׁ. The verb
בּוֹא, to come, conjugates like קוּם, save that it has ו
instead of י. Hence the imperfect is יָבוֹא, and the
infinitive construct is בּוֹא(לְ). שׁוּב is found in an
idiomatic form meaning "to do over again". The
phrase, and he arose again, would thus be rendered
וַיָּשָׁב וַיָּקָם, *i.e.*, and he returned and arose. Some
verbs have Poʿlel as an intensive to replace the Piʿel,
e.g., קוֹמֵם (imperfect יְקוֹמֵם), and occasionally a Pilpel,
כִּלְכֵּל (כּוּל).

VOCABULARY

מוּת to die ; (Hiph.) put to death.	בּוֹא to come ; (Hiph.) to bring.	שׁוּב to return ; (Hiph.) to restore.

יָטַב to be good.　　יָשֵׁן to sleep.　　בּוֹשׁ to be
　　　　　　　　　　　　　　　　　　ashamed.

נַחַל stream.　　נְבֵלָה corpse (f).　　זַיִת olive.

נוּחַ to rest.　　קוּם to arise.　　יָצָא to go out.

אֵלִיָּהוּ Elijah.　　שֹׁמְרוֹן Samaria.　　פָּצַר בְּ to urge.

Exercise 22

Translate :

1. וַיֵּלֶךְ וַיֵּשֶׁב בַּנַּחַל אֲשֶׁר עַל־פְּנֵי הָעִיר．2. וַיָּקָם וַיֵּלֶךְ אֶל־
נַפְשׁוֹ וַיָּבוֹא עַד־הַמִּדְבָּר．3. קוּם אֱכָל כִּי רַב מִמְּךָ הַדָּרֶךְ．
4. וַיֹּאמֶר יהוה אֵלָיו לֵךְ שׁוּב לְדַרְכְּךָ מִדְבָּרָה 5. וַתֹּאמֶר לָהּ
בַּת־פַּרְעֹה הוֹלִיכִי אֶת־הַיֶּלֶד הַזֶּה וְהֵינִקִהוּ 6. וַיֹּאמֶר לֹא־
יֵרֵד בְּנִי עִמָּכֶם כִּי־אָחִיו מֵת 7. וְאַתָּה תֶּחֱזֶה מִכָּל־הָעָם
אַנְשֵׁי־חַיִל יִרְאֵי אֱלֹהִים 8. וְהַדָּגָה אֲשֶׁר בַּיְאֹר תָּמוּת 9. יִשָּׂא
פַרְעֹה אֶת־רֹאשְׁךָ וַהֲשִׁיבְךָ עַל־הַהֵיכָל 10. כִּי אָנֹכִי מֵת בָּאָרֶץ
הַזֹּאת וְאַתֶּם עֹבְרִים וִירִשְׁתֶּם אֶת־הָאָרֶץ הַטּוֹבָה הַזֹּאת.

1. And he said, Go out and stand upon the mountain.
2. Go, return, for what have I done to thee ? 3. And he
arose and went after Elijah. 4. And they urged him
until (עַד) he was ashamed, and he said, Send. 5. And
the king died, and he was brought to Samaria, and
they buried the king in Samaria. 6. And all the men of
valour arose and went all the night and took the corpse
of Saul. 7. And the woman took the boy and nursed (יָנַק)
him. 8. And they shall fear the name of Jehovah in the
city. 9. His seed shall inherit the earth. 10. And he
said, I will certainly return to thee in the day of evil.

Translate : 1 Kings 17, verses 10-12.

CHAPTER XXIV

DOUBLE 'AYIN, LAMEDH HE, AND
DOUBLY WEAK VERBS

DOUBLE 'Ayin verbs are very similar to the 'Ayin Waw class in many respects, exhibiting a weakness in the second and third radicals, which are identical. Some authorities think that the stems are in fact only biliteral, since the two radicals in question are frequently written as one letter, *e.g.*, קלל becomes קל in the perfect Qal. Where these forms take endings, dagheš forte is used to indicate the presence of a double letter. Hence קטטו becomes קטטו, and so קטו, but the dagheš is omitted in simple forms.

From this it appears that there are two forms of perfect Qal. The longer one, *e.g.*, סָבַב, is conjugated like קָטַל, but seldom appears except in the third person singular and plural. A shorter form, סַב, is much more common, and takes dagheš forte in the ב, and full holem, as will be seen from the paradigm. The longer form is transitive, the shorter one intransitive.

The imperfect Qal has two forms also, one of which reflects affinity with ע״ו verbs. This is the most common, and using the previous verb would be יָסֹב, with the original "a" vowel under the prefix, as in

ע״ו verbs. With waw consecutive the accent falls on the yodh, leaving the last syllable shut, e.g., וַיָּסָב, wayyaṣobh. A resemblance to פ״ן verbs is seen in the alternate form יִסֹּב, with the first radical doubled instead of the second.

The original "a" vowel occurs in the perfect Niph'al, נָסַב, whilst the imperfect, יִסַּב, is similar to the imperfect Qal. The Hiph'il perfect is like the Niph'al perfect except that it has two çere vowels, הֵסֵב, which appear also in the participle, מֵסֵב. Intensive forms such as the Po'el (סוֹבֵב), Pilpel (גִּלְגֵּל) and Hithpalpel, (הִתְגַּלְגֵּל), are sometimes found. A reduplication of the first radical, similar to that found in Aramaic, occurs in the imperfect of some verbs, e.g., יִתַּם from תָּמַם, and יִקֹּד from קָדַד.

Lamedh He verbs originally ended in yodh or waw, e.g., גָּלָה derives from an original גָּלַי, and שָׁלָה from שָׁלַו. The final ה is really a vowel-letter, since were it a consonant it would of course take mappiq, and thus bring the verb into the Lamedh guttural class.

The third masculine singular perfect in all forms terminates in ה, but otherwise the ה disappears. All imperfects terminate in הֶ֖ in the third masculine singular, but this disappears before a vowel afformative e.g., יִגְלוּ. The original third radical, yodh, survives as a quiescent letter in the second and first persons perfect of the Qal (גָּלִיתָ, גָּלִיתִי) and Niph'al

(נִגְלֵיתָ, נִגְלֵיתִי). The jussive is formed throughout by
dropping the הָ- of the imperfect by a process called
"apocopation". Such forms are known as "apocopated forms", *i.e.*, "cut off". Thus the jussive Qal
becomes יִגֶל, the Niph'al יִגָל, and so on, with sᵉghol
as an auxiliary vowel where two consonants would
occur together. The cohortative הָ- is never attached
to ל״ה verbs ; instead the simple imperfect is employed to express the cohortative concept.

Before a mute second radical (ד, כ, ק, ת) a monosyllabic apocopation takes place, *e.g.*, וַיֵּשְׁתְּ, from שָׁתָה,
and וַיֵּבְךְ, from בָּכָה. Pe Guttural verbs which are
also ל״ה in class will retain pathah in apocopated
forms, and so the imperfect Qal and Hiph'il of עָלָה
are יַעֲלֶה, apoc. יַעַל. The verb רָאָה, to see, has an
imperfect יִרְאֶה, and a jussive יֵרֶא, but in the waw
consecutive the א quiesces, וַיַּרְא. The common verb
הָיָה, to be, has its imperfect יִהְיֶה, and the jussive יְהִי,
or in pause יֶהִי. A similar verb חָיָה, to live, is formed
in exactly the same way.

שׁחה, to bow down, is used in the Hithpa'lel,
reflecting the original terminal radical waw. The
perfect is הִשְׁתַּחֲוָה (with the ת and שׁ interchangeable
by rule) ; imperfect is יִשְׁתַּחֲוֶה, and the apocopated
form is יִשְׁתַּחוּ. Apocopation of the Hiph'il imperative
takes place chiefly in the verb רָפָה, as illustrated by
the phrase, הֶרֶף מִמֶּנִּי, let me alone.

Doubly weak verbs have more than one weak radical, as with נָשָׂא, to lift up, which is both פ״נ and ל״א. Some of the more common verbs and their principal formations are as follows :

יָצָא, to go out. imp. יֵצֵא, imperat. צֵא, Hiph. הוֹצִיא, הוֹצֵאתָ, etc. (ל״א and פ״י).

בּוֹא, to come. perf. בָּא, בָּאתָ, etc. impf. יָבוֹא, imperat. בּוֹא, Hiph. הֵבִיא, with suff. generally הֲבִיאוֹ (ל״א and ע״י).

נָשָׂא, to lift. impf. יִשָּׂא. imperat. שָׂא (with suff. שָׂאֵהוּ etc.), infin. cstr. שְׂאֵת (בִּשְׂאֵת etc.). (ל״א and פ״נ)

נָגַע, to touch. impf. יִגַּע. imperat. גַּע. Hiph. perf. הִגִּיע, Hiph. impf. יַגִּיע (פ״נ and ל gt.).

Defective verbs are those which function in part only, but deficiencies may be supplemented by allied defective verbs which differ in one radical only, e.g., יָצַב and נָצַב, to place. The commonly used defective verbs are :

הָלַךְ, to go. perf. הָלַךְ. imperf. יֵלֵךְ, imperat. לֵךְ ; Hiph. הוֹלִיךְ (from ילך).

טוֹב, to be good. perf., particip. and infinitive from טוֹב (ע״י) ; impf. יִיטַב and Hiph. הֵיטִיב (from יטב).

שָׁתָה, to drink. regular in Qal ; Hiph. הִשְׁקָה, etc. (from שקה).

יָכֹל, to be able. perfect like קָטֹן, infin. cstr. יְכֹלֶת;
impf. יוּכַל (thought to be an imperfect Hoph'al,
but probably a modification of יוּכַל or יוּכַל).

בּוֹשׁ, to be ashamed. perf. בּוֹשׁ, imperf. יֵבוֹשׁ, imperat.
בּוֹשׁ, Hiph. (regular) הֵבִישׁ; Hiph. also הוֹבִישׁ
(from יבשׁ).

VOCABULARY

עָלָה to go up.	בָּכָה to weep.	רָבָה to multiply.
הָרָה to conceive.	חָנַן to pity.	שָׁבָה to take captive.
סָבַב to turn, turn away.	מָאוֹר luminary.	נְשָׁמָה breath, life (*f*).
תֹּהוּ desolation.	יַבָּשָׁה dry land (*f*).	רָחַף to hover, soar.
הָיָה to be, become.	חָיָה to live.	פָּרָה to be fruitful.
קָלַל to be light, trifling ; (Pi.) to curse.	כַּד earthen jar, pitcher (*f*).	יָתַר (Niph.) to remain.

Exercise 23

Translate :

‎1. הָאִישׁ אֲשֶׁר יְקַלֵּל אֶת־אָבִיו וְאֶת־אִמּוֹ מוֹת יוּמָת‎. ‎2. אָרוּר‎
‎אַתָּה בְּבֹאֶךָ וְאָרוּר אַתָּה בְּצֵאתֶךָ‎. ‎3. יִשָּׂא יהוה פָּנָיו אֵלֶיךָ וְיָשֵׂם‎
‎לְךָ שָׁלוֹם‎. ‎4. וַתֹּאמֶר שְׁתֵה אֲדֹנִי וַתֵּרֶד כַּדָּהּ עַל־יָדָהּ בַּבְּאֵר‎

5. וַיֹּאמֶר אֱלֹהִים יְהִי אוֹר וַיְהִי־אוֹר 6. וַיְהִי־עֶרֶב וַיְהִי־בֹקֶר

יוֹם חֲמִישִׁי 7. כִּי־יִבְכּוּ עָלַי לֵאמֹר תְּנָה־לָּנוּ בָשָׂר 8. וַיְהִי

הָלְיוֹ חָזָק מְאֹד עַד אֲשֶׁר לֹא־נוֹתְרָה־בּוֹ נְשָׁמָה 9. כִּי הִנֵּה

הָעִיר אֲשֶׁר נִקְרָא שְׁמִי עָלֶיהָ אָנֹכִי מֵחֵל לְהָרַע בָּיּוֹם הַזֶּה

10. וַיַּרְא אֱלֹהִים כִּי־טוֹב

1. And he said to her, fear not, go, do according to your word. 2. And they called on the name of their god saying, Baal, hear us, and there was no voice and no one answering them. 3. And the word of the Lord came to him saying, Arise, go to the desert. 4. And a messenger of Jehovah came to the woman and said to her, Behold, now, thou dost bear not, but thou shalt conceive a son. 5. Let there be luminaries in the firmament of the heaven. 6. Be ye fruitful and multiply and replenish the earth. 7. And he said unto Joseph, Behold, I die, but God will be with you, and will bring you again to the land of your fathers. 8. And thou shalt keep all that I am commanding thee (*part.*) to-day. 9. And he went up and looked towards the sea. 10. And the king did according to all that God commanded him.

Translate : Genesis 1, verses 1-8.

VOCABULARIES

Numbers in brackets refer to the chapters where the words in question receive their principal treatment. Declensions of nouns are indicated numerically where they might not be obvious, and nouns unmarked as to gender are masculine

ENGLISH TO HEBREW

A

Aaron, אַהֲרֹן

able, to be, יָכֹל (24)

above, up, מֵעַל

Abraham, אַבְרָהָם

accusative, sign of, אֵת (אֶת־) (12)

after, behind, אַחֲרֵי ,אַחַר

age, duration, עוֹלָם

alas ! אֲהָהּ

all, כֹּל

allow, leave, to, נָטַשׁ, *Impf.* יִטֹּשׁ

also, moreover, אַף

altar, מִזְבֵּחַ

among, within, בְּתוֹךְ

Anathoth, עֲנָתוֹת

and, וְ (*conj.*)

angry, to be, קָצַף

anoint, to, מָשַׁח

answer, to, עָנָה (24)

arise, stand, to, קוּם (23)

arm, an, זְרֹעַ *f.*

army, valour, force, חַיִל

ashamed, to be, בּוֹשׁ (23, 24)

ask, to, שָׁאַל

ass, an, חֲמוֹר

avenge, to, נָקַם (21)

B

Baal, lord, husband, בַּעַל

Babylon, בָּבֶל

bad, רַע

bare, to lay (lead captive)

barley, שְׂעוֹרָה *f.*

battle, war, מִלְחָמָה *f.*

be, to, become, הָיָה, *impf.* יִהְיֶה, *apoc.* יְהִי

beasts, cattle, בְּהֵמָה *f.* 1

before, לִפְנֵי

begin, to, חָלַל, *Hiph.*
(24) (הֵחֵל)

behind, (after)

behold, הֵן, הִנֵּה

between, בֵּין (*prep.*)

bind, gird, to, חָבַשׁ

bird, fowl, 2 עוֹף

birthright, בְּכוֹרָה *f.*

bless, to, *Pi.* ברך

blessing, בְּרָכָה *f.*

blood, דָּם

blot out, to, (destroy)

book, 2 סֵפֶר

bow, קֶשֶׁת *f.* 2

boy, 2 יֶלֶד (18) ; 2 נַעַר

bread, 2 לֶחֶם

break down, to, נָתַץ (22)

breath, life, נְשָׁמָה *f.*

brother, אָח (18)

build, to, בָּנָה

burn, to, שָׂרַף

burnt-offering, עוֹלָה *f.*

bury, to, קָבַר

C

cake, מָעוֹג

calf, 2 עֵגֶל

captain (prince)

captive, to lead, lay bare,
גָּלָה ; take captive, שָׁבָה

capture, to, a city, לָכַד

cast, to (send)

cattle (beasts)

cease, to, leave off, חָדַל

choose, to, בָּחַר ; search
out, חָזָה (23)

city, עִיר *f.* 2

clean, to be, become pure,
טָהֵר ; *Pi.* to cleanse

collect, gather, to, קָשַׁשׁ

come, to בּוֹא ; *Hiph.*
(הֵבִיא), to bring (23, 24)

command, to, *Pi.* צוה (24)

command, a, מִצְוָה *f.* 1

companion (friend)

corpse, נְבֵלָה *f.*

corrupted, to be (destroy)

couch, עֶרֶשׂ *f.* 2

counsel, עֵצָה *f.*

count, write, to, סָפַר ; *Pi.*
to recount

courage, to take, (strong)

covenant, בְּרִית *f.* 2

cover, to, *Pi.* כסה

create, fashion, to, בָּרָא

cross, pass over, to, עָבַר (21)

cry, call, to, קָרָא ; cry out, זָעַק

curse, to אָרַר (24) ; Pi. קלל

cut off, cut down, to, כָּרַת

D

darkness, חֹשֶׁךְ 2

daughter, בַּת f. 2 (18)

David, דָּוִד, דָּוִיד

day, יוֹם 2 (18)

dead, מֵת

death, put to, kill, to מות (23)

deliver, to, Hiph. נצל (הִצִּיל) (21)

desert, מִדְבָּר

desolation, תֹּהוּ

despise, reject, to, מָאַס

destroy, blot out, to, מָחָה ; Hiph. שָׁמַד ; to be corrupted, שָׁחַת

dig, to, כָּרָה

disease, sickness, חֳלִי 2

distant, to be, withdraw, to, רָחַק

divide, to, חָלַק ; Hiph. בדל

do, make, to, עָשָׂה ; פָּעַל (poet.) (22)

door, דֶּלֶת f. 2

dove, יוֹנָה f. (9)

draw near, to, נגש, impf. on'y in Qal; Niph. to draw near (21)

dream, to, חָלַם (21)

dream, a, חֲלוֹם

drink, to, שָׁתָה

dry land, יַבָּשָׁה f. 1

duration (age)

dust, עָפָר 1

dwell, sit, to, יָשַׁב ; שָׁכַן

E

ear, אֹזֶן f. 2

earth, land, אֶרֶץ f. 2, pl. אֲרָצוֹת

earthen jar (pitcher)

east, קֶדֶם

eat, to, אָכַל

Egypt, מִצְרַיִם

Elijah, אֵלִיָּהוּ

enemy, אֹיֵב 3

evening, עֶרֶב 2

ever, for, עַד־עוֹלָם

evil, to do, Hiph. רעע

evil, רָעָה f. 2 ; רָשָׁע (adj.)

except, כִּי אִם

eye, עַיִן f. 2

F

face, פָּנִים 1

fall, to, נָפַל (21)

fashion, to, (create)

father, אָב (18)

fear, to, יָרֵא, *impf.* יִירָא (23)

few, a, little, מְעַט

fight, to, *Niph.* לחם

fig tree, תְּאֵנָה *f.*

find, to, מָצָא (22)

fire, אֵשׁ *f.* 2

firmament, רָקִיעַ 1

firstborn, בְּכוֹר

fish, a, דָּג 1

flesh, בָּשָׂר

food, אֹכֶל 2 (אָכְלָה *f.* 2)

foot, רֶגֶל *f.* 2

force (army)

forget, to, שָׁכַח

four, אַרְבַּע (19)

fowl (bird)

friend, רֵעַ (רֵעֶה)

fruitful, to be, פָּרָה (24)

full, to be, מָלֵא; *Pi.* to fill

G

garden, גַּן 2

gate, opening, פֶּתַח

gather, to, אָסַף, *impf.* יֶאֱסֹף; collect, קָבַץ קָשַׁשׁ

gird, bind, to, חָבַשׁ

girl, נַעֲרָה *f.* 2

give, set, to, נָתַן (21)

glory, כָּבוֹד

go, to, הָלַךְ; *Hith.* to walk (24); go down, יָרַד; go out, יָצָא, *impf.* יֵצֵא (23, 24); go up, עָלָה, *impf.* יַעֲלֶה *apoc.* יַעַל

God, אֱלֹהִים

gold, זָהָב

good, to be, יָטַב (23)

good, טוֹב

goodness, טוֹבָה *f.*

good things, goodness, טוּב

grave, קֶבֶר 2

great, to be, grow, גָּדַל; *Pi.* to magnify

great, גָּדוֹל; great, much, רַב

greatness, גֹּדֶל

grievous (strong)

ground, אֲדָמָה *f.* 1

guilty, רָשָׁע

H

half, חֲצִי

hand, יָד f. 1

handmaid, שִׁפְחָה f.

hate, to, שָׂנֵא (22)

head, רֹאשׁ

health (peace)

hear, to, שָׁמַע

heart, לֵב 2, לֵבָב 1

heaven, שָׁמַיִם 1

heavy, to be, כָּבֵד; Pi. to
    harden, honour; Hiph. be
    honoured

hero, mighty man, גִּבּוֹר

hide, to, Pi. and Hiph.
    סתר

high, lofty, רָם

hill, mountain, הַר 2

hither, הֲלֹם

holiness, קֹדֶשׁ

holy, to be, קָדַשׁ; Pi. to
    hallow, sanctify

holy, קָדוֹשׁ

horn, קֶרֶן f. 2

horse, סוּס 2

house, בַּיִת 2 (18)

hover, to, רָחַף

how? how! מָה, אֵיךְ

how much? כַּמָּה

husband (Baal)

I

I, אֲנִי (10)

if, whether, אִם

image, likeness, צֶלֶם 2

inherit, possess, to יָרַשׁ;
    Hiph. (הוֹרִישׁ), to dis-
    possess

inheritance (possession)

iniquity (sin)

in order than, לְמַעַן (prep.)

Isaac, יִצְחָק

Israel, יִשְׂרָאֵל

is, there, are, was, were, יֵשׁ,
    יֶשׁ־

J

Jacob, יַעֲקֹב

Jehovah, יהוה

Jonathan, יְהוֹנָתָן

Joseph, יוֹסֵף

Joshua, יְהוֹשֻׁעַ, יְהוֹשׁוּעַ

Judah, יְהוּדָה

judge, to, שָׁפַט

justice, ordinance, מִשְׁפָּט

K

keep, to, שָׁמַר

kill, slay, to, הָרַג; put to
  death, מוּת (23); kill
  smite, Hiph. נכה (הִכָּה),
  impf. apoc. יַךְ (21, 24)

kindness (mercy)

king, to be, מָלַךְ; Hiph. to
  make king

king, מֶלֶךְ 2

kiss, to, נָשַׁק (with לְ of
  persons)

knee, בֶּרֶךְ f. 2, dual בִּרְכַּיִם

know, to, יָדַע

L

land (earth)

law, תּוֹרָה f.

lead captive, to, lay bare,
  to, (captive)

Leah, לֵאָה

lean, to, Niph. שען

leave, to, (allow)

leave off, to, (cease)

lest, פֶּן־

let go, to (send)

lie down, to (sleep)

life (breath)

lift up, to, נָשָׂא (22, 24)

light, insignificant, to be,
  קָלַל; Pi. to curse (24)

light, אוֹר 2

likeness (image)

lion, אֲרִי 2

lip, שָׂפָה f.

little, a, (few)

live, to, חָיָה (24)

living, חַי

lofty (high)

look, to, Hiph. נבט (הִבִּיט)
  (22)

lord (Baal); lord, master,
  אָדוֹן 1

love, to, אָהַב. impf. יֶאֱהַב

luminary, מָאוֹר

M

magnify, to, (great)

make, do, to, עָשָׂה

male, זָכָר 1

man, mankind, אָדָם; man
  אִישׁ

master (lord)

meal-offering, מִנְחָה f. 2

mercy, kindness, חֶסֶד 2

messenger, מַלְאָךְ

middle, תָּוֶךְ

mighty man (hero)

month, חֹדֶשׁ 2

moreover (also)

morning, בֹּקֶר 2

Moses, מֹשֶׁה

mother, אֵם f. 2

mountain (hill)

much (great)

multiply, to, רָבָה

N

name, שֵׁם 3

new, חָדָשׁ 1

night, לַיְלָה 2, pl. לֵילוֹת

no, none, אַיִן ; no, not,
    אַל־ (with prohib.) ; not,
    לֹא

north, צָפוֹן f. 1

now, shortly, עַתָּה

number, מִסְפָּר

O

oil, שֶׁמֶן

old, old man, זָקֵן

old age, זְקֻנִים (זְקֻנָה f.)

old, from of, מֵעוֹלָם

olive, זַיִת

one, אֶחָד (19)

opening (gate)

ordinance (justice)

over, upon, עַל־ (prep.)

ox, שׁוֹר

P

palace (temple)

pass over, to, (cross)

peace, health, שָׁלוֹם

Pekah, פֶּקַח

people, עַם 2

perfect, תָּמִים

Pharaoh, פַּרְעֹה

piece, a, פַּת f.

pitcher, earthen jar, כַּד f.

pity, to, חָנַן

place, set, to, שִׂים, שׂוּם (23)

place, a, מָקוֹם

poor, אֶבְיוֹן 1

possess, to (inherit)

possession, inheritance,
    נַחֲלָה f.

pour out, to, יָצַק

powerful, עָצוּם

prayer, תְּפִלָּה f.

priest, כֹּהֵן 3

prince, captain, שַׂר

prison, (כְּלֶא) כְּלוּא

promise, to, (say)

prophesy, to, *Niph.* נבא

prophet, נָבִיא 1

pursue, to, רָדַף

Q

queen, מַלְכָּה *f.* 2

R

Rachel, רָחֵל

reach, touch, to, נָגַע (24)

refuse, be unwilling, to, *Pi.*
מאן

reject, to, (despise)

remain, to, *Niph.* יתר

remember, to זָכַר ; *Hiph.* to
bring to remembrance

repent, to, *Niph.* נחם (22)

rest, to, נוּחַ (23) ; שָׁבַת

return, to, שׁוּב (23)

righteousness, צֶדֶק 2

river, יְאֹר ; נָהָר (of Nile)

rule, to, מָשַׁל (over, בְּ)

S

sacrifice, slaughter, to, זָבַח

sacrifice, a, זֶבַח

Samaria, שֹׁמְרוֹן

Samuel, שְׁמוּאֵל

sanctify, to, (holy)

satisfied, to be, שָׂבַע ; *Hiph.*
to satisfy

Saul, שָׁאוּל

say, to, promise, אָמַר (21)

saying (word)

sceptre, tribe, שֵׁבֶט

sea, יָם 2

search out, to, (choose)

see, to, רָאָה

seed, זֶרַע 2

seek, to, *Pi.* בקשׁ

sell, to, מָכַר

send, let go, to, שָׁלַח

seraph, שָׂרָף 1

servant, slave, עֶבֶד 2

serve, till the ground, to,
עָבַד (21)

set, to (give) ; (place)

shed, to, שָׁפַךְ

shepherd, רֹעֶה

short, קָצַר

shortly (now)

sickness (disease)

side, יַרְכָה *f.* 2

sign, אוֹת

silver, כֶּסֶף 2

sin, to, חָטָא (21)

sin, iniquity, עָוֹן 1

sit, to (dwell)

skin, עוֹר

slay, to (kill)

sleep, to, יָשֵׁן, *Impf.* יִישַׁן ;
   lie down, שָׁכַב

smite, to (kill)

soar (hover)

Solomon, שְׁלֹמֹה

son, בֵּן 3 (18)

song, שִׁיר

soul, life, נֶפֶשׁ *f.* 2

south, נֶגֶב

speak, to, *Pi.* דבר

spear, חֲנִית *f.*

spirit (wind)

staff, מַקֵּל

stand, to, עָמַד ; *Hiph.* to
   place, set (21) ; (arise)

steal, to, גָּנַב

stone, אֶבֶן *f.* 2 (18)

stream, torrent, נַחַל 2

strong, to be, חָזַק ; *Hith.* to
   take courage ; אָמַץ ; *Pi.*
   to strengthen

strong, grievous, חָזָק

sun, שֶׁמֶשׁ

swear, to, *Niph.* שבע

sword, חֶרֶב *f.* 2

T

table, שֻׁלְחָן

take, to, לָקַח

tall, גָּבֹהַּ

temple, palace, הֵיכָל

terebinth, אֵלָה *f.*

thence, מִשָּׁם

there, שָׁם

thing (word)

this, זֶה (10)

thither, שָׁמָּה

throne, seat, כִּסֵּא

thus, כֹּה

till the ground, to (serve)

tomorrow, מָחָר

tongs (dual), מֶלְקָחַיִם

tongue, לָשׁוֹן *f.* 1

torrent (stream)

touch, to, (reach)

towards (unto)

tree, twig, עֵץ 1

tribe (sceptre)

trumpet, שׁוֹפָר

trust, to, בָּטַח

truth, אֱמֶת f. 2

turn, turn away, to, סָבַב (24)

U

unction, מִשְׁחָה f.

under, תַּחַת

until, unto, ־עַד (prep.)

unto, towards, ־אֶל (prep.)

unwilling, to be, (refuse)

up (above)

upon (over)

upright, יָשָׁר

urge, to, פָּצַר בְּ

V

valour (army)

vengeance, נְקָמָה f. 1

very, מְאֹד ; very good, טוֹב מְאֹד

vineyard, כֶּרֶם 2

violence, חָמָס 1

visit, to, פָּקַד

voice, קוֹל 2

W

walk, to, (go)

war (battle)

water(s) מַיִם

way, דֶּרֶךְ 2

weep, to, בָּכָה

well, בְּאֵר f. 2

wheat, חִטָּה f. (9)

where ? אַיֵּה

wherein ? בַּמָּה

whether (if)

who, which, אֲשֶׁר (10)

why ? לָמָה

widow, אַלְמָנָה f.

wind, spirit, רוּחַ

wisdom, חָכְמָה f. 2

wise, to be, חָכַם

wise, חָכָם

with, אֵת (prep.).

withdraw, to, (be distant)

within (among)

woman, אִשָּׁה f.

word, thing, דָּבָר ; saying, מִלָּה f.

write, to, כָּתַב

Y

year, שָׁנָה f.

youth, עֲלוּמִים

HEBREW TO ENGLISH

'Aleph

אָב father (18)

אֶבְיוֹן poor

אֶבֶן stone f. 2 (18)

אַבְרָהָם Abraham

אָדָם man, mankind

אֲדָמָה ground f. 1

אָדוֹן lord, master

אָהֵב to love, *impf.* יֶאֱהַב

אֲהָהּ alas!

אַהֲרֹן Aaron

אוֹר light 2

אוֹת sign

אֹזֶן ear f. 2

אָח brother (18)

אֶחָד one (19)

אַחֲרֵי, אַחַר after, behind

אֹיֵב enemy 3

אַיֵּה where ?

אֵיךְ how ? how!

אַיִן no, none

אִישׁ man

אִשָּׁה woman f.

אָכַל to eat

אֹכֶל food 2 (אָכְלָה f. 2)

אַל־ no, not

אֶל (*prep.*) unto,

towards

אֵלָה terebinth f.

אֱלֹהִים God (*pl.*)

אֵלִיָּהוּ Elijah

אַלְמָנָה widow f.

אִם if, whether

אֵם mother f. 2

אָמֵץ to be strong; *pi.*

to strengthen

אָמַר to say, promise

(21)

אֱמֶת truth f. 2

אֲנִי I (10)

אָסַף to gather, *impf.*

יֶאֱסֹף

אַף also, moreover

אַרְבַּע four (19)

אֲרִי lion 2

אֶרֶץ earth, land f. 2

(*pl.* אֲרָצוֹת)

אָרַר to curse (24)

אֵשׁ fire f. 2

אֲשֶׁר who, which (10)

אֵת (אֶת־) sign of accus.
(12)

אֵת (*prep.*) with

Beth

בְּאֵר well *f.* 2

בָּבֶל Babylon

בדל *Hiph.* to divide

בְּהֵמָה beasts, cattle *f.* 1

בּוֹא to come ; *Hiph.*
(הֵבִיא) to bring
(23, 24)

בּוֹשׁ to be ashamed
(23, 24)

בָּחַר to choose

בָּטַח to trust

בֵּין (*prep.*) between

בַּיִת house 2 (18)

בָּכָה to weep

בְּכוֹר firstborn

בְּכוֹרָה birthright *f.* 1

בַּמָּה wherein ?

בֵּן son 3 (18)

בָּנָה to build

בַּעַל lord, husband, Baal

בֹּקֶר morning 2

בקשׁ *Pi.* to seek

בָּרָא to create, fashion

בְּרִית covenant *f.*

בֶּרֶךְ knee *f.* 2 (dual
בִּרְכַּיִם)

ברך *Pi.* to bless

בְּרָכָה blessing

בָּשָׂר flesh

בַּת daughter *f.* 2 (18)

בְּתוֹךְ within, among

Gimel

גָּבֹהַּ tall

גִּבּוֹר hero, mighty man

גָּדַל to be great, grow ;
Pi. to magnify

גֹּדֶל greatness

גָּדוֹל great

גָּלָה to lay bare, *Hiph.*
to lead captive

גָּנַב to steal

Daleth

דבר *Pi.* to speak

דָּבָר word, thing

דָּג a fish

דָּוִיד, דָּוִד David

דֶּלֶת door *f.* 2

דָּם blood

דֶּרֶךְ way 2

He

הִיא, הוּא pronoun (10)
הָיָה to be, become, *Impf.* יִהְיֶה, *apoc.* יְהִי
הֵיכָל temple, palace
הָלַךְ to go; *Hith.* to walk (24)
הֲלֹם hither
הִנֵּה הֵן behold
הַר mountain, hill 2
הָרַג to kill, slay

Waw

וְ (*conj.*) and

Zayin

זָבַח to sacrifice, slaughter
זֶבַח a sacrifice 2
זֶה this (10)
זָהָב gold
זַיִת olive 2
זָכַר to remember; *Hiph.* to bring to remembrance
זָכָר male
זָעַק to cry out
זָקֵן old, old man
זְקֻנִים old age (זִקְנָה *f.*)
זְרוֹעַ an arm *f.*
זֶרַע seed

Heth

חבא *Hith.* to hide oneself
חָבַשׁ to bind, gird
חָדַל to cease, leave off
חָדָשׁ new
חֹדֶשׁ month 2
חָזָה to search out, choose (23)
חָזַק to be strong; *Hith.* to take courage
חָזָק strong, grievous
חָטָא to sin (21)
חִטָּה wheat *f.* (9)
חָיָה to live (24)
חַי living
חַיִּים life
חַיִל force, army, valour
חָכַם to be wise
חָכָם wise
חָכְמָה wisdom *f.* 2
חֳלִי disease, sickness 2

חָלַל *Hiph.* (הֵחֵל) to begin (24)

חָלַם to dream (21)

חֲלוֹם a dream

חָלַק to divide

חֲמוֹר an ass

חָמָס violence

חֲנִית spear *f.*

חָנַן to pity

חֶסֶד kindness, mercy 2

חֲצִי half

חֶרֶב sword *f.* 2

חֹשֶׁךְ darkness 2

Teth

טָהֵר to be clean, become pure; *Pi.* to cleanse

טוֹב good

טוּב good things, goodness

טוֹבָה goodness *f.*

Yodh

יְאֹר river

יַבָּשָׁה dry land *f.* 1

יָד hand *f.* 1

יָדַע to know

יְהוּדָה Judah

יהוה Jehovah

יְהוֹנָתָן Jonathan

יְהוֹשֻׁעַ, יְהוֹשׁוּעַ Joshua

יוֹם day 2 (18)

יוֹנָה dove *f.* (9)

יוֹסֵף Joseph

יָטַב to be good (23)

יָכֹל to be able (24)

יֶלֶד boy 2 (18)

יָם sea 2

יַעֲקֹב Jacob

יָצָא to go out, *Impf.* יֵצֵא (23, 24)

יִצְחָק Isaac

יָצַק to pour out

יָרֵא to fear, *Impf.* יִירָא (23)

יָרַד to go down

יַרְכָה side *f.* 2

יָרַשׁ to inherit, possess; *Hiph.* (הוֹרִישׁ) to dispossess

יֵשׁ, יֶשׁ־ there is, are, was, were

יָשַׁב to sit, dwell

יָשֵׁן to sleep, *Impf.* יִישַׁן

יָשָׁר upright

יִשְׂרָאֵל Israel

יתר Niph. to remain

Kaph

כָּבֵד to be heavy; Pi.
to harden,
honour; Niph.
to be honoured

כָּבוֹד glory

כַּד earthen jar,
pitcher f.

כֹּה thus

כֹּהֵן priest 3

כִּי אִם except

כָּלָא prison

כֹּל all

כַּמָּה how much?

כִּסֵּא seat, throne

כסה Pi. to cover

כֶּסֶף silver 2

כָּרָה to dig

כֶּרֶם vineyard 2

כָּרַת to cut off, down

כָּתַב to write

Lamedh

לֹא not

לֵאָה Leah

לֵב, לֵבָב heart 2

לחם Niph. to fight

לֶחֶם bread 2

לַיְלָה night 2 (pl. לֵילוֹת)

לָכַד to capture (city)

לָמָּה why?

לְמַעַן (prep.) in order that

לִפְנֵי before

לָקַח to take

לָשׁוֹן tongue f.

Mem

טוֹב מְאֹד very; מְאֹד
very good

מָאוֹר luminary

מאן Pi. to be unwilling,
refuse

מָאַס to reject, despise

מִדְבָּר desert

מות Hiph. to kill, put to
death (23)

מִזְבֵּחַ altar 3

מָחָה to destroy, blot out

מָחָר tomorrow

מַיִם waters

מָכַר to sell

מָלֵא to be full; Pi. to
fill

מַלְאָךְ messenger

מִלָּה saying, word *f.*

מִלְחָמָה battle, war *f.*

מָלַךְ to be king; *Hiph.*
to make king

מֶלֶךְ king 2

מַלְכָּה queen *f.* 2

מֶלְקָחַיִם tongs (dual)

מִנְחָה meal offering *f.* 2

מִסְפָּר number

מָעוֹג cake

מֵעוֹלָם from of old

מְעַט a little, few

מֵעַל above, up

מָצָא to find (22)

מִצְוָה command *f.*

מִצְרַיִם Egypt

מָקוֹם place

מַקֵּל staff

מֹשֶׁה Moses

מָשַׁח to anoint

מִשְׁחָה unction *f.*

מָשַׁל (בְּ) to rule (over)

מִשָּׁם thence

מִשְׁפָּט ordinance, justice

מֵת dead

Nun

נבא *Niph.* to prophesy

נָבִיא prophet 1

נבט *Hiph.* (הִבִּיט) to
look (22)

נְבֵלָה corpse *f.*

נֶגֶב south

נָגַע to touch, reach (24)

נגש only *Impf.* in *Qal.*
(יִגַּשׁ); *Niph.* to
draw near (21)

נָהָר river

נוּחַ to rest (23)

נַחַל torrent, stream 2

נַחֲלָה inheritance,
possession

נחם *Niph.* to repent
(22)

נָטַשׁ to leave, allow,
Impf. יִטּשׁ

נָכָה *Hiph.* (הִכָּה) to
smite, kill, *Impf.*
apoc. יַךְ (21, 24)

נַעַר lad 2

נַעֲרָה girl *f.* 2

נָפַל to fall (21)

נֶפֶשׁ soul, life *f.* 2

נצל *Hiph.* (הִצִּיל) to deliver(21)

נָקַם to avenge (21)

נְקָמָה vengeance *f.*

נְשָׁמָה breath, life *f.*

נָשַׁק to kiss (with לְ of persons) (21)

נָשָׂא to lift up (22, 24)

נָתַן to give, set (21)

נָתַץ to break down (22)

Samekh

סָבַב to turn, turn away (24)

סוּס horse 2

סָפַר to count, write ; *Pi.* to recount

סֵפֶר book 2

סתר *Pf.* and *Hiph.* to hide

Ayin

עָבַד to serve, till the ground (21)

עֶבֶד servant, slave 2

עָבַר to pass over, cross (21)

עֵגֶל calf 2

עַד־ (*prep.*) until, unto

עוֹלָה burnt offering *f.*

עוֹלָם age, duration (עַד־עוֹלָם, for ever)

עָוֹן sin, iniquity 1

עוֹף fowl, bird 2

עוֹר skin

עַיִן eye *f.* 2

עִיר city *f.* 2

עַל־ (*prep.*) upon, over

עָלָה to go up, *Impf.* יַעַל *apoc.* יַעֲלֶה (24)

עֲלוּמִים youth

עַם people 2

עָמַד to stand ; *Hiph.* to place, set (21)

עָנָה to answer (24)

עֲנָתוֹת Anathoth

עָפָר dust 1

עֵץ tree, twig 1

עֵצָה counsel *f.*

עָצוּם powerful

עֶרֶב evening 2

עֶרֶשׂ couch *f.* 2

עָשָׂה to do, make

עַתָּה now, shortly

Pe

פֶּן־ lest

פָּנִים face (*pl.*)

פָּעַל to do (22)

פָּצַר בְּ to urge

פָּקַד to visit

פֶּקַח Pekah

פָּרָה to be fruitful (24)

פַּרְעֹה Pharaoh

פַּת a piece

פֶּתַח opening, gate

Çadhe

צֶדֶק righteousness 2

צוה *Pi.* to command (24)

צֶלֶם image, likeness 2

צָפוֹן north *f.* 1

Qoph

קָבַץ to gather

קָבַר to bury

קֶבֶר grave 2

קָדוֹשׁ holy

קֶדֶם east

קָדַשׁ to be holy; *Pi.* to hallow, sanctify

קֹדֶשׁ holiness 2

קוֹל voice 2

קוּם to arise, stand (23)

קָלַל to be light, insignificant; *Pi.* to curse (24)

קָצַף to be angry

קָצֵר short

קָרָא to call cry

קָרַב to draw near

קֶרֶן horn *f.* 2

קָשַׁשׁ to gather, collect

קֶשֶׁת bow *f.* 2

Resh

רָאָה to see

רֹאשׁ head

רַב great, much

רָבָה to multiply

רֶגֶל foot *f.* 2

רָדַף to pursue

רוּחַ wind, spirit *f.*

רעע *Hiph.* to do evil

רָחֵל Rachel

רָחַף to hover, soar

רָחַק to be distant, withdraw

רָם high

רַע bad

רֵעַ friend, companion

רָעָב famine

רָעָה evil *f.*

רֹעֶה shepherd

רָקִיעַ firmament

רָשָׁע wicked, guilty, evil

Sin

שָׂבַע to be satisfied ;
    Hiph. to satisfy

שִׂים, שׂוֹם to place, set (23)

שָׂנֵא to hate (22)

שְׂעוֹרָה barley *f.*

שָׂפָה lip *f.*

שַׂר prince, captain

שָׂרַף to burn

שָׂרָף seraph

Šin

שָׁאוּל Saul

שָׁאַל to ask

שָׁבָה to take captive

שֵׁבֶט tribe, sceptre

שבע *Niph.* to swear

שָׁבַת to rest

שׁוּב to return

שׁוֹפָר trumpet

שׁוֹר ox

שָׁחַת to destroy, be
    corrupted

שִׁיר song

שָׁכַב to sleep, lie down

שָׁכַח to forget

שָׁכַן to dwell

שָׁלוֹם peace, health

שָׁלַךְ to send, let go

שֻׁלְחָן table

שְׁלֹמֹה Solomon

שָׁם there

שֵׁם name

שמד *Hiph.* to destroy

שָׁמָּה thither

שְׁמוּאֵל Samuel

שָׁמַיִם heaven (*pl.*)

שֶׁמֶן oil

שָׁמַע to hear

שָׁמַר to keep

שֹׁמְרוֹן Samaria

שֶׁמֶשׁ sun

שָׁנָה year

שָׁעַן *Niph.* to lean

שִׁפְחָה handmaid *f.*

שָׁפַט to judge

שָׁפַךְ to shed

שָׁתָה to drink

Taw

תּוֹרָה law *f.*	
תְּאֵנָה fig tree *f.*	תַּחַת under
תֹּהוּ desolation	תָּמִים perfect
תָּוֶךְ middle	תְּפִלָּה prayer *f.*

PARADIGMS

The Regular Verb

	Qal Active	Qal Stative		Niph'al
Perfect.				
Sing. 3 m.	קָטַל	כָּבֵד	קָטֹן	נִקְטַל
3 f.	קָטְלָה	כָּבְדָה	קָטְנָה	נִקְטְלָה
2 m.	קָטַלְתָּ	כָּבַדְתָּ	קָטֹנְתָּ	נִקְטַלְתָּ
2 f.	קָטַלְתְּ	כָּבַדְתְּ	קָטֹנְתְּ	נִקְטַלְתְּ
1 c.	קָטַ֫לְתִּי	כָּבַדְתִּי	קָטֹנְתִּי	נִקְטַלְתִּי
Plur. 3 c.	קָטְלוּ	כָּבְדוּ	קָטְנוּ	נִקְטְלוּ
2 m.	קְטַלְתֶּם	כְּבַדְתֶּם	קְטָנְתֶּם	נִקְטַלְתֶּם
2 f.	קְטַלְתֶּן	כְּבַדְתֶּן	קְטָנְתֶּן	נִקְטַלְתֶּן
1 c.	קָטַ֫לְנוּ	כָּבַ֫דְנוּ	קָטֹ֫נוּ	נִקְטַ֫לְנוּ
Imperfect.				
Sing. 3 m.	יִקְטֹל	יִכְבַּד	יִקְטַן	יִקָּטֵל
3 f.	תִּקְטֹל	תִּכְבַּד	etc.	תִּקָּטֵל
2 m.	תִּקְטֹל	תִּכְבַּד		תִּקָּטֵל
2 f.	תִּקְטְלִי	תִּכְבְּדִי		תִּקָּטְלִי
1 c.	אֶקְטֹל	אֶכְבַּד		אִקָּטֵל¹
Plur. 3 m.	יִקְטְלוּ	יִכְבְּדוּ		יִקָּטְלוּ
3 f.	תִּקְטֹ֫לְנָה	תִּכְבַּ֫דְנָה		תִּקָּטַ֫לְנָה
2 m.	תִּקְטְלוּ	תִּכְבְּדוּ		תִּקָּטְלוּ
2 f.	תִּקְטֹ֫לְנָה	תִּכְבַּ֫דְנָה		תִּקָּטַ֫לְנָה
1 c.	נִקְטֹל	נִכְבַּד		נִקָּטֵל

1. or אָקָטֵל

158

THE REGULAR VERB

Pi'el	Pu'al	Hiph'il	Hoph'al	Hithpa'el
² קִטֵּל	קֻטַּל	הִקְטִיל	הָקְטַל	הִתְקַטֵּל ¹
קִטְּלָה	קֻטְּלָה	הִקְטִילָה	הָקְטְלָה	הִתְקַטְּלָה
קִטַּלְתָּ	קֻטַּלְתָּ	הִקְטַלְתָּ	הָקְטַלְתָּ	הִתְקַטַּלְתָּ
קִטַּלְתְּ	קֻטַּלְתְּ	הִקְטַלְתְּ	הָקְטַלְתְּ	הִתְקַטַּלְתְּ
קִטַּלְתִּי	קֻטַּלְתִּי	הִקְטַלְתִּי	הָקְטַלְתִּי	הִתְקַטַּלְתִּי
קִטְּלוּ	קֻטְּלוּ	הִקְטִילוּ	הָקְטְלוּ	הִתְקַטְּלוּ
קִטַּלְתֶּם	קֻטַּלְתֶּם	הִקְטַלְתֶּם	הָקְטַלְתֶּם	הִתְקַטַּלְתֶּם
קִטַּלְתֶּן	קֻטַּלְתֶּן	הִקְטַלְתֶּן	הָקְטַלְתֶּן	הִתְקַטַּלְתֶּן
קִטַּלְנוּ	קֻטַּלְנוּ	הִקְטַלְנוּ	הָקְטַלְנוּ	הִתְקַטַּלְנוּ
יְקַטֵּל	יְקֻטַּל	יַקְטִיל	יָקְטַל	יִתְקַטֵּל
תְּקַטֵּל	תְּקֻטַּל	תַּקְטִיל	תָּקְטַל	תִּתְקַטֵּל
תְּקַטֵּל	תְּקֻטַּל	תַּקְטִיל	תָּקְטַל	תִּתְקַטֵּל
תְּקַטְּלִי	תְּקֻטְּלִי	תַּקְטִילִי	תָּקְטְלִי	תִּתְקַטְּלִי
אֲקַטֵּל	אֲקֻטַּל	אַקְטִיל	אָקְטַל	אֶתְקַטֵּל
יְקַטְּלוּ	יְקֻטְּלוּ	יַקְטִילוּ	יָקְטְלוּ	יִתְקַטְּלוּ
תְּקַטֵּלְנָה	תְּקֻטַּלְנָה	תַּקְטֵלְנָה	תָּקְטַלְנָה	תִּתְקַטֵּלְנָה
תְּקַטְּלוּ	תְּקֻטְּלוּ	תַּקְטִילוּ	תָּקְטְלוּ	תִּתְקַטְּלוּ
תְּקַטֵּלְנָה	תְּקֻטַּלְנָה	תַּקְטֵלְנָה	תָּקְטַלְנָה	תִּתְקַטֵּלְנָה
נְקַטֵּל	נְקֻטַּל	נַקְטִיל	נָקְטַל	נִתְקַטֵּל

2. or קֻטַּל   3. or הִתְקַטֵּל

The Regular Verb

	Qal. Active	Qal Stative		Niph'al
Cohort. 1 sg.	אֶקְטְלָה	אֶכְבְּדָה		אֶקָּטְלָה
Juss. 3 sg. m.	יִקְטֹל	יִכְבַּד		יִקָּטֵל
Waw cons. impft.	וַיִּקְטֹל	וַיִּכְבַּד		וַיִּקָּטֵל
waw cons. pft.	וְקָטַלְתָּ	וְכָבַדְתָּ		וְנִקְטַלְתָּ
Imperative				
Sing. 2 m.	קְטֹל¹	כְּבַד		הִקָּטֵל
2 f.	קִטְלִי	כִּבְדִי		הִקָּטְלִי
Plur. 2 m.	קִטְלוּ	כִּבְדוּ		הִקָּטְלוּ
2 f.	קְטֹלְנָה	כְּבַדְנָה		הִקָּטַלְנָה
Infinitive				
constr.	קְטֹל	כְּבַד		הִקָּטֵל
absol.	קָטוֹל	כָּבוֹד		הִקָּטֹל, נִקְטֹל
Participle				
active	קֹטֵל	כָּבֵד	קָטֹן	
passive	קָטוּל			נִקְטָל

1. קָטְלָה (emphatic imperative).

The Regular Verb

Pi'el	Pu'al	Hiph'il	Hoph'al	Hithpa'el
אֲקַטְּלָה		אַקְטִילָה		אֶתְקַטְּלָה
יְקַטֵּל	יְקֻטַּל	יַקְטֵל	יָקְטַל	יִתְקַטֵּל
וַיְקַטֵּל	וַיְקֻטַּל	וַיַּקְטֵל	וַיָּקְטַל	וַיִּתְקַטֵּל
וְקִטַּלְתָּ		וְהִקְטַלְתָּ		
קַטֵּל		הַקְטֵל		הִתְקַטֵּל
קַטְּלִי		הַקְטִילִי		הִתְקַטְּלִי
קַטְּלוּ		הַקְטִילוּ		הִתְקַטְּלוּ
קַטֵּלְנָה		הַקְטֵלְנָה		הִתְקַטֵּלְנָה
קַטֵּל		הַקְטִיל	(הָקְטַל)	הִתְקַטֵּל
קַטֵּל, קַטֹּל	קֻטֹּל	הַקְטֵל	(הָקְטֵל)	הִתְקַטֵּל
מְקַטֵּל		מַקְטִיל		מִתְקַטֵּל
	מְקֻטָּל		מָקְטָל	

F

The Regular Verb with Suffixes
Perfect Qal

	3 sg. m. קָטַל	3 sg. f. קָטְלָה	2 sg. m. קָטַלְתָּ	2 sg. f. קָטַלְתְּ
Suffixes				
sing. 1 c.	קְטָלַנִי	קְטָלַתְנִי	קְטַלְתַּנִי	קְטַלְתִּינִי
2 m.	קְטָלְךָ	קְטָלַתְךָ		
2 f.	קְטָלֵךְ	קְטָלָתֶךְ		
3 m.	קְטָלוֹ	קְטָלַתְהוּ	קְטָלַתְהוּ	קְטַלְתִּיהוּ
	קְטָלָהוּ	קְטָלַתּוּ	קְטַלְתּוֹ	
3 f.	קְטָלָהּ	קְטָלָתָהּ	קְטַלְתָּהּ	קְטַלְתִּיהָ
plur. 1 c.	קְטָלָנוּ	קְטָלַתְנוּ	קְטַלְתָּנוּ	קְטַלְתִּינוּ
2 m.	קְטַלְכֶם			
2 f.	קְטַלְכֶן			
3 m.	קְטָלָם	קְטָלָתַם	קְטַלְתָּם	קְטַלְתִּים
3 f.	קְטָלָן	קְטָלָתַן	קְטַלְתָּן	קְטַלְתִּין

THE REGULAR VERB WITH SUFFIXES
PERFECT QAL

	1 sg. c. קָטַלְתִּי	3 pl. c. קָטְלוּ	2 pl. m. קְטַלְתֶּם	1 pl. c. קָטַלְנוּ
Suffixes				
sing. 1 c.		קְטָלוּנִי	קְטַלְתּוּנִי	
2 m.	קְטַלְתִּיךָ	קְטָלוּךָ		קְטַלְנוּךָ
2 f.	קְטַלְתִּיךְ	קְטָלוּךְ		קְטַלְנוּךְ
3 m.	קְטַלְתִּיהוּ	קְטָלוּהוּ	קְטַלְתּוּהוּ	קְטַלְנוּהוּ
	קְטַלְתִּיו		etc.	etc.
3 f.	קְטַלְתִּיהָ	קְטָלוּהָ		
plur. 1 c.		קְטָלוּנוּ		
2 m.	קְטַלְתִּיכֶם			
2 f.	קְטַלְתִּיכֶן			
3 m.	קְטַלְתִּים	קְטָלוּם		
3 f.	קְטַלְתִּין	קְטָלוּן		

THE REGULAR VERB WITH SUFFIXES

	Imperfect Qal		Imperative		Infin. Constr.
	3 sg. m.	3 pl. m.	sing.	plur.	
	יִקְטֹל	יִקְטְלוּ	קְטֹל	קִטְלוּ	קְטֹל

Suffixes

	3 sg. m.	3 pl. m.	sing.	plur.	Infin. Constr.
sg. 1 c.	יִקְטְלֵנִי	יִקְטְלוּנִי	קָטְלֵנִי	קְטְלוּנִי	קָטְלִי, קְטְלֵנִי
2 m.	יִקְטָלְךָ	יִקְטָלוּךָ			קָטְלְךָ, קְטָלְךָ
2 f.	יִקְטְלֵךְ	יִקְטְלוּךְ			קָטְלֵךְ
3 m.	יִקְטְלֵהוּ	יִקְטְלוּהוּ	קָטְלֵהוּ		קָטְלוֹ
3 f.	יִקְטְלֶהָ	יִקְטְלוּהָ	קָטְלֶהָ	etc.	קָטְלָה
pl. 1 c.	יִקְטְלֵנוּ	יִקְטְלוּנוּ	קָטְלֵנוּ		קָטְלֵנוּ
2 m.	יִקְטָלְכֶם	יִקְטָלוּכֶם			קָטְלְכֶם, קְטָלְכֶם
2 f.	יִקְטָלְכֶן	יִקְטָלוּכֶן			קָטְלְכֶן, קְטָלְכֶן
3 m.	יִקְטְלֵם	יִקְטְלוּם	קָטְלֵם		קָטְלֵם
3 f.	יִקְטְלֵן	יִקְטְלוּן	קָטְלֵן		קָטְלֵן

THE REGULAR VERB WITH SUFFIXES

		Pi‘el		Hiph·il	
		Perfect 3 sg. m. קִטֵּל	Imperfect 3 sg. m. יְקַטֵּל	Perfect 3 sg. m. הִקְטִיל	Imperfect 3 sg. m. יַקְטִיל
Suffixes					
sg.	1 c.	קְטָלַנִי	יְקַטְלֵנִי	הִקְטִילַנִי	יַקְטִילֵנִי
	2 m.	קְטֶלְךָ	יְקֶטֶלְךָ	הִקְטִילְךָ	יַקְטִילְךָ
	2 f.	קְטָלֵךְ	יְקַטְלֵךְ	הִקְטִילֵךְ	יַקְטִילֵךְ
	3 m.	קְטָלוֹ	יְקַטְלֵהוּ	etc.	etc.
	3 f.	קְטָלָהּ	יְקַטְלָהּ		
pl.	1 c.	קְטָלָנוּ	יְקַטְלֵנוּ		
		etc.	etc.		

F 2

Pe Nun Verb

		Qal		Niph'al	Hiph'il
Perfect					
Sing.	3 m.	(נָגַשׁ)	נָפַל	נִגַּשׁ	הִגִּישׁ
	3 f.		regular	נִגְּשָׁה	הִגִּישָׁה
	2 m.			נִגַּשְׁתָּ	הִגַּשְׁתָּ
	2 f.			נִגַּשְׁתְּ	הִגַּשְׁתְּ
	1 c.			נִגַּשְׁתִּי	הִגַּשְׁתִּי
Plur.	3 c.			נִגְּשׁוּ	הִגִּישׁוּ
	2 m.			נִגַּשְׁתֶּם	הִגַּשְׁתֶּם
	2 f.			נִגַּשְׁתֶּן	הִגַּשְׁתֶּן
	1 c.			נִגַּשְׁנוּ	הִגַּשְׁנוּ
Imperfect					
Sing.	3 m.	יִגַּשׁ	יִפֹּל	יִנָּגֵשׁ	יַגִּישׁ
	3 f.	תִּגַּשׁ	תִּפֹּל	etc.	תַּגִּישׁ
	2 m.	תִּגַּשׁ	תִּפֹּל		תַּגִּישׁ
	2 f.	תִּגְּשִׁי	תִּפְּלִי		תַּגִּישִׁי
	1 c.	אֶגַּשׁ	אֶפֹּל		אַגִּישׁ
Plur.	3 m.	יִגְּשׁוּ	יִפְּלוּ		יַגִּישׁוּ
	3 f.	תִּגַּשְׁנָה	תִּפֹּלְנָה		תַּגֵּשְׁנָה
	2 m.	תִּגְּשׁוּ	תִּפְּלוּ		תַּגִּישׁוּ
	2 f.	תִּגַּשְׁנָה	תִּפֹּלְנָה		תַּגֵּשְׁנָה
	1 c.	נִגַּשׁ	נִפֹּל		נַגִּישׁ

PE NUN VERB

		Hoph'al	Qal		Niph'al	
Perfect						
Sing.	3 m.	הֻגַּשׁ	נָתַן	לָקַח	נִלְקַח	נִתַּן
	3 f.	הֻגְּשָׁה	נָתְנָה		נִתְּנָה	
	2 m.	הֻגַּשְׁתָּ	נָתַתָּ		נִתַּתָּ	
	2 f.		נָתַתְּ	regular	regular	
	1 c.	etc.	נָתַתִּי			
Plur.	3 c.		נָתְנוּ			
	2 m.		נְתַתֶּם			
	2 f.		נְתַתֶּן			
	1 c.		נָתַנּוּ			
Imperfect						
Sing.	3 m.	יֻגַּשׁ	יִתֵּן	יִקַּח	יִלָּקַח	יִנָּתֵן
	3 f.	תֻּגַּשׁ	תִּתֵּן	תִּקַּח		
	2 m.	תֻּגַּשׁ	תִּתֵּן	תִּקַּח		
	2 f.	etc.	תִּתְּנִי	תִּקְחִי	etc.	
	1 c.		אֶתֵּן	אֶקַּח		
Plur.	3 m.		יִתְּנוּ	יִקְחוּ		
	3 f.		(תִּתֵּנָּה)	תִּקַּחְנָה		
	2 m.		תִּתְּנוּ	תִּקְחוּ		
	2 f.		(תִּתֵּנָּה)	תִּקַּחְנָה		
	1 c.		נִתֵּן	נִקַּח		

PE NUN VERB

	Qal		Niph'al	Hiph'il
Cohor. 1 sg.	אֶגְּשָׁה	אֶפְּלָה		אַגִּישָׁה
Juss. 3 sg. m.	יִגַּשׁ	יִפֹּל		יַגֵּשׁ
Waw cons. imp.	וַיִּגַּשׁ	וַיִּפֹּל		וַיַּגֵּשׁ
Waw cons. pft.		וְנָפַלְתָּ		
Imperative				
Sing. 2 m.	גַּשׁ (גְּשָׁה)	נְפֹל	הִנָּגֵשׁ	הַגֵּשׁ
2 f.	גְּשִׁי	נִפְלִי	הִנָּגְשִׁי	הַגִּישִׁי
Plur. 2 m.	גְּשׁוּ	נִפְלוּ	הִנָּגְשׁוּ	הַגִּישׁוּ
2 f.	גַּשְׁנָה	נְפֹלְנָה	הִנָּגַשְׁנָה	הַגֵּשְׁנָה
Infinitive constr.	גֶּשֶׁת	נְפֹל	הִנָּגֵשׁ	הַגִּישׁ
absol.	נָגוֹשׁ	נָפֹל	הִנָּגֵשׁ	הַגֵּשׁ
Participle active	(נֹגֵשׁ)	נֹפֵל	נִגָּשׁ	מַגִּישׁ
passive	(נָגוּשׁ)			

Pe Nun Verb

	Hoph'al		Qal		Niph'al
Cohor. 1 sg.			אֶתְּנָה	אֶקְחָה	
Juss. 3 sg. m.	יֻגַּשׁ		יִתֵּן	יִקַּח	
Waw cons. imp.	וַיֻּגַּשׁ		וַיִּתֵּן	וַיִּקַּח	
Waw cons. pft.			וְנָתַתָּ		
Imperative					
Sing. 2 m.			תֵּן, תְּנָה	קַח, קְחָה	הִלָּקַח הִנָּתֵן
2 m.			תְּנִי	קְחִי	etc.
Plur. 2 m.			תְּנוּ	קְחוּ	
2 f.			(תֵּנָּה)	(קְחֶנָה)	
Infinitive constr.	הֻגַּשׁ		תֵּת¹	קַחַת²	הִלָּקַח הִנָּתֵן
absol.	הֻגֵּשׁ		נָתוֹן	לָקוֹחַ	הִלָּקֹם הִנָּתֹן
Participle active			נֹתֵן	לֹקֵחַ	
passive	מֻגָּשׁ		נָתוּן	לָקוּם	נִלְקָח נִתָּן

1. with suffixes תִּתִּי etc.   2. with suffixes קַחְתִּי etc.

Pe Guttural Verbs

	Qal		Niph'al	Hiph'il
Perfect	Active	Stative		
Sing. 3 m.	עָמַד	חָזַק	נֶעֱמַד	הֶעֱמִיד
3 f.	עָמְדָה	etc.	נֶעֶמְדָה	הֶעֱמִידָה
2 m.	עָמַדְתָּ		נֶעֱמַדְתָּ	הֶעֱמַדְתָּ
2 f.	עָמַדְתְּ		נֶעֱמַדְתְּ	הֶעֱמַדְתְּ
1 c.	עָמַדְתִּי		נֶעֱמַדְתִּי	הֶעֱמַדְתִּי
Plur. 3 c.	עָמְדוּ		נֶעֶמְדוּ	הֶעֱמִידוּ
2 m.	עֲמַדְתֶּם		נֶעֱמַדְתֶּם	הֶעֱמַדְתֶּם
2 f.	עֲמַדְתֶּן		נֶעֱמַדְתֶּן	הֶעֱמַדְתֶּן
1 c.	עָמַדְנוּ		נֶעֱמַדְנוּ	הֶעֱמַדְנוּ
Imperfect				
Sing. 3 m.	יַעֲמֹד	יֶחֱזַק	יֵעָמֵד	יַעֲמִיד
3 f.	תַּעֲמֹד	תֶּחֱזַק	תֵּעָמֵד	תַּעֲמִיד
2 m.	תַּעֲמֹד	תֶּחֱזַק	תֵּעָמֵד	תַּעֲמִיד
2 f.	תַּעַמְדִי	תֶּחֶזְקִי	תֵּעָמְדִי	תַּעֲמִידִי
1 c.	אֶעֱמֹד	אֶחֱזַק	אֵעָמֵד	אַעֲמִיד
Plur. 3 m.	יַעַמְדוּ	יֶחֶזְקוּ	יֵעָמְדוּ	יַעֲמִידוּ
3 f.	תַּעֲמֹדְנָה	תֶּחֱזַקְנָה	תֵּעָמַדְנָה	תַּעֲמֵדְנָה
2 m.	תַּעַמְדוּ	תֶּחֶזְקוּ	תֵּעָמְדוּ	תַּעֲמִידוּ
2 f.	תַּעֲמֹדְנָה	תֶּחֱזַקְנָה	תֵּעָמַדְנָה	תַּעֲמֵדְנָה
1 c.	נַעֲמֹד	נֶחֱזַק	נֵעָמֵד	נַעֲמִיד

PE GUTTURAL VERBS

		Hophʻal	Qal
Perfect			
Sing.	3 m.	הָעֳמַד	אָכַל
	3 f.	הָעָמְדָה	regular
	2 m.	הָעֳמַדְתָּ	
	2 f.	הָעֳמַדְתְּ	
	1 c.	הָעֳמַדְתִּי	
Plur.	3 c.	הָעָמְדוּ	
	2 m.	הָעֳמַדְתֶּם	
	2 f.	הָעֳמַדְתֶּן	
	1 c.	הָעֳמַדְנוּ	
Imperfect			
Sing.	3 m.	יָעֳמַד	יֹאכַל
	3 f.	תָּעֳמַד	תֹּאכַל
	2 m.	תָּעֳמַד	תֹּאכַל
	2 f.	תָּעָמְדִי	תֹּאכְלִי
	1 c.	אָעֳמַד	אֹכַל
Plur.	3 m.	יָעָמְדוּ	יֹאכְלוּ
	3 f.	תָּעֳמַדְנָה	תֹּאכַלְנָה
	2 m.	תָּעָמְדוּ	תֹּאכְלוּ
	2 f.	תָּעֳמַדְנָה	תֹּאכַלְנָה
	1 c.	נָעֳמַד	נֹאכַל

Pe Guttural Verbs

	Qal		Niph'al	Hiph'il
Cohor. 1 sg.	אֶעֶמְדָה			אַעֲמִידָה
Juss. 3 sg. m.	יַעֲמֹד	יֶחֱזַק		יַעֲמֵד
Waw cons. imp.	וַיַּעֲמֹד	וַיֶּחֱזַק		וַיַּעֲמֵד
Waw cons. pft.	וְעָמַדְתָּ			וְהַעֲמַדְתָּ
Imperative				
Sing. 2 m.	עֲמֹד	חֲזַק	הֵעָמֵד	הַעֲמֵד
2 f.	עִמְדִי	חִזְקִי	הֵעָמְדִי	הַעֲמִידִי
Plur. 2 m.	עִמְדוּ	חִזְקוּ	הֵעָמְדוּ	הַעֲמִידוּ
2 f.	עֲמֹדְנָה	חֲזַקְנָה	הֵעָמַדְנָה	הַעֲמֵדְנָה
Infinitive constr.	עֲמֹד		הֵעָמֵד	הַעֲמִיד
absol.	עָמוֹד		נַעֲמֹד	הַעֲמֵד
Participle active	עֹמֵד		נֶעֱמָד	מַעֲמִיד
passive	עָמוּד			

Pe Guttural Verbs

	Hoph'al	Qal
Cohor. 1 sg.		אֹכְלָה
Juss. 3 sg. m.		יֹאכַל
Waw cons. impft.		וַיֹּאכַל
Waw cons. pft.		וְאָכַלְתָּ
Imperative Sing. 2 m.		אֱכֹל
2 f.		אִכְלִי
Plur. 2 m.		אִכְלוּ
2 f.		אֱכֹלְנָה
Infinitive constr.		אֱכֹל
absol.	הָעֳמֵד	אָכוֹל
Participle active		אֹכֵל
passive	מֳעֳמָד	אָכוּל

'Ayin Guttural Verbs

		Qal	Niph'al	Pi'el	Pu'al	Hithpa'el
Perfect						
sing.	3 m.	בָּחַר	נִבְחַר	בֵּרֵךְ	בֹּרַךְ	הִתְבָּרֵךְ
	3 f.	בָּחֲרָה	נִבְחֲרָה	בֵּרֲכָה	בֹּרְכָה	הִתְבָּרֲכָה
	2 m.	בָּחַרְתָּ	נִבְחַרְתָּ	בֵּרַכְתָּ	בֹּרַכְתָּ	הִתְבָּרַכְתָּ
	2 f.	בָּחַרְתְּ	etc.	בֵּרַכְתְּ	etc.	הִתְבָּרַכְתְּ
	1 c.	בָּחַרְתִּי		בֵּרַכְתִּי		הִתְבָּרַכְתִּי
plur.	3 c.	בָּחֲרוּ		בֵּרֲכוּ		הִתְבָּרֲכוּ
	2 m.	בְּחַרְתֶּם		בֵּרַכְתֶּם		הִתְבָּרַכְתֶּם
	2 f.	בְּחַרְתֶּן		בֵּרַכְתֶּן		הִתְבָּרַכְתֶּן
	1 c.	בָּחַרְנוּ		בֵּרַכְנוּ		הִתְבָּרַכְנוּ
Imperfect						
sing.	3 m.	יִבְחַר	יִבָּחֵר	יְבָרֵךְ	יְבֹרַךְ	יִתְבָּרֵךְ
	3 f.	תִּבְחַר	תִּבָּחֵר	תְּבָרֵךְ	תְּבֹרַךְ	תִּתְבָּרֵךְ
	2 m.	תִּבְחַר	תִּבָּחֵר	תְּבָרֵךְ	תְּבֹרַךְ	תִּתְבָּרֵךְ
	2 f.	תִּבְחֲרִי	תִּבָּחֲרִי	תְּבָרֲכִי	תְּבֹרְכִי	תִּתְבָּרֲכִי
	1 c.	אֶבְחַר	אֶבָּחֵר	אֲבָרֵךְ	אֲבֹרַךְ	אֶתְבָּרֵךְ
plur.	3 m.	יִבְחֲרוּ	יִבָּחֲרוּ	יְבָרֲכוּ	יְבֹרְכוּ	יִתְבָּרֲכוּ
	3 f.	תִּבְחַרְנָה	תִּבָּחַרְנָה	תְּבָרֵכְנָה	תְּבֹרַכְנָה	תִּתְבָּרֵכְנָה
	2 m.	תִּבְחֲרוּ	תִּבָּחֲרוּ	תְּבָרֲכוּ	תְּבֹרְכוּ	תִּתְבָּרֲכוּ
	2 f.	תִּבְחַרְנָה	תִּבָּחַרְנָה	תְּבָרֵכְנָה	תְּבֹרַכְנָה	תִּתְבָּרֵכְנָה
	1 c.	נִבְחַר	נִבָּחֵר	נְבָרֵךְ	נְבֹרַךְ	נִתְבָּרֵךְ

'Ayin Guttural Verbs

	Qal	Niph'al	Pi'el	Pu'al	Hithpa'el
Cohor. 1 sg.	אֶבְחֲרָה	אֶבָּחֲרָה	אֲבָרֲכָה		
Juss. 3 sg. m.	יִבְחַר	יִבָּחֵר	יְבָרֵךְ		
Waw cons. imp.	וַיִּבְחַר	וַיִּבָּחֵר	וַיְבָרֶךְ		
Waw cons. pf.	וּבָחַרְתָּ	וְנִבְחַרְתָּ			
Imperative					
sing. 2 m.	בְּחַר	הִבָּחֵר	בָּרֵךְ		הִתְבָּרֵךְ
2 f.	בַּחֲרִי	הִבָּחֲרִי	בָּרְכִי		הִתְבָּרְכִי
plur. 2 m.	בַּחֲרוּ	הִבָּחֲרוּ	בָּרְכוּ		הִתְבָּרְכוּ
2 f.	בְּחַרְנָה	הִבָּחַרְנָה	בָּרֵכְנָה		הִתְבָּרֵכְנָה
Infinitive					
constr.	בְּחֹר	הִבָּחֵר	בָּרֵךְ	בֹּרַךְ	הִתְבָּרֵךְ
absol.	בָּחוֹר	נִבְחֹר	בָּרֵךְ		
Participle					
active	בֹּחֵר		מְבָרֵךְ		מִתְבָּרֵךְ
passive	בָּחוּר	נִבְחָר		מְבֹרָךְ	

LAMEDH GUTTURAL VERBS

		Qal	Niph'al	Pi'el
Perfect				
sing.	3 m.	שָׁלַח	נִשְׁלַח	שִׁלַּח
	3 f.	שָׁלְחָה	נִשְׁלְחָה	שִׁלְּחָה
	2 m.	שָׁלַחְתָּ	נִשְׁלַחְתָּ	שִׁלַּחְתָּ
	2 f.	שָׁלַחַתְּ	etc.	etc.
	1 c.	שָׁלַחְתִּי		
plur.	3 c.	שָׁלְחוּ		
	2 m.	שְׁלַחְתֶּם		
	2 f.	שְׁלַחְתֶּן		
	1 c.	שָׁלַחְנוּ		
Imperfect				
sing.	3m.	יִשְׁלַח	יִשָּׁלַח	יְשַׁלַּח
	3 f.	תִּשְׁלַח	תִּשָּׁלַח	תְּשַׁלַּח
	2 m.	תִּשְׁלַח	תִּשָּׁלַח	תְּשַׁלַּח
	2 f.	תִּשְׁלְחִי	תִּשָּׁלְחִי	תְּשַׁלְּחִי
	1 c.	אֶשְׁלַח	אֶשָּׁלַח	אֲשַׁלַּח
plur.	3 m.	יִשְׁלְחוּ	יִשָּׁלְחוּ	יְשַׁלְּחוּ
	3 f.	תִּשְׁלַחְנָה	תִּשָּׁלַחְנָה	תְּשַׁלַּחְנָה
	2 m.	תִּשְׁלְחוּ	תִּשָּׁלְחוּ	תְּשַׁלְּחוּ
	2 f.	תִּשְׁלַחְנָה	תִּשָּׁלַחְנָה	תְּשַׁלַּחְנָה
	1 c.	נִשְׁלַח	נִשָּׁלַח	נְשַׁלַּח

LAMEDH GUTTURAL VERBS

		Pu'al	Hiph'il	Hoph'al	Hithpa'el
Perfect					
sing.	3 m.	שֻׁלַּח	הִשְׁלִיחַ	הָשְׁלַח	הִשְׁתַּלַּח
	3 f.	שֻׁלְּחָה	הִשְׁלִיחָה	הָשְׁלְחָה	הִשְׁתַּלְּחָה
	2 m.	שֻׁלַּחְתָּ	הִשְׁלַחְתָּ	הָשְׁלַחְתָּ	הִשְׁתַּלַּחְתָּ
	2 f.	etc.	הִשְׁלַחַתְּ	etc.	etc.
	1 c.		הִשְׁלַחְתִּי		
plur.	3 c.		הִשְׁלִיחוּ		
	2 m.		הִשְׁלַחְתֶּם		
	2 f.		הִשְׁלַחְתֶּן		
	1 c.		הִשְׁלַחְנוּ		
Imperfect					
sing.	3 m.	יְשֻׁלַּח	יַשְׁלִיחַ	יָשְׁלַח	יִשְׁתַּלַּח
	3 f.	תְּשֻׁלַּח	תַּשְׁלִיחַ	תָּשְׁלַח	תִּשְׁתַּלַּח
	2 m.	תְּשֻׁלַּח	תַּשְׁלִיחַ	תָּשְׁלַח	תִּשְׁתַּלַּח
	2 f.	etc.	תַּשְׁלִיחִי	etc.	etc.
	1 c.		אַשְׁלִיחַ		
plur.	3 m.		יַשְׁלִיחוּ		
	3 f.		תַּשְׁלַחְנָה		
	2 m.		תַּשְׁלִיחוּ		
	2 f.		תַּשְׁלַחְנָה		
	1 c.		נַשְׁלִיחַ		

LAMEDH GUTTURAL VERBS

	Qal	Niph'al	Pi'el
Cohor. 1 sg.	אֶשְׁלְחָה	אֶשָּׁלְחָה	אֲשַׁלְּחָה
Juss. 3 sg. m.	יִשְׁלַח	יִשָּׁלַח	יְשַׁלַּח
Waw cons. imp.	וַיִּשְׁלַח	וַיִּשָּׁלַח	וַיְשַׁלַּח
Waw cons. pf.	וְשָׁלַחְתָּ		
Imperative			
sing. 2 m.	שְׁלַח	הִשָּׁלַח	שַׁלַּח
2 f.	שִׁלְחִי	הִשָּׁלְחִי	שַׁלְּחִי
plur. 2 m.	שִׁלְחוּ	הִשָּׁלְחוּ	שַׁלְּחוּ
2 f.	שְׁלַחְנָה	הִשָּׁלַחְנָה	שַׁלַּחְנָה
Infinitive constr.	שְׁלֹחַ	הִשָּׁלַח	שַׁלַּח
absol.	שָׁלוֹחַ	נִשְׁלֹחַ	שַׁלֵּחַ
Participle active	שֹׁלֵחַ		מְשַׁלֵּחַ
passive	שָׁלוּחַ	נִשְׁלָח	

Lamedh Guttural Verbs

	Pu'al	Hiph'il	Hoph'al	Hithpa'el
Cohor. 1 sg.		אַשְׁלִיחָה		
Juss. 3 sg. m.		יַשְׁלַח		
Waw cons. imp		וַיַּשְׁלַח		
Waw cons. pf.				
Imperative				
sing. 2 m.		הַשְׁלַח		הִשְׁתַּלַּח
2 ff.		הַשְׁלִיחִי		הִשְׁתַּלְּחִי
plural 2 m.		הַשְׁלִיחוּ		הִשְׁתַּלְּחוּ
2 f.		הַשְׁלַחְנָה		הִשְׁתַּלַּחְנָה
Infinitive				
constr.		הַשְׁלִיחַ		הִשְׁתַּלַּח
absol.		הַשְׁלֵחַ	הָשְׁלֵחַ	
Participle				
active		מַשְׁלִיחַ		מִשְׁתַּלֵּחַ
passive	מְשֻׁלָּח		מָשְׁלָה	

LAMEDH 'ALEPH VERBS
Qal

		Active	Stative	Niph'al	Pi'el
Perfect					
sing.	3 m.	מָצָא	מָלֵא	נִמְצָא	מִצֵּא
	3 f.	מָצְאָה	מָלְאָה	נִמְצְאָה	מִצְּאָה
	2 m.	מָצָאתָ	מָלֵאתָ	נִמְצֵאתָ	מִצֵּאתָ
	2 f.	מָצָאת	מָלֵאת	נִמְצֵאת	etc.
	1 c.	מָצָאתִי	מָלֵאתִי	נִמְצֵאתִי	as Niph.
plur.	3 c.	מָצְאוּ	מָלְאוּ	נִמְצְאוּ	
	2 m.	מְצָאתֶם	מְלֵאתֶם	נִמְצֵאתֶם	
	2 f.	מְצָאתֶן	מְלֵאתֶן	נִמְצֵאתֶן	
	1 c.	מָצָאנוּ	מָלֵאנוּ	נִמְצֵאנוּ	
Imperfect					
sing.	3 m.	יִמְצָא	יִמְלָא	יִמָּצֵא	יְמַצֵּא
	3 f.	תִּמְצָא	etc.	תִּמָּצֵא	תְּמַצֵּא
	2 m.	תִּמְצָא		תִּמָּצֵא	תְּמַצֵּא
	2 f.	תִּמְצְאִי		תִּמָּצְאִי	תְּמַצְּאִי
	1 c.	אֶמְצָא		אֶמָּצֵא	אֲמַצֵּא
plur.	3 m.	יִמְצְאוּ		יִמָּצְאוּ	etc.
	3 f.	תִּמְצֶאנָה		תִּמָּצֶאנָה	as
	2 m.	תִּמְצְאוּ		תִּמָּצְאוּ	Niph.
	2 f.	תִּמְצֶאנָה		תִּמָּצֶאנָה	
	1 c.	נִמְצָא		נִמָּצֵא	

LAMEDH ʾALEPH VERBS

	Puʿal	Hiphʿil	Hophʿal	Hithpaʿel
Perfect				
sing. 3 m.	מֻצָּא	הִמְצִיא	הֻמְצָא	הִתְמַצֵּא
3 f.	מֻצְּאָה	הִמְצִיאָה	הֻמְצְאָה	הִתְמַצְּאָה
3 m.	מֻצֵּאתָ	הִמְצֵאתָ	הֻמְצֵאתָ	הִתְמַצֵּאתָ
2 f.	etc.	הִמְצֵאת	etc.	etc.
1 c.	as	הִמְצֵאתִי	as	as
	Niph.		Niph.	Niph.
plur. 3 c.		הִמְצִיאוּ		
2 m.		הִמְצֵאתֶם		
2 f.		הִמְצֵאתֶן		
1 c.		הִמְצֵאנוּ		
Imperfect				
sing. 3 m.	יֻמְצָּא	יַמְצִיא	יֻמְצָא	יִתְמַצֵּא
3 f.	תֻּמְצָּא	תַּמְצִיא	תֻּמְצָא	תִּתְמַצֵּא
2 m.	תֻּמְצָּא	תַּמְצִיא	תֻּמְצָא	תִּתְמַצֵּא
2 f.	etc.	תַּמְצִיאִי	etc.	etc.
1 c.	as	אַמְצִיא	as	as
plur. 3 m.	Qal	יַמְצִיאוּ	Qal	Niph.
3 f.		תַּמְצֶאנָה		
2 m.		תַּמְצִיאוּ		
2 f.		תַּמְצֶאנָה		
1 c.		נַמְצִיא		

Lamedh 'Aleph Verbs

Qal

	Active	Stative	Niph'al	Pi'el
Cohor. 1 sg.	אֶמְצָאָה		אִמָּצְאָה	
Juss. 3 sg. m.	יִמְצָא		יִמָּצֵא	
Waw cons. imp.	וַיִּמְצָא		וַיִּמָּצֵא	
Waw cons. pf.	וּמָצָאתָ			
Imperative				
sing. 2 m.	מְצָא		הִמָּצֵא	מַצֵּא
2 f.	מִצְאִי		הִמָּצְאִי	etc.
plur. 2 m.	מִצְאוּ		הִמָּצְאוּ	as
				Niph.
2 f.	מְצֶאנָה		הִמָּצֶאנָה	
Infinitive				
constr.	מְצֹא		הִמָּצֵא	מַצֵּא
absol.	מָצוֹא		נִמְצֹא	מַצֹּא
Participle				
active	מֹצֵא			מְמַצֵּא
passive	מָצוּא		נִמְצָא	

Lamedh 'Aleph Verbs

	Pu'al	Hiph'il	Hoph'al	Hithpa'el
Cohor. 1 sg.		אַמְצִיאָה		
Juss. 3 sg. m.		יַמְצֵא		
Waw cons. imp.		וַיַּמְצֵא		
Waw cons. pf.				
Imperative				
sing. 2 m.		הַמְצֵא		הִתְמַצֵּא
2 f.		הַמְצִיאִי		הִתְמַצְּאִי
plur. 2 m.		הַמְצִיאוּ		etc.
				as
2 f.		הַמְצֶאנָה		Niph.
Infinitive				
constr.		הַמְצִיא	הָמְצָא	הִתְמַצֵּא
absol.		הַמְצֵא		
Participle				
active		מַמְצִיא		מִתְמַצֵּא
passive	מְמְצָא		מָמְצָא	

Pe Waw and Pe Yodh Verbs

		Qal		Niph'al	Hiph'il	Hoph'al
Perfect						
sing.	3 m.	יָרֵא	יָשַׁב	נוֹשַׁב	הוֹשִׁיב	הוּשַׁב
	3 f.		יָשְׁבָה	נוֹשְׁבָה	הוֹשִׁיבָה	הוּשְׁבָה
	2 m.		יָשַׁבְתָּ	נוֹשַׁבְתָּ	הוֹשַׁבְתָּ	הוּשַׁבְתָּ
	2 f.		etc.	etc.	etc.	etc.
	1 c.					
plur.	3 c.					
	2 m.					
	2 f.					
	1 c.					
Imperfect						
sing.	3 m.	יִירָא	יֵשֵׁב	יִוָּשֵׁב	יוֹשִׁיב	יוּשַׁב
	3 f.		תֵּשֵׁב	תִּוָּשֵׁב	תּוֹשִׁיב	תּוּשַׁב
	2 m.		תֵּשֵׁב	תִּוָּשֵׁב	תּוֹשִׁיב	תּוּשַׁב
	2 f.		תֵּשְׁבִי	תִּוָּשְׁבִי	תּוֹשִׁיבִי	etc.
	1 c.		אֵשֵׁב	אִוָּשֵׁב	אוֹשִׁיב	
plur.	3 m.		יֵשְׁבוּ	יִוָּשְׁבוּ	יוֹשִׁיבוּ	
	3 f.		תֵּשַׁבְנָה	תִּוָּשַׁבְנָה	(תּוֹשֵׁבְנָה)	
	2 m.		תֵּשְׁבוּ	תִּוָּשְׁבוּ	תּוֹשִׁיבוּ	
	2 f.		תֵּשַׁבְנָה	תִּוָּשַׁבְנָה	(תּוֹשֵׁבְנָה)	
	1 c.		נֵשֵׁב	נִוָּשֵׁב	נוֹשִׁיב	

Pe Waw and Pe Yodh Verbs

		Qal.	Hiph'il
Perfect			
sing.	3 m.	יָטַב	הֵיטִיב
	3 f.	יָטְבָה	הֵיטִיבָה
	2 m.	etc.	הֵיטַבְתָּ
	2 f.		הֵיטַבְתְּ
	1 c.		הֵיטַבְתִּי
plur.	3 c.		הֵיטִיבוּ
	2 m.		הֵיטַבְתֶּם
	2 f.		הֵיטַבְתֶּן
	1 c.		הֵיטַבְנוּ
Imperfect			
sing.	3 m.	יִיטַב	יֵיטִיב
	3 f.	תִּיטַב	תֵּיטִיב
	2 m.	תִּיטַב	תֵּיטִיב
	2 f.	תִּיטְבִי	תֵּיטִיבִי
	1 c.	אִיטַב	אֵיטִיב
plur.	3 m.	יִיטְבוּ	יֵיטִיבוּ
	3 f.	תִּיטַבְנָה	תֵּיטֵבְנָה
	2 m.	תִּיטְבוּ	תֵּיטִיבוּ
	2 f.	תִּיטַבְנָה	תֵּיטֵבְנָה
	1 c.	נִיטַב	נֵיטִיב

G

Pe Waw and Pe Yodh Verbs

	Qal	Niph'al	Hiph'il	Hoph'al
Cohor. 1 sg.	אֵשְׁבָה			
Juss. 3 sg. m.	יֵשֵׁב		יוֹשֵׁב	
Waw cons. imp.	וַיֵּשֶׁב		וַיּוֹשֵׁב	
Waw cons. pf.	וְיָשַׁבְתָּ			
Imperative				
sing. 2 m.	יְרָא שֵׁב (שְׁבָה)	הִוָּשֵׁב	הוֹשֵׁב	
2 f.	שְׁבִי	הִוָּשְׁבִי	הוֹשִׁיבִי	
plur. 2 m.	שְׁבוּ	הִוָּשְׁבוּ	הוֹשִׁיבוּ	
2 f.	שֵׁבְנָה	הִוָּשַׁבְנָה	הוֹשֵׁבְנָה	
Infinitive constr.	יִרְאָה שֶׁבֶת	הִוָּשֵׁב	הוֹשִׁיב	הוּשַׁב
absol.	יָשׁוֹב		הוֹשֵׁב	
Participle active	יָרֵא יֹשֵׁב		מוֹשִׁיב	
passive	יָשׁוּב	נוֹשָׁב		מוּשָׁב

PE WAW AND PE YODH VERBS

	Qal	Hiph'il
Cohor. 1 sg.		
Juss. 3 sg. m.	יֵיטַב	יֵיטֵב
Waw cons. imp.	וַיֵּיטַב	וַיֵּיטֶב
Waw cons. pf.		
Imperative		
sing. 2 m.		הֵיטֵב
2 f.		הֵיטִיבִי
plur. 2 m.		הֵיטִיבוּ
2 f.		הֵיטַבְנָה
Infinitive constr.	(יְטֹב)	הֵיטִיב
absol.	יָטוֹב	הֵיטֵב
Participle active	יֹטֵב	מֵיטִיב
passive	יָטוּב	

'Ayin Waw and 'Ayin Yodh Verbs

		Qal			Niph'al
		Active	**Stative**		
Perfect					
sing.	3 m.	קָם	מֵת	בּוֹשׁ	נָקוֹם
	3 f.	קָ֫מָה	מֵ֫תָה	בּוֹשָׁה	נָק֫וֹמָה
	2 m.	קַ֫מְתָּ	מַ֫תָּה	בֹּשְׁתָּ	נְקוּמֹ֫תָ
	2 f.	קַמְתְּ	מַתְּ	בֹּשְׁתְּ	נְקוּמֹת
	1 c.	קַ֫מְתִּי	מַ֫תִּי	בֹּשְׁתִּי	נְקוּמֹ֫תִי
plur.	3 c.	קָ֫מוּ	מֵ֫תוּ	בּוֹשׁוּ	נָק֫וֹמוּ
	2 m.	קַמְתֶּם	מַתֶּם	בָּשְׁתֶּם	נְקוּמֹתֶם
	2 f.	קַמְתֶּן	מַתֶּן	בָּשְׁתֶּן	נְקוּמֹתֶן
	1 c.	קַ֫מְנוּ	מַ֫תְנוּ	בֹּשְׁנוּ	נְקוּמֹ֫נוּ
Imperfect					
sing.	3 m.	יָקוּם	יָמוּת	יֵבוֹשׁ	יִקּוֹם
	3 f.	תָּקוּם	etc.	תֵּבוֹשׁ	תִּקּוֹם
	2 m.	תָּקוּם		תֵּבוֹשׁ	תִּקּוֹם
	2 f.	תָּק֫וּמִי		תֵּב֫וֹשִׁי	תִּקּ֫וֹמִי
	1 c.	אָקוּם		אֵבוֹשׁ	אֶקּוֹם
plur.	3 m.	יָק֫וּמוּ		יֵב֫וֹשׁוּ	יִקּ֫וֹמוּ
	3 f.	תְּקוּמֶ֫ינָה		תֵּבֹ֫שְׁנָה	
	2 m.	תָּק֫וּמוּ		תֵּב֫וֹשׁוּ	תִּקּ֫וֹמוּ
	2 f.	תְּקוּמֶ֫ינָה		תֵּבוֹשְׁ֫נָה	
	1 c.	נָקוּם		נֵבוֹשׁ	נִקּוֹם

'Ayin Waw and 'Ayin Yodh Verbs

		Hiph'il	Hoph'al	'Ayin Yodh Verb Qal
Perfect				
sing.	3 m.	הֵקִים	הוּקַם	שָׂם
	3 f.	הֵקִימָה	הוּקְמָה	שָׂמָה
	2 m.	הֲקִימֹ֫תָ	הוּקַ֫מְתָּ	שַׂ֫מְתָּ
	2 f.	הֲקִימֹת	הוּקַמְתְּ	
	1 c.	הֲקִימֹ֫תִי	הוּקַ֫מְתִּי	etc. as קָם
plur.		הֵקִ֫ימוּ	הוּקְמוּ	
	2 m.	הֲקִימֹתֶם	הוּקַמְתֶּם	
	2 f.	הֲקִימֹתֶן	הוּקַמְתֶּן	
	1 c.	הֲקִימֹ֫נוּ	הוּקַ֫מְנוּ	
Imperfect				
sing.	3 m.	יָקִים	יוּקַם	יָשִׂים
	3 f.	תָּקִים	תּוּקַם	תָּשִׂים
	2 m.	תָּקִים	תּוּקַם	תָּשִׂים
	2 f.	תָּקִ֫ימִי	תּוּקְמִי	תָּשִׂ֫ימִי
	1 c.	אָקִים	אוּקַם	אָשִׂים
plur.	3 m.	יָקִ֫ימוּ	יוּקְמוּ	יָשִׂ֫ימוּ
	3 f.	תָּקֵ֫מְנָה[1]	תּוּקַ֫מְנָה	תָּשֵׂ֫מְנָה[2]
	2 f.	תָּקִ֫ימוּ	תּוּקְמוּ	תָּשִׂ֫ימוּ
	2 f.	תָּקֵ֫מְנָה	תּוּקַ֫מְנָה	תָּשֵׂ֫מְנָה[2]
	1 c.	נָקִים	נוּקַם	נָשִׂים

1. Or, תָּקִימֶ֫ינָה   2. Or, תָּשִׂימֶ֫ינָה

'AYIN WAW AND 'AYIN YODH VERBS

Qal

	Active	Stative		Niph'al
Cohor. 1 sg.	אָקוּמָה	אָמוּתָה	אֵבוֹשָׁה	
Juss. 3 sg. m.	יָקֹם	יָמֹת	יֵבוֹשׁ	
Waw cons. imp.	וַיָּקָם	וַיָּמָת	וַיֵּבוֹשׁ	
Waw cons. pf.	וְקַמְתָּ			
Imperative				
sing. 2 m.	קוּם	מוּת	בּוֹשׁ	הִקּוֹם
2 f.	קוּמִי	etc.	בּוֹשִׁי	הִקּוֹמִי
plur. 2 m.	קוּמוּ		בּוֹשׁוּ	הִקּוֹמוּ
2 f.	קֹמְנָה		בֹּשְׁנָה	הִקֹּמְנָה
Infinitive constr.	קוּם	מוּת	בּוֹשׁ	הִקּוֹם
absol.	קוֹם	מוֹת	בּוֹשׁ	נָקוֹם
Participle active	קָם	מֵת	בּוֹשׁ	¹נָקוֹם
passive	קוּם			

1. fem. נָקוֹמָה

'Ayin Waw and 'Ayin Yodh Verbs

	Hiph'il	Hoph'al	'Ayin Yodh Verb Qal
Cohor. 1 sg.	אָקִימָה		אָשִׂימָה
Juss. 3 sg. m.	יָקֵם		יָשֵׂם
Waw cons. imp.	וַיָּקֶם		וַיָּשֶׂם
Waw cons. pf.	וַהֲקִימֹתָ		וְשַׂמְתָּ
Imperative			
sing. 2 m.	הָקֵם		שִׂים
2 f.	הָקִימִי		שִׂימִי
plur. 2 m.	הָקִימוּ		שִׂימוּ
2 f.	הֲקֵמְנָה		
Infinitive constr.	הָקִים	הוּקַם	שִׂים
absol.	הָקֵם		שׂוֹם
Participe active	מֵקִים		שָׂם
passive		מוּקָם	

DOUBLE ʻAYIN VERBS

Qal

		Active		Stative	

Perfect

sing.	3 m.	סַב	סָבַב	קַל	מַל
	3 f.	סַבָּה	סָבְבָה	קַלָּה	etc.
	2 m.		סַבּוֹתָ	קַלּוֹתָ	
	2 f.		סַבּוֹת	קַלּוֹת	
	1 c.		סַבּוֹתִי	קַלּוֹתִי	
plur.	3 c.	סַבּוּ	סָבְבוּ	קַלּוּ	
	2 m.		סַבּוֹתֶם	קַלּוֹתֶם	
	2 f.		סַבּוֹתֶן	קַלּוֹתֶן	
	1 c.		סַבּוֹנוּ	קַלּוֹנוּ	

Imperfect

sing.	3 m.	יָסֹב	יִסֹּב	יֵקַל	יִמַּל
	3 f.	תָּסֹב	תִּסֹּב	תֵּקַל	תִּמַּל
	2 m.	תָּסֹב	תִּסֹּב	תֵּקַל	תִּמַּל
	2 f.	תָּסֹבִּי	תִּסֹּבִי	תֵּקְלִי	תִּמְּלִי
	1 c.	אָסֹב	אֶסֹּב	אֵקַל	אֶמַּל
plur.	3 m.	יָסֹבּוּ	יִסֹּבוּ	יֵקַלּוּ	יִמְּלוּ
	3 f.	תָּסֻבֶּינָה	תִּסֹּבְנָה	תְּקַלֶּינָה	תִּמַּלְנָה
	2 m.	תָּסֹבּוּ	תִּסֹּבוּ	תֵּקַלּוּ	תִּמְּלוּ
	2 f.	תָּסֻבֶּינָה	תִּסֹּבְנָה	תְּקַלֶּינָה	תִּמַּלְנָה
	1 c.	נָסֹב	נִסֹּב	נֵקַל	נִמַּל

Double 'Ayin Verbs

		Niph'al	Hiph'il	Hoph'al
Perfect				
sing.	3 m.	נָסַב	הֵסֵב	יוּסַב
	3 f.	נָסַבָּה	הֵסַבָּה	הוּסַבָּה
	2 m.	נְסַבּוֹתָ	הֲסִבּוֹתָ	הוּסַבּוֹתָ
	2 f.	נְסַבּוֹת	הֲסִבּוֹת	etc.
	1 c.	נְסַבּוֹתִי	הֲסִבּוֹתִי	
plur.	3 c.	נָסַבּוּ	הֵסֵבּוּ	
	2 m.	נְסַבּוֹתֶם	הֲסִבּוֹתֶם	
	2 f.	נְסַבּוֹתֶן	הֲסִבּוֹתֶן	
	1 c.	נְסַבּוֹנוּ	הֲסִבּוֹנוּ	
Imperfect				
sing.	3 m.	יִסַּב	יָסֵב יָסֵב	יוּסַב יָסַב
	3 f.	תִּסַּב	תָּסֵב	תּוּסַב
	2 m.	תִּסַּב	תָּסֵב	תּוּסַב
	2 f.	תִּסַּבִּי	תָּסֵבִּי	etc.
	1 c.	אֶסַּב	אָסֵב	
plur.	3 m.	יִסַּבּוּ	יָסֵבּוּ יָסֵבּוּ	
	3 f.	תִּסַּבֶּינָה	תְּסִבֶּינָה	
	2 m.	תִּסַּבּוּ	תָּסֵבּוּ	
	2 f.	תִּסַּבֶּינָה	תְּסִבֶּינָה	
	1 c.	נִסַּב	נָסֵב	

Double 'Ayin Verbs

Qal

	Active		Stative	
Cohor. 1 sg.	אָסֹבָּה	אֶסֹּבָה		
Juss. 3 sg. m.	יָסֹב	יִסֹּב	יֵקַל	יֵמַל
Waw cons. imp.	וַיָּסָב	וַיִּסֹּב	וַיֵּקַל	
Waw cons. pf.	וְסַבֹּתָ			
Imperative sing. 2 m.		סֹב		
2 f.		סֹבִּי		
plur. 2 m.		סֹבּוּ		
2 f.		סֻבֶּינָה		
Infinitive constr.		סֹב	קַל, קָל	
absol.		סָבוֹב	קָלוֹל	
Participle active		סֹבֵב	קַל, קָלֶה	
passive		סָבוּב		

Double 'Ayin Verbs

	Niph'al	Hiph'il	Hoph'al
Cohor. 1 sg.			
Juss. 3 sg. m.	יָסֵב	יָסֵב	
Waw cons. imp.	וַיִּסֵּב	וַיָּסֶב	
Waw cons. pf.			
Imperative			
sing.　2 m.	הִסֵּב	הָסֵב	
2 f.	הִסַּבִּי	הָסֵבִּי	
plur.　2 m.	הִסַּבּוּ	הָסֵבּוּ	
2 f.	הִסַּבֶּינָה	הֲסִבֶּינָה	
Infinitive constr.	הִסֵּב	הָסֵב	הוּסַב
absol.	הִסּוֹב	הָסֵב	
Participle active	נָסָב	מֵסֵב	
passive			מוּסָב

1. fem. sing. נָסַבָּה

LAMEDH HE (LAMEDH YODH AND WAW) VERBS

		Qal	Niph'al	Pi'el
Perfect				
sing.	3 m.	גָּלָה	נִגְלָה	גִּלָּה
	3 f.	גָּלְתָה	נִגְלְתָה	גִּלְּתָה
	2 m.	גָּלִיתָ	נִגְלֵיתָ	גִּלִּיתָ
	2 f.	גָּלִית	נִגְלֵית	etc.
	1 c.	גָּלִיתִי	נִגְלֵיתִי	
plur.	3 c.	גָּלוּ	נִגְלוּ	
	2 m.	גְּלִיתֶם	נִגְלֵיתֶם	
	2 f.	גְּלִיתֶן	נִגְלֵיתֶן	
	1 c.	גָּלִינוּ	נִגְלֵינוּ	
Imperfect				
sing.	3 m.	יִגְלֶה	יִגָּלֶה	יְגַלֶּה
	3 f.	תִּגְלֶה	תִּגָּלֶה	תְּגַלֶּה
	2 m.	תִּגְלֶה	תִּגָּלֶה	תְּגַלֶּה
	2 f.	תִּגְלִי	תִּגָּלִי	etc.
	1 c.	אֶגְלֶה	אֶגָּלֶה	
plur.	3 m.	יִגְלוּ	יִגָּלוּ	
	3 f.	תִּגְלֶינָה	תִּגָּלֶינָה	
	2 m.	תִּגְלוּ	תִּגָּלוּ	
	2 f.	תִּגְלֶינָה	תִּגָּלֶינָה	
	1 c.	נִגְלֶה	נִגָּלֶה	

Lamedh He (Lamedh Yodh and Waw) Verbs

		Puʻal	Hiphʻil	Hophʻal	Hithpaʻel
Perfect					
sing.	3 m.	גֻּלָּה	הִגְלָה	הָגְלָה	הִתְגַּלָּה
	3 f.	גֻּלְּתָה	הִגְלְתָה	הָגְלְתָה	הִתְגַּלְּתָה
	2 m.	גֻּלֵּיתָ	הִגְלֵיתָ	הָגְלֵיתָ	הִתְגַּלֵּיתָ
	2 f.	etc.	etc.	etc.	etc.
	1 c.				
plur.	3 c.				
	2 m.				
	2 f.				
	1 c.				
Imperfect					
sing.	3 m.	יְגֻלֶּה	יַגְלֶה	יָגְלֶה	יִתְגַּלֶּה
	3 f.	תְּגֻלֶּה	תַּגְלֶה	תָּגְלֶה	תִּתְגַּלֶּה
	2 m.	תְּגֻלֶּה	תַּגְלֶה	תָּגְלֶה	תִּתְגַּלֶּה
	2 f.	etc.	etc.	etc.	etc.
	1 c.				
plur.	3 m.				
	3 f.				
	2 m.				
	2 f.				
	1 c.				

LAMEDH HE (LAMEDH YODH AND WAW) VERBS

	Qal	Niph'al	Pi'el
Cohor. 1 sg.			
Juss. 3 sg. m.	יִגֶל	יִגָּל	יְגַל
Waw cons, imp.	וַיִּגֶל	וַיִּגָּל	וַיְגַל
Waw cons. pf.	וְגָלִיתָ	וְנִגְלֵיתָ	
Imperative			
sing. 2 m.	גְּלֵה	הִגָּלֵה	גַּלֵּה (גַּל)
2 f.	גְּלִי	הִגָּלִי	גַּלִּי
plur. 2 m.	גְּלוּ	הִגָּלוּ	גַּלּוּ
2 f.	גְּלֶינָה	הִגָּלֶינָה	גַּלֶּינָה
Infinitive constr.	גְּלוֹת	הִגָּלוֹת	גַּלּוֹת
absol.	גָּלֹה	נִגְלֹת	
Participle active	גֹּלֶה	נִגְלֶה	מְגַלֶּה
passive	גָּלוּי		

LAMEDH HE (LAMEDH YODH AND WAW) VERBS

	Pu'al	Hiph'il	Hoph'al	Hithpa'el
Cohor. 1 sg.				
Juss. 3 sg. m.		יֶגֶל		יִתְגַּל
Waw cons. imp.	וַיְגֻלֶּה	וַיֶּגֶל		וַיִּתְגַּל
Waw cons. pf.				
Imperative				
sing. 2 m.		הַגְלֵה		הִתְגַּלֵּה
2 f.		הַגְלִי		הִתְגַּלִּי
plur. 2 m.		etc.		etc.
2 f.				
Infinitive constr.	גֻּלּוֹת	הַגְלוֹת	הָגְלוֹת	הִתְגַּלּוֹת
absol.	גֻּלֹּה	הַגְלֵה	הָגְלֵה	הִתְגַּלֵּה
Participle active		מַגְלֶה		מִתְגַּלֶּה
passive	מְגֻלֶּה		מָגְלֶה	

KEY TO EXERCISES

Exercise 1

(a) 1. 'thph   2. blnw.   3. qṭlm.   4. slḥyny.   5. mšlkḥ.
6. ʿrbhynw.   7. zphsln.   8. klwthy.   9. çlʿphʾ.   10. zrghḥm.
11. tlṭmʿyn.   12. hwkhlʿym.   13. ḥphʿzyq.   14. ṭyrʾš.
15. slqʿlw.   16. dphṭʾnyn.   17. ʿlysmw.   18. ṣmṭšbh.
19. kçphʿyl.   20. ḥzqhms.

(b) 1. חטשם 2. לפאש 3. צרמיו 4. סנטחלי 5. תּאקלעמי

6. שׁבוי 7. קפסעטץ 8. דערמאלי 9. פמחטשאֻֻן

10. כרמעספקי 11. אזוענגא 12. טרשדמו 13. בגלסחע

14. צהוגלע 15. קמתוי 16. אנצעלין 17. חנבטש

18. תצאנסאם 19. אמינעטו 20. גרקלאמיו.

Exercise 2

(a) 1. lî or lê.   2. mâ or mĕh.   3. kî or kê.   4. šâ.   5. lâlô
or lâlû.   6. mîmô or mîmû or mêmô or mêmû.   7. ḥôlê
or ḥûlê or ḥôlî or ḥûlî.   8. nâmî or nàmê.   9. ṣênû or
ṣînû or ṣênô or ṣînô.   10. lômî or lûmî or lômê or lûmê.

(b) 1. להלה 2. לילו 3. לולה 4. בהנה 5. מולו

6. נילו 7. מוני 8. לילי 9. קינה 10. ליני.

(c) 1. û. 2. ē. 3. ĕ. 4. î. 5. ā or ŏ. 6. ŭ. 7. ê.
8. ô. 9. ĭ. 10. ō. 11. ă. 12. ŏ or ā.

(d) 1. ַ 2. וֹ 3. ָ 4. ֵ 5. ֹ 6. וּ 7. ֶ 8. ָ
9. ֶ 10. ַ 11. ִי 12. ִי.

(e) 1. בֵּן 2. בֶּן 3. גוּר 4. מֵם 5. אָכַל 6. צָפוֹן
7. אִישׁ 8. מֶחֶן 9. אֱמֶת 10. קֹטֶל 11. חָשִׁים 12. סֵפֶר
13 גָּדוֹל 14. הוּא 15. שׁוּרְק 16. מָלֵינוּ 17. עָפָר
18. הִיא 19. עֵינֵי 20. אֶבֶן.

(f) 1. 'ādhām. 2. 'ĕrîth. 3. šālôm. 4. mîmê. 5.
çāphônâ. 6. 'îr. 7. băth. 8. 'ĕlômî. 9. lānû. 10. măyĭm.
11. qārā'. 12. kôkhābhîm. 13. yĕlĕth. 14. gămānû.
15. 'ĕlĕm. 16. 'āçûm. 17. yārē'. 18. kōphĕr. 19. šôr.
20. māḥāh.

Exercise 3

(a) 1. 'adhōnî. 2. mĭšpāṭ. 3. ṭôbhîm. 4. yĭqbᵉrû.
5. ḥānăn. 6. mălkᵉkhā. 7. ḥôlênû. 8. 'āmᵉdhû. 9. 'ᵉmôr.
10. gᵉdhôlê. 11. kôhᵃnîm. 12. yᵉdhāmēr. 13. lᵉbhābhām.
14. šā'ᵃlû. 15. 'ᵃnāšîm. 16. 'ĕlōhîm. 17. hĕḥᵉtî.
18. tᵉnâ. 19. 'ᵃšĕr. 20. măḥᵃnĕh.

(b) 1. שְׁלָמִי 2. יִקְטְלוּ 3. דְּבַר 4. בְּנֵי 5. אֲלֵיכֶם
6. כְּנַעַן 7. יִרְאוּ 8. יַעֲזֹב 9. חֲזָקָה 10. אַחֲרֵנִי
11. הַחֲלוֹם 12. אֲנַחְנוּ 13. מִשְׁמַר 14. בִּרְכַּת 15. חֲזָקוֹת
16. בְּעֵינֵי 17. אֵלָיו 18. יַעֲשֶׂה 19. עֲדַת 20. בְּכוֹרִי.

Exercise 4

(a) 1. בְּנֵי 2. יִשְׂכְּלוּ 3. קֶרֶב 4. שָׂרִים 5. יָדַגְתִּי

6. גָּדוֹל 7. אָדְנָם 8. כְּבַדְתֶּן 9. בְּתוֹרוּ 10. כָּלְפָּם.

(b) 1. הַלֵּי 2. מְלְקֶכַת 3. מֶכֶב 4. שַׂגֵּר 5. מַלְכְּכוּ

6. בְּכֶם 7. לַעֲרַת 8. יָבָם 9. מְדְבְּרוּ 10. כְּפֵנִי.

Exercise 5

1. לֶאֱמֶת 2. חֲכָמִים 3. שָׂרִים 4. מִשְׁחֲדוּ 5. רוּחוּ

6. הַיֵלֵךְ 7. מֵאָדָם 8. זֶבַח 9. בַּעֲלִי 10. לַעֲבִיר.

As pronounced:

1. lĕʾᵉmĕth. 2. ḥᵃkhāmîm. 3. sārîm. 4. mĭšḥᵃdhû.
5. rûḥô. 6. hᵃyēlēkh. 7. mēʾādhām. 8. zĕbhăḥ.
9. bāʿᵃlî. 10. lăʿᵃbhîr.

Exercise 6

1. הָאִישׁ 2. הָעָם 3. הַמַּיִם 4. הַיּוֹם 5. הַמֶּלֶךְ

6. הָרָקִיעַ 7. הַקּוֹל 8. הַחֹשֶׁךְ 9. הָעַיִן 10. הַבֹּקֶר

11. אִשָּׁה 12. יוֹם 13. הֶעָפָר 14. הָאוֹר.

Exercise 7

(*a*) 1. The prophet is good. 2. The good prophet.
3. The great and good morning. 4. The mountain is high.
5. The man and the prophet. 6. The temple is great and
good. 7. The night and the day. 8. The daughter and
the woman. 9. The man is the king. 10. The gold is good.

(*b*) 1. הָאִישׁ הַגָּדוֹל 2. הַיּוֹם 3. הָעֶרֶב וְהַבֹּקֶר 4. זָהָב
5. הַמֶּלֶךְ גָּדוֹל וְטוֹב 6. הַיָּד וְהָעַיִן 7. הָאִשָּׁה
8. גָּדוֹל הָעָם 9. הֶחָלִי וְהַנָּבִיא 10. הַיּוֹם הַגָּדוֹל
וְהַלַּיְלָה הָרָע.

Exercise 8

(*a*) 1. Words. 2. A pair of horses. 3. Fathers. 4. The
two hands. 5. The two sides. 6. Old age. 7. Hearts.
8. Wells. 9. Cities. 10. Two feet.

(*b*) 1. שְׁלָחֲנוֹת 2. אֲבָנִים 3. שְׁנָתַיִם 4. שׁוֹפָרוֹת 5. הַסּוּס
6. אָבוֹת טוֹבִים 7. גְּדוֹלָה הַשָּׂרָה 8. עֵינַיִם
וְהַסּוּסָה
וְאָזְנַיִם 9. טוֹבִים וְטוֹבוֹת 10. בָּנִים וּבָנוֹת·

Exercise 9

(a) 1. I am the man. 2. The great darkness is the night. 3. Thou art the good daughter. 4. That is a good man. 5. What is it ? 6. These heroes. 7. What is this that he has done? 8. That fair daughter. 9. How lofty is this place ! 10. Is he very powerful ?

(b) 1. אֵ֫לֶּה הָאֲנָשִׁים הַחֲכָמִים 2. הַשָּׁמַ֫יִם הַהֵ֫מָּה 3. טוֹבָה 4. הָאִישׁ הַטּוֹב הַזֶּה 5. זֶה הָאִישׁ הַטּוֹב 6. מַה־עִיר 7. מַה־הֵיכָל 8. הוּא הָאִישׁ הָאִשָּׁה הַזֹּאת וְהֶעָצוּם 9. אֲנִי הַמֶּ֫לֶךְ הֶעָצוּם אֲשֶׁר עַל־הָאָ֫רֶץ אֲשֶׁר עַל־הַבַּ֫יִת 10. אֵ֫לֶּה הַשָּׁמַ֫יִם וְהָאָ֫רֶץ וְהַיָּם. הַגְּדוֹלָה

Exercise 10

(a) 1. In peace. 2. Like Jehovah. 3. For sickness. 4. To Samuel. 5. Day and night are in the heavens. 6. The king has a son. 7. Bread and water are very good. 8. From darkness until the day. 9. Dust from the ground are we. 10. God is in this temple.

(b) 1. בֵּאלֹהִים 2. כַּאֲרִי 3. לִיהוֹשֻׁעַ 4. יהוה הוּא בַּשָּׁמַ֫יִם 5. מִן־הָהָר 6. הַבֵּן הוּא כַּמֶּ֫לֶךְ 7. בָּהָר הָרָם בַּבֹּ֫קֶר 8. הַהֵיכָל הוּא לַמֶּ֫לֶךְ 9. הָעָם הֶחָכָם הוּא בַּהֵיכָל בָּעֶ֫רֶב 10. בַּת וּבֵן לַנָּבִיא.

Exercise 11

(a) 1. I have heard the prophet. 2. The woman did not hear the voice in the great garden. 3. I remember the man who shed the blood in the desert. 4. I wrote in the book in this day. 5. These are the bad mares which we killed on the ground. 6. May he keep the good queen in the palace. 7. And behold, the man took this woman for a wife. 8. And the man Isaac was very great in the land. 9. You shall keep the commands which God has given. 10. The man whom God created is good.

(b) 1. אֶכְתֹּב בְּסֵפֶר 2. מִי הַגִּבּוֹרִים וְהַנְּבִיאִים הָאֵלֶּה 3. קָרָא

4. אָכַלְתָּ מִן־הָעֵץ וְאָמַר גָּדוֹל יהוה זֶה אֶל־זֶה 5. יִשְׁמַע

6. הֲלֹא נָתַן הָאֱלֹהִים דָּם אֲשֶׁר לֹא־יִשָׁפֵּךְ אֶת־הָאִישׁ יהוה

בֶּן וּבַת לַנָּבִיא 7. תִּשְׁמֹרְנָה אֶת־הַדְּבָרִים אֲשֶׁר בַּסֵּפֶר

8. בָּרָא אֱלֹהִים טוֹב וָרַע וְיוֹם וְלָיְלָה 9. זָכַרְתִּי אֶת־אֲשֶׁר

שָׁמַעְתִּי בַּהֵיכָל 10. לֹא יִשְׁמֹר אֶת־הַדְּבָרִים אֲשֶׁר נָתַן הַנָּבִיא

לָעָם בַּמִּדְבָּר׃

Exercise 12

(a) 1. The good mares of the king. 2. The prophet took a horse belonging to the king. 3. These are the days of the years of the life of the bad king. 4. God set the sun in the firmament of the heaven. 5. He said, I am the servant of Abraham. 6. And in the presence of all the prophets shall he dwell. 7. Thou hast kept the heart of the great king from evil. 8. The people did not hear the words of the prophet of the Lord. 9. The sword of gold is in the hand of the mighty man. 10. You did not remember the words which the sons of the prophets of the Lord spake.

1. (b) אֱלֹהֵי הַשָּׁמַיִם וֵאלֹהֵי הָאָרֶץ   2. קוֹל הָאֱלֹהִים בָּעִיר
דָּוִד   3. עֵינֵי הָאִישׁ עַל־סוּסֵי פַרְעֹה   4. דִּבְרֵי הָעָם הֵם
רָעִים מְאֹד בְּאָזְנֵי הַנָּבִיא   5. הַסּוּס אֲשֶׁר לַמֶּלֶךְ הַטּוֹב בַּמִּדְבָּר
6. הָרַג גִּבּוֹר שָׁאוּל אֶת־נְבִיאֵי יהוה בַּמָּקוֹם אֲשֶׁר יָשַׁב דָּוִד
שָׁם   7. לֹא נָבִיא אָנִי וְלֹא בֶן־נָבִיא   8. אָמַר אָנֹכִי אֱלֹהֵי אַבְרָהָם
אֱלֹהֵי יִצְחָק וֵאלֹהֵי יַעֲקֹב   9. תּוֹרַת יהוה הִיא טוֹבָה בְּעֵינֵי
הָעָם   10. הֲאָכַלְתָּ מִן־הָעֵץ אֲשֶׁר בְּגַן יהוה.

Exercise 13

(a) 1. From you. 2. From him, or, from us. 3. After
thee(f). 4. With her. 5. Before the man. 6. Their(f)
horses. 7. Their(m) mares. 8. Your(f) righteousnesses.
9. I have heard their(m) words. 10. Your(m) hands.
11. To them(m). 12. Their(m) words are evil in the sight
of Jehovah. 13. The prophet sent his sons and his
daughters toward the desert. 14. We have heard thy
voice in the temple of the Lord. 15. Between me and
thee. 16. And I did not pursue after the sons of Jacob.
17. For I have kept the ways of Jehovah the God of Israel.
18. In the book of the kings of Israel and Judah. 19. They
have not kept the commandments of Jehovah which he
gave to them on the mountain. 20. And all his judgments
are before thee.

1. (b) לְפָנַי   2. אַחֲרֵיהֶן   3. עָלָיו   4. מִמְּךָ   5. אֲלֵיכֶם
6. לִפְנֵיכֶם   7. לְפָנֶיךָ   8. פָּנַי   9. יָדֵינוּ   10. שְׁפָתַיִךְ
11. צִדְקוֹתֵיהֶן   12. דְּבָרֵינוּ   13. סוּסָם   14. סוּסֵיכֶן
15. סוּסוֹתֵיכֶן   16. בֵּינֵינוּ   17. תַּחְתָּיו   18. הִנְנִי   19. שְׂפָתֵיהֶם
20. יָדְךָ הַחֲזָקָה הִיא בָּעָם.

Exercise 14

(*a*) 1. Be not (ye) angry. 2. Thou shalt not steal. 3. Speak, I beg. 4. And God said, fall thou down before me, and I will not be angry with thee for ever. 5. Pursue ye after him. 6. Let him not write in the book of the law of Jehovah, the God of Israel. 7. I went and sold the boy. 8. The man forgot the words of the prophet and did not keep the law of Jehovah. 9. And he set him over all the land of Egypt. 10. He will surely keep the law of God. 11. And when the prophet remembered these words he said, Pursue (thou) after them northwards. 12. Ye are remembering the words of God which I spoke in that day. 13. Behold, I am sending the prophet towards the city.

(*b*) 1. תִּשְׁמֹר אֶת־מִצְוֹתַי 2. יִשְׁמֹר אֹתְךָ מִכָּל־רַע בָּאָרֶץ

3. אֵלְכָה־נָא אֶל־בֵּית הַנָּבִיא 4. וַיַּעַשׂ אֱלֹהִים אֶת־הָרָקִיעַ בֵּין הַמַּיִם אֲשֶׁר תַּחַת לָרָקִיעַ וּבֵין הַמַּיִם אֲשֶׁר עַל־הָרָקִיעַ

5. אֶשְׁמְרָה אֶת־מִצְוֹתֶיךָ 6. הָלַךְ הָלוֹךְ אֶל־בֵּית יוֹסֵף 7. אֶשְׁמֹר שָׁמוֹר אֶת־מִצְוֹתֶיךָ 8. חָדְלוּ לִסְפֹּר אֶת־כּוֹכְבֵי הַשָּׁמָיִם

9. יָרְדוּ מִצְרַיְמָה לִשְׁבָּר־אֹכֶל בַּמָּקוֹם הַהוּא 10. וְהִנֵּה שָׁלַח אֶת־הַיֶּלֶד לִשְׁמוֹר אֶת־עִיר הַגִּבּוֹרִים 11. יהוה הוּא שֹׁמְרֶךָ בְּיוֹם הָרָע 12. הַנְּבִיאִים שֹׁמְרִים אֶת־תּוֹרַת יהוה אֱלֹהֵי יִשְׂרָאֵל 13. הַמֶּלֶךְ מָשַׁל בָּעָם בָּאָרֶץ.

Exercise 15

(a) 1. And Jehovah said unto me, Say unto them, do not fight. 2. And we rested in that place many days. 3. And Jehovah repented that he had made man on the earth. 4. And all the great mountains were covered, which were under all the heavens. 5. The sacrifices of God are a broken spirit. 6. Thou wilt send to thy servant an attentive (hearing) heart to judge this thy people. 7. Son of man, I have broken the arm of Pharaoh, king of Egypt, and behold, it has not been bound up. 8. Thou hast said, seek ye my face, thy face will I seek. 9. And now thou art cursed from the ground which the Lord has made. 10. And Pharaoh hardened his heart and did not let the people go.

(b) 1. וַיִּשְׁלַח הָאֱמֹרִי הַיֹּשֵׁב בָּהָר הַהוּא וַיִּרְדְּפוּ אֶתְכֶם 2. לֹא תִּלָּחֲמוּ אֶת־קָטֹן וְאֶת־גָּדוֹל כִּי־אִם־אֶת־מֶלֶךְ יִשְׂרָאֵל 3. וַיֹּאמֶר יהוה הַמְכַסֶּה מֵאַבְרָהָם אֲשֶׁר עָשִׂיתִי 4. שֹׁפֵךְ דַּם הָאָדָם בָּאָדָם דָּמוֹ יִשָּׁפֵךְ כִּי בְּצֶלֶם אֱלֹהִים עָשָׂה אֶת־הָאָדָם 5. וּבְסִפְרֵי בֵית־יִשְׂרָאֵל לֹא יִכָּתֵבוּ 6. הֵן שָׁלַחְתָּ אֹתִי הַיּוֹם מֵעַל פְּנֵי הָאֲדָמָה וּמִפָּנֶיךָ אֶסָּתֵר׃ 7. לֹא יָכְלוּ לִשְׁתֹּת מִמֵּימֵי הַיְאֹר 8. וְאָמַרְתָּ אֶל־פַּרְעֹה כֹּה אָמַר יהוה בְּנִי בְכֹרִי יִשְׂרָאֵל 9. וְשָׁמְעוּ לְקֹלֶךָ וּבָאתָ אַתָּה וְזִקְנֵי יִשְׂרָאֵל אֶל־מֶלֶךְ מִצְרַיִם וַאֲמַרְתֶּם אֵלָיו נֵלְכָה־נָּא בַּמִּדְבָּר וְנִזְבְּחָה לַיהוה אֱלֹהֵינוּ 10. וַיְדַבֵּר אַהֲרֹן אֶת־כָּל־הַדְּבָרִים אֲשֶׁר דִּבֶּר יהוה אֶל־מֹשֶׁה׃

Exercise 16

(a) 1. And Jehovah said to Samuel, listen to their voice and make a king for them. 2. And he came to the gate of the city, and behold there a woman gathering sticks. 3. As for you, you have caused many to stumble at the law of Jehovah. 4. And behold, their lord was fallen down dead on the ground. 5. And thou art cast out of heaven with everyone who does evil. 6. And Jacob said to his sons, Why do you look upon one another, behold, I have heard that there is bread in Egypt. 7. And they said, we have walked to and fro in the earth, and behold, all the earth is still. 8. She is the city to be visited by the hand of Jehovah the God of Israel. 9. And as the prophet heard these words he took courage. 10. I saw the wicked buried and they were forgotten in the city where they had so done.

(b) 1. בָּא אִישׁ מֵהָעָם לְהַשְׁחִית אֶת־הַמֶּלֶךְ 2. בָּאתָ אֵלַי לְהַזְכִּיר אֶת־עֲוֹנִי וּלְהָמִית אֶת־בְּנִי 3. אֵלֶּה הַמְּאֹרֹת בִּרְקִיעַ הַשָּׁמַיִם לְהַבְדִּיל בֵּין הַיּוֹם וּבֵין הַלָּיְלָה 4. וְהִשָּׁכַב בְּקִבְרוֹ בַּמָּקוֹם אֲשֶׁר נָתַן הַמֶּלֶךְ לוֹ 5. וַיֹּאמֶר יְהוֹשֻׁעַ אֶל־הָעָם הִתְקַדְּשׁוּ כִּי יהוה בַּמָּקוֹם הַזֶּה 6. מָשְׁלָךְ רֹאשׁוֹ עַל־הָאֲדָמָה בְּיַד הַגִּבּוֹר 7. וַיִּשְׁמְעוּ אֶת־קוֹל יהוה מִתְהַלֵּךְ בַּגָּן 8. וַיִּתְחַבְּאוּ הָאָדָם וְאָשְׁתּוֹ מִפְּנֵי יהוה אֱלֹהִים בְּתוֹךְ עֲצֵי הַגָּן 9. וַיֹּאמֶר פַּרְעֹה הֵן רַבִּים עַם הָאָרֶץ וְהִשְׁבַּתֶּם אֹתָם בַּמָּקוֹם הַזֶּה 10. וַיִּתְנַבְּאוּ עַד־הָעֶרֶב וְאֵין־קוֹל.

210

Exercise 17

(a) 1. Two feet. 2. His messengers. 3. Their years.
4. Your places. 5. In his heart. 6. Thy(*f*) calf. 7. Our
counsels. 8. Their (*m*) women. 9. Their (*m*) waters.
10. Their (*f*) oxen. 11. Thy (*m*) handmaidens. 12. Your
(*m*) mouth. 13. Their (*f*) cities. 14. My vineyard. 15. Two
knees.

(b) 1. עֵינַיִם 2. אָזְנַיִם 3. יְדֵיהֶם 4. בִּרְכַתְכֶם 5. דִּבְרֵיהֶם

6. אֲחִיכֶם 7. בָּתֵּיהֶן 8. בְּנֹתֵיהֶם 9. אַחִי 10. רָאשֵׁיהֶם

11. צִדְקוֹ 12. עֶגְלֵיהֶם 13. גָּדְלִי 14. מַלְכְּכֶם 15. חֲיָלֵינוּ

Exercise 18

(a) 1. Younger than his brother. 2. David is the
greatest of his brothers. 3. His youngest son. 4. The
most servile slave. 5. I will be greater than thou. 6. I
am taller than he. 7. One of thy tribes. 8. His three
sons. 9. On the fifteenth day. 10. The eighteenth year
of Solomon. 11. In the second year of Pekah. 12. In the
twelfth month in the third year. 13. In the eighteenth
year of the king of Israel. 14. Those two. 15. Two by two.

(b) 1. טוֹב מִזָּהָב 2. בִּתּוֹ הַקְּטַנָּה 3. גָּבֹהַּ הוּא מֵאִשְׁתּוֹ

4. מִגְּדוֹלָם וְעַד־קְטַנָּם 5. יֶאֱהַב יַעֲקֹב אֶת־רָחֵל מִלֵּאָה

6. לֹא־טוֹב אָנֹכִי מֵאֲבֹתַי 7. שְׁנֵי הֶהָרִים 8. שָׁלֹשׁ בְּנוֹתֶיהָ

9. חֲמִשָּׁה עָשָׂר בָּנִים 10. שְׁתַּיִם וְשִׁשִּׁים שָׁנָה 11. עֶשְׂרִים

וְשִׁבְעָה or שִׁבְעָה וְעֶשְׂרִים 12. אַחַת עֶשְׂרֵה שָׁנָה 13. הָאָרֶץ

הָרִאשׁוֹנָה 14. הַחֹדֶשׁ הָעֲשִׂירִי 15. בַּשָּׁנָה הַשֵּׁנִית.

Exercise 19

(a) 1. He will seek me. 2. Our keeping, or, keeping us.
3. He will make me king. 4. They (m) will keep you (f).
5. You (f) have kept me. 6. Thou (f) hast kept me. 7. He
has kept them (f). 8. After they had made a covenant.
9. We have sought thee in the temple. 10. Seek him
in the morning. 11. When he kept thy words. 12. Make
him king over this people. 13. He who justifies me is God.
14. He will destroy me in that day. 15. For those who
honour me I will honour.

1. (b) הִמְלִיכְתַּנִי 2. שְׁמַרְתִּיךָ 3. שְׁמָרוּם 4. הַמְלִיכֵנִי 5. יְבַקְשׁוּנִי

6. בְּקַשְׁתּוּנִי 7. שְׁמָרְנוּךָ 8. בְּשָׁמְרֶךָ 9. כִּזְכֹר הָאִישׁ אֶת־

תּוֹרָתֶךָ 10. בְּיוֹם פָּקְדִי אֹתָם 11. יְכַבְּדֵנִי בָּעִיר הַהִיא

12. אֶשְׁפְּטֶךָ כִּדְרָכֶיךָ 13. שְׁלָחַנִי אֱלֹהִים לִפְנֵיכֶם 14. בְּקַשְׁהוּ

בְּכָל־לְבָבָם 15. הַמֹּצְאַתַנִי אֹיְבִי.

Exercise 20

(a) 1. And he said to me, Son of man, stand upon thy feet and I will speak with thee. 2. I will serve thee seven years for Rachel thy younger daughter. 3. And the elders of his city will send and take him from there, and will give him into the hand of the king. 4. Thus saith Jehovah unto the men of Anathoth who are seeking thy life, saying, Do not prophesy in the name of Jehovah. 5. And Pharaoh dreamed and behold he stood by the river. 6. And Jonathan spoke good of David unto Saul his father, and said unto him, Let not the king sin against his servant. 7. And thou shalt serve thine enemies which Jehovah shall send against thee. 8. In the day of evil I will call upon thee, for thou wilt answer me. 9. Thou hast not allowed me to kiss my sons and my daughters. 10. And he divided himself against them by night, he and his servants.

(b) 1. תַּעַבְדוּן אֶת־אֱלֹהִים עַל־הָהָר הַזֶּה 2. וְאַתָּה בֶּן־אָדָם הִנָּבֵא אֶל־הָרֵי יִשְׂרָאֵל 3. וַיַּחַלְמוּ חֲלוֹם בְּלַיְלָה אֶחָד 4. וַיֹּאמֶר גְּשׁוּ הֲלֹם כֹּל הָעָם 5. כִּי הַמָּקוֹם אֲשֶׁר אַתָּה עֹמֵד עָלָיו אַדְמַת־קֹדֶשׁ הִיא 6. וְלֹא תֶחֱטִיא אֶת־הָאָרֶץ אֲשֶׁר יהוה אֱלֹהֶיךָ נֹתֵן לְךָ נַחֲלָה 7. כֹּה אָמַר יהוה שַׁלַּח אֶת־עַמִּי וְיַעַבְדֻנִי 8. וְצִוָּה יהוה וְאָמַר לְעַמּוֹ הִנְנִי שֹׁלֵחַ לָכֶם לֶחֶם בַּמִּדְבָּר 9. בְּכָל הַדְּבָרִים הָאֵלֶּה לֹא חָטָא בִּשְׂפָתָיו 10. וַיֹּאמֶר אֵלָיו אָבִיו גְּשָׁה־נָא וּשְׁקָה־לִי בְּנִי.

Exercise 21

(a) 1. And Jehovah said to Moses, Pharaoh's heart is heavy, he is unwilling to let the people go. 2. And the earth was corrupt before God, and the earth was full of violence. 3. And thou shalt speak unto everyone who is wise of heart, whom I have filled with the spirit of wisdom. 4. And he refused, and said unto his master's wife, Behold, my lord does not know, and everything which he has he has given into my hand. 5. And how shall I do this great evil, and sin against God? 6. As for me, I hate him, because he does not prophesy good unto me. 7. And if it is evil in your sight to serve Jehovah, choose ye to-day whom ye will serve. 8. And ye shall cry out in that day because of your king whom ye have chosen for yourselves. 9. He will not destroy thee, nor forget the covenant of thy fathers which he sware unto them. 10. And thou shalt anoint for me the one whom I shall tell unto thee.

(b) 1. וַיְבָרֶךְ אֱלֹהִים אֶת־יוֹם הַשְּׁבִיעִי וַיְקַדֵּשׁ אֹתוֹ   2. לֹא יִנָּחֵם כִּי לֹא אָדָם הוּא לְהִנָּחֵם   3. יִשְׁלַח אֶת מַלְאָכוֹ לְפָנֶיךָ   4. וַיִּשָּׁבַע לוֹ עַל־הַדְּבָרִים הָאֵלֶּה   5. וְהִנֵּה שָׁאוּל נִשְׁעָן עַל־חֲנִיתוֹ   6. וְדַם־זְבָחֶיךָ יִשָּׁפֵךְ עַל־מִזְבַּח יהוה אֱלֹהֶיךָ וְהַבָּשָׂר תֹּאכֵל   7. אֶבְיוֹנֶיהָ אַשְׂבִּיעַ לָחֶם   8. וַיֹּאמֶר אֶל־יַעֲקֹב לֹא מְצָאתִיהָ   9. לֹא תִשְׂנָא אֶת־אָחִיךָ בִּלְבָבֶךָ   10. וְלָקַחְתָּ אֶת־שֶׁמֶן הַמִּשְׁחָה וְיָצַקְתָּ עַל־רֹאשׁוֹ וּמָשַׁחְתָּ אֹתוֹ.

Exercise 22

(a) 1. And he went and dwelt by the stream which is before the city. 2. And he arose, and went for his life, and came unto the desert. 3. Arise, eat, for the way is too difficult for thee. 4. And Jehovah said unto him, go, return on thy way towards the desert. 5. And the daughter of Pharaoh said unto her, cause this child to go away, and nurse it for me. 6. And he said, my son shall not go down with you, for his brother is dead. 7. And thou shalt choose from all the people men of valour, fearing God. 8. And the fish which is in the river shall die. 9. Pharaoh will lift up thy head, and will restore thee to the palace. 10. For I am to die in this land, but ye shall go over and possess this good land.

1. (b) וַיֹּאמֶר צֵא וְעָמַדְתָּ בָּהָר   2. לֵךְ שׁוּב כִּי מֶה עָשִׂיתִי לָךְ

3. וַיָּקָם וַיֵּלֶךְ אַחֲרֵי אֵלִיָּהוּ   4. וַיִּפְצְרוּ עַד־בֹּשׁ וַיֹּאמֶר שָׁלַח

5. וַיָּמָת הַמֶּלֶךְ וַיּוּבָא שֹׁמְרוֹן וַיִּקְבְּרוּ אֶת־הַמֶּלֶךְ בְּשֹׁמְרוֹן   6. וַיָּקוּמוּ

כָּל־אַנְשֵׁי־חַיִל וַיֵּלְכוּ כָּל־הַלַּיְלָה וַיִּקְחוּ אֶת־נִבְלַת שָׁאוּל   7. וַתִּקַּח

הָאִשָּׁה אֶת־הַיֶּלֶד וַתְּנִיקֵהוּ   8. וַיִּרְאוּ אֶת־שֵׁם יהוה בָּעִיר

9. זַרְעוֹ יִירַשׁ אֶת־הָאָרֶץ   10. וַיֹּאמֶר שׁוּב אָשׁוּב אֵלֶיךָ בְּיוֹם

הָרָע.

Exercise 23

(*a*) 1. The man who curses his father or his mother shall surely be put to death. 2. Cursed shall you be when you come in, and cursed shall you be when you go out. 3. May Jehovah lift up his countenance upon you and give you peace. 4. And she said, drink, my lord, and she let down her pitcher upon her hand in the well. 5. And God said, let there be light, and there was light. 6. And the evening and the morning were the fifth day. 7. For they weep unto me saying, give us flesh. 8. And his disease was very grievous, so that there was no breath left in him. 9. For behold, on the city which is called by my name I am beginning to do evil in this day. 10. And God saw that it was good.

(*b*) 1. וַיֹּאמֶר אֵלֶיהָ אַל־תִּירְאִי בֹּאִי עֲשִׂי כִדְבָרֵךְ 2. וַיִּקְרְאוּ בְשֵׁם־אֱלֹהֵיהֶם לֵאמֹר הַבַּעַל עֲנֵנוּ וְאֵין קוֹל וְאֵין עֹנֶה אֹתָם. 3. וַיְהִי דְבַר־יְהוָה אֵלָיו לֵאמֹר קוּם לֵךְ מִדְבָּרָה 4. וַיָּבֹא מַלְאַךְ־יְהוָה אֶל הָאִשָּׁה וַיֹּאמֶר אֵלֶיהָ הִנֵּה־נָא לֹא יָלַדְתְּ וְהָרִית בֵּן 5. יְהִי מְאֹרֹת בִּרְקִיעַ הַשָּׁמָיִם 6. פְּרוּ וּרְבוּ וּמִלְאוּ אֶת־הָאָרֶץ 7. וַיֹּאמֶר אֶל־יוֹסֵף הִנֵּה אָנֹכִי מֵת וְהָיָה אֱלֹהִים עִמָּכֶם וְהֵשִׁיב אֶתְכֶם אֶל־אֶרֶץ אֲבֹתֵיכֶם 8. וְשָׁמַרְתָּ אֶת־כָּל־אֲשֶׁר אָנֹכִי מְצַוְּךָ הַיּוֹם 9. וַיַּעַל וַיַּבֵּט אֶל־הַיָּם 10. וַיַּעַשׂ הַמֶּלֶךְ כְּכָל־אֲשֶׁר צִוָּה אֹתוֹ אֱלֹהִים.

INDEX

ING & PUBLICITY   ALGEBRA   AMATEUR ACTING   ANATO
EPING   BRICKWORK   BRINGING UP CHILDREN   BUSINESS
CHINESE   COMMERCIAL ARITHMETIC   COMMERCIAL ART
MUSIC   CONSTRUCTIONAL DETAILS   CONTRACT BRIDGE
RDS   ECONOMIC GEOGRAPHY   ECONOMICS   ELECTRI
GRAMMAR   LITERARY APPRECIATION   ENGLISH RENASCE
VICTORIAN AGE   CONTEMPORARY LITERATURE   ETCHIN
CE WRITING   FRENCH   FRENCH DICTIONARY   FRENCH
THINGS   GEOLOGY   GEOMETRY   GERMAN   GERMAN
ONTROL OF INSECT PESTS   GOOD CONTROL OF PLANT DISEA
ARMING BY MACHINE   GOOD FARM WORKMANSHIP   GOOD
ARKET GARDENING   GOOD MILK FARMING   GOOD PIG KEE
NGLISH   GREEK   GREGG SHORTHAND   GUIDEBOOK TO TH
BOLIVAR   BOTHA   CATHERINE THE GREAT   CHATHAM   CLEM
M   HENRY V   JOAN OF ARC   JOHN WYCLIFFE   LENIN   LOUIS X

HASTINGS
EPAIRS
IVE INSTRUCTION   ND TOOL
LCRAFT
TO A WISE MAN...   FICIENCY
DESIGN
NG   RE

OOK   SAILING   SALESMANSHIP   SECRETA   ACTICE
SPELLING   STAMP COLLECTING   STUDE   DE   ST
ITING   USE OF GEOGRAPHY   WAY TO POETR   WRIT
Y FOR GIRLS   DOGS AS PETS FOR BOYS AND GIRLS   KNIT
RAPHY FOR BOYS AND GIRLS   RADIO FOR BOYS   RIDING
OR BOYS   STAMP COLLECTING FOR BOYS AND GIRLS   WO
ANATOMY   ARABIC   ASTRONOMY   BANKING   BEE
BUSINESS ORGANISATION   CALCULUS   CANASTA   C
AL ART   COMMERCIAL CORRESPONDENCE   COMMER
T BRIDGE   COOKING   CRICKET   DRAWING   DRESS
ICS   ELECTRICITY   ELECTRICITY IN THE HOUSE   ELOCU
RENASCENCE   ENGLISH RENASCENCE TO THE ROMANTIC
URE   ETCHING   EVERYDAY FRENCH   TO EXPRESS YOURS
ARY   FRENCH PHRASE BOOK   GARDENING   GAS IN T
GERMAN DICTIONARY   GERMAN GRAMMAR   GERMAN
L OF PLANT DISEASES   GOOD FARM ACCOUNTING   G
ARM WORKMANSHIP   GOOD FRUIT FARMING   GOOD GRA
MILK FARMING   GOOD PIG KEEPING   GOOD POULTRY KEE
SHORTHAND   GUIDEBOOK TO THE BIBLE   HINDUSTANI
NE THE GREAT   CHATHAM CLEMENCEAU CONSTANTINE CO
HN WYCLIFFE   LENIN   LOUIS XIV   MILTON   PERICLES   PETER TH
HISTORY   WARREN HASTINGS   WOODROW WILSON   HOCKE
OLD ELECTRICITY   HOUSE REPAIRS   ITALIAN   JOINERY
EMENT   MATHEMATICS   HAND TOOLS   ENGINEERING
HTSMANSHIP   METEOROLOGY   MODELCRAFT   MODERN DA
NORWEGIAN   PERSONAL EFFICIENCY   PHILOSOPHY   PHO
HAND   PLANNING AND DESIGN   PLUMBING   POLISH   PO

OVERTIS
OOK-KE
HESS
OMPOS
EEDWO
NGLISH
EVIVAL
REELAN
VING
OOD C
OOD F
OOD M
OOD E
REAT
BERALI
OBES
OUS
WRITE
ECH
OTC
HYSI
DMI
HR
DEBAT
YPEWR
OOKER
HOTOGF
OCCER F
CTING
CHILDREN
OMMERC
ONTRAC
CONOM
NGLISH
ITERAT
ICTION
GERMAN
ONTR
OOD
OOD
GREGG
ATHER
ARC JO
SE OF
OUSE
MANAG
DRAUG
MUSIC
SHORTH